Clothing Goes to War

Clothing Goes to War

Creativity Inspired by Scarcity in World War II

Nan Turner

intellect
Bristol, UK / Chicago, USA

First published in the UK in 2022 by
Intellect, The Mill, Parnall Road, Fishponds, Bristol, BS16 3JG, UK

First published in the USA in 2022 by
Intellect, The University of Chicago Press, 1427 E. 60th Street,
Chicago, IL 60637, USA

A catalogue record for this book is available from
the British Library.

Copy editor: MPS Limited
Cover designer: Aleksandra Szumlas
Cover image: Joseph Earl Turner
Production managers: Aimée Bates, Georgia Earl, and Debora Nicosia
Typesetter: MPS Limited
Printed and bound by CPI Group (UK) Ltd, Croydon, CR0 4YY

Paperback ISBN 978-1-78938-346-1
ePDF ISBN 978-1-78938-347-8
ePUB ISBN 978-1-78938-348-5

This is a peer-reviewed publication.

This book is dedicated to my parents, Joseph Earl and Patricia Jean Ford Turner, who would never have met in college in Emporia, Kansas without the disruption of World War II.

Contents

Acknowledgments ix
Introduction 1

1. Rationale for Rationing: The Demanding War 16
2. Textiles Go to War: Military Uniforms Prioritized 42
3. Gender Defined by Clothing: Women in Slacks 63
4. Home Front Handicrafts: Creativity Inspired by Restrictions 91
5. Feed Sack Fashion: Nothing Was Wasted 121
6. Wartime Weddings: Falling in Love During Wartime 128
7. Costumes Go to War: Clothing in Hollywood and British Film 154
8. Clothing as Commerce: Hoarding, Bartering, and the Black Market 173
9. Make-Do and Mend: Once Forgotten, Now Reborn 193
10. Epilogue: Global Pandemic of 2020 Forces Revivals of 1940s Handicrafts 211

Bibliography 217
Index 239

Acknowledgments

As I finish *Clothing Goes to War*, I think back on this long journey that started with a box of photos documenting my father's WWII experience. I am so appreciative of all the people who believed in this project and shared their experiences, knowledge, and expertise.

First of all, I am grateful to my professor, Dr. Susan B. Kaiser at the University of California, Davis, who suggested that I turn my interest in WWII into a master's thesis. She, along with Joan Chandler, Ann Savageau, and Dr. Margaret H. Rucker, guided me through my research and graduate study. Also at the University of California, Davis I would like to thank Amy Clark and David Masiel in the University Writing Program who generously shared their writing expertise. Daniel Goldstein, David Michalski, and Roberto Delgadillo, University of California, Davis librarians, generously met with me numerous times to help me find resources.

Deprivation Fashion: Creative Sustainability Inspired by Clothing Restrictions during WWII, my thesis and the preliminary research for this book, was completed in June 2012. After completing my master's degree, I found the subject so interesting, and the urgency of documenting the stories of the dwindling numbers of primary resources so compelling, that I continued my research.

I am indebted to so many people who shared their wartime experience with me. Especially, the women in Weston-super-Mare, UK whose parents invited my father to Christmas lunch in 1944 and extended an invitation to me in 2011 to stay in their home. I know they were just as curious as I was to exchange information. Their first question about the nice young American soldier they became friends with during the few months he was stationed in their village was if he had gone to medical school after the war. I was happy to report that he had as well as suppling other information that the "loose lips sink ships" war era protocol had not allowed him to share.

My thanks for shared experiences, all kinds of help, inspiration, and giving me the confidence that I could finish this project to:

- Dennis Wile, the photographer for the 1270th Engineer Combat Battalion, along with his wife Virginia and son Dennis Wile Jr, who graciously hosted me at their home in Trussville, Alabama and shared his professional photographs and experiences.

- The members of the World War II War Brides Association and the Bay Area War Brides chapter who warmly welcomed me to their monthly lunches and several national conventions. The members, hailing from a wide range of countries, were very generous in sharing their stories.
- Edward and Ludmilla Trautt who invited me over for tea on many occasions and shared their WWII memories with me.
- Jillian Azevedo, Karen Quail, Therese Poletti, Jennifer Coile, and Kristine Mietzner, my preliminary editors and friends, who helped with organization, format, grammar, and moral support and were always quick to answer my questions.
- Rosemond Rowe Sleigh who spent many hours helping me find my voice and improve my writing.
- The Normandy Veterans' Association members and their wives who I met in London at the 2014 commemorative ceremony of the 1944 Normandy invasion.
- Dorothy Sheridan, director of the Mass Observation Archive, who I met at the 75th Anniversary Conference of MO.
- The American Historical Association (AHA) who generously awarded me a Bernadotte Schmitt Grant.
- Peter Winning and Lisa Redlinski at St. Peter's House library in Brighton, UK which owns a priceless collection of WWII magazines.
- Generous longtime friends: Lois Breida, Sally Calabrese, Ellen Miller Coile, Will and Patti Collins, Virginia Fry, Doris Gilpin, Marilyn Kren, Leila Ruddick, Elizabeth Sosic, and Rosemary Smith who shared their stories of growing up during the Great Depression and living through World War II.

For help obtaining permissions to use images that added so much to the story, I would like to thank:

- David Abbott, Head of Brand Partnerships, TI Media;
- Marie Alm, daughter of WWII nurse, May Buelow Alm;
- Sandy Antelme, author of *Se Chausser Sous l'Occupation. 1940-1944,* for her help obtaining the shoe images from the Musée des Métiers de la Chaussure, Sèvremoine, France;
- David Bagwell, Brand Identity & Heritage Manager, Michelin North America;
- Tiffany Boodram, Assistant Manager, Condé Nast Licensing;
- Caroline Berton, Photo Syndication Manager, Condé Nast, Paris;
- Gillian Collins of gilliancollinsartist.com;
- John Grover, Deputy General Counsel, Hanesbrands;
- Franklin Habit of franklinhabit.com;

- Suzanne Isaacs, Community Manager, National Archives Catalog;
- Mary Palmer Linnemann, Digital Imaging Coordinator, Hargrett Rare Book and Manuscript Library, University of Georgia;
- Eirlys Penn of http://www.scrapiana.com;
- Kay Peterson, Rights and Reproductions Coordinator, National Museum of American History;
- Emmanuel Petrakis, Chairman of the Maritime Museum of Crete;
- Mary-Jo Miller, Assistant Curator, Nebraska State Historical Society;
- Scott Olsen, Permissions Department, King Features Syndicate;
- Pete Pitman, Deputy Curator and David Coxon, Director, Tangmere Military Aviation Museum;
- Lauren Steinke, SVP Brand Management, Iconix Brand Group;
- Shelley Tobin, Costume Curator, Killerton House © National Trust;
- Andrew Webb, Media Sales & Licensing Executive, Imperial War Museum;
- Ruth Woods of craftschooloz.com.

I am so thankful for the time and efforts of my peer editors: Dr. Susan B. Kaiser, Dr. Margaret Ordoñez, and Dr. Denise N. Rall. They graciously offered thoughtful constructive criticism and challenges that made an immeasurably improvement to my work.

Finally, thank you to my editors, Aimee Bates, Georgia Earl, and Debora Nicosia, at Intellect Books, Bristol, UK, who made this book possible.

Introduction

> All we wore were hand-me-downs and old clothes.
>
> Emma (born 1925, Auckland, New Zealand)[1]

Valerie Maier, a young seamstress born in 1922, was desperate for fabric to make herself a new dress in war-torn Germany during World War II. She lived in Fürstenfeldbruck, a town in Bavaria so small that it did not even have a clothing store. It would not have mattered anyway since as the war progressed, all stores were either empty or bombed out. It was impossible to find fabric, so Valerie often used unrationed or unexpected textiles to sew up dresses for herself and her sister Ingrid, seven years younger. Ingrid described a rather risky action Valerie took to find fabric: "In the last year, 1944–45, there was a store that sold material and among other things, they sold the German flags. My sister bought quite a few of the flags and cut out the insignia. She made dresses out of them." Desecrating the German flag was a criminal offense. Ingrid was afraid of the consequences of wearing a dress made from the German flag. "I remember once I was walking from the place that I worked at the time and I saw, a block away, there was a woman with a red dress. I guess at that time the color was not really worn. And my friend said, 'Oh, look at that! There is someone wearing a red dress!' And I knew it was my sister, but I did not say anything." Ingrid was afraid of the possible stigma attributed to her relationship to the woman in the problematic red dress.

Recently, another story about clothing made from a German flag appeared in the Canadian newspaper, *National Post*. Thom Cholowski, a World War II historian, bought a red skirt similar to the dress made for Ingrid on the auction site eBay. The online seller had purchased the skirt from a collector who bought it from the original wearer. Cholowski knew that the skirt was made by a German woman for her daughter from a Third Reich banner at the end of the war. He explained why the flag was used as dress material in the *National Post* article:

> The war ended in Europe May 8, 1945, but the struggle for survival for millions of people didn't stop there. [...] So you made do with what you had. And in this case, the Nazis had been defeated, this flag was useless, but fabric was still good.
>
> ("Searching for the Girl Who Wore This Dress" 2016)

The *Saskatoon StarPhoenix* videotaped Cholowski appealing to the public to help him find the now grown German girl. She was purported to live in Manitoba or Saskatchewan, Canada. Cholowski expressed his emotions about the symbolism of the skirt in the video:

> It tells a story that is not covered by the history books. You can read about all the major battles but it's the stories of the individuals. This is the story of displaced people. And especially the story of those on the losing side, [which] does not really get told. And what drew me to it, is to take a symbol of oppression, hatred and violence and to turn it into a thing of joy and hope is very compelling.
>
> (Charlton 2018)

Cholowski searched the internet for clues about the origin of the skirt. He discovered a postwar film showing life in Hamburg, Germany in which he was amazed to see a little girl wearing a skirt very similar to the one he owned. "It is virtually impossible to definitively confirm that this is indeed the same dress currently in my possession, however it is positive proof that Nazi flags were repurposed into clothing after WW2."[2]

Ingrid's red dress and the little girl's red skirt are examples of the stories that clothing can tell. As Cholowski said in the video, these stories are not in history books but are the personal narratives of the interplay of wartime and civilian life.

The past, the present, and sometimes even the future can be interpreted by analyzing the clothing of an era. Dominique Veillon, in *Fashion Under the Occupation* (2002), stated: "Fashion is an expression of every aspect of life; it is a way of existing and behaving, and is, in fact, an observation point from which to view the political, economic and cultural environment of an historical period" (vii). The silhouette, color, line, fabric, and construction of clothing holds clues about the owner and the time in which it was worn. Wartime clothing can reveal cultural norms and represent themes of politics, scientific discovery, gender identity, creativity, hope, art, and sometimes dishonesty.

Starting My Search

My interest in World War II, and ultimately the research that became this book, was inspired by the contents of a large cardboard box containing the photos my father had taken while serving in the 1270th Engineer Combat Battalion in Europe.[3] His souvenirs of five years in the military. He started the war as a bugler in the 161th Field Artillery Band and after three years was accepted in a flight training program. When the program was cancelled, Joe was reassigned as an intelligence officer in the 1270th and sailed off to England in October 1944.

I spent many hours sorting the photos in the box, trying to put them in chronological order following the battalion's itinerary that I was fortunate to receive from the U.S. National Archives and Records Administration. One photo of a group of civilians dressed in classic British sartorial garb (Figure 0.1) and another larger group outside a church, maybe a wedding photo (Figure 0.2), grabbed my attention. Joe was in the wedding photo, tall and handsome in his dress uniform. I was sure these photos told a story; one I wished I had asked my father before he died. Like most men of his generation, Joe rarely spoke about the five years he had spent in the military during the war. As children, we had seen the photos but did not know to ask more questions, and now it was too late.

Through careful searching, I found three photos of Joe with two of the people pictured in the smaller group. They looked like they were having fun, joking, and eating ice cream while it was snowing. My guess was that the photos were taken while he was stationed in Weston-super-Mare, Somerset, UK. I remember my mother telling me that he liked the people he met there.

In the wedding photo, Joe stands next to another soldier who has his arm around the waist of a pretty young woman dressed in a suit. She wears a large corsage pinned to her lapel. From her dress and their posture, I assumed she was

FIGURE 0.1: *Kath, Roger, Sophie, Mrs. and Mr. Eastlake after Christmas lunch*, Weston-super-Mare, UK, December 25, 1944. Courtesy Turner family.

FIGURE 0.2: *Robert (Bob) J. Miller and Peggy Pearce's wedding photo*, Holy Trinity Church, Weston-super-Mare, UK, March 5, 1945. Courtesy Turner family.

the bride. They are surrounded by a group of men, women, and children, dressed in winter coats, suits, and hats, standing outside a church.

Thanks to the internet, it was easy to contact the Weston-super-Mare historian and ask if they could possibly help me locate the people in the photo. Their answer was not hopeful; 65 years had passed and much had changed, but they would try. Holy Trinity Church on Atlantic Road, Weston-super-Mare, still standing, was easily identified as the location for the wedding photo. One half hour later, I received a second communication. Through luck or fate, the historian's husband had glanced at the computer screen and recognized his former riding instructor: Kath Eastlake. She is the woman on the left, standing by her brother and sister, all three still living in Weston-super-Mare in the same house where the photo was taken.

I wrote to Kath hoping she would remember my father, the young American soldier who had been stationed for six months in her village. I was thrilled to receive a letter back. The following is an excerpt:

Dear Nan,

What a wonderful surprise to see the notice in our local newspaper wishing to contact the family who invited your father Joe to Christmas lunch. This was with three or

> *four other USA servicemen who were stationed at the Cairo Hotel in town, about 5 miles from the countryside where our farmhouse lies. It was the Christmas before the big invasion of Europe and my mother came up with the idea of inviting four or five USA soldiers stationed in Weston-super-Mare for Christmas lunch. She did not quite know how to go about it, but eventually telephoned the commanding officer at the Cairo or his second in command. I can remember to this day, she said, much to the embarrassment of my sister and I, "Would four or five of your nice soldiers like to accept our invitation to Christmas lunch?" In reply, he said, "They are all nice, Ma'am."*
>
> *We made open house to any of the five men who came and I remember what a cold, dreadful winter it was. If they passed by the farmhouse at any time they often stepped in and warmed themselves by our enormous open fire which went all day long.*[4]

Kath Eastlake and I exchanged several letters, from which came an invitation to visit Weston-super-Mare. I started to plan my June 2011 research trip to Europe, which would include attending the 65th anniversary of D-Day in Normandy, several days in Paris, and a visit to Weston-super-Mare.

At that time I was working on my master's degree in textiles and clothing and had started developing a topic based on clothing use during World War II. Dominique Veillon's book *Fashion Under the Occupation* (2002), originally published in French as *La Mode Sous l'Occupation*, was one of the first of many books that I read. I contacted Mme. Veillon in Paris to see if she might meet with me to discuss my research. She generously agreed and kindly put up with my French, acquired when I lived in Paris from 1978 to 1981 working in the fashion industry. Mme. Veillon influenced my decision to focus my research on the struggles of average people, from a range of countries and economic status, dealing with clothing scarcity.

During the second part of the trip, in London, I happened upon a formal remembrance celebration for British veterans who had participated in D-Day, members of the now disbanded Normandy Veteran's Association (Color Plate 1). A rather sizable group of men in their 80s, dressed in military uniforms, chests ablaze with metals, were assembled at The Cenotaph, the UK's official national war memorial on Whitehall in London (Mavin 2018). Their wives waited on the sidelines. Before the procession started, several women told me their stories of hardships and accomplishments while making do during the war. This was the first of many opportunities I had to talk to people about their wartime experience.

In Weston-super-Mare, I stayed at the old stone farmhouse where my father had been invited for Christmas lunch in 1944. I got to know Kath, her sister Sophie, and sister-in-law Sarah, and recorded their comments about clothing rationing during World War II.

They had been very friendly with Joe while he was stationed in their town, but knew nothing about the wedding he had been in. Still eager to find the identity of the wedding couple, I made an appointment with the town registrar to see the marriage certificate. I was allowed a glimpse of the original signatures in the 1945 civil registry book. There was my father's familiar handwriting, confirming my hunch that he was the best man. The couple's names were Bob J. Miller and Peggy Pearce. I wondered what had become of them and if I could find them or any of the others in the wedding party.

Later that summer, back in California, I started to search for more women who had firsthand experience of clothing scarcity during World War II. It became apparent that the USA, due to its vast resources and late entry into the war, suffered fewer clothing shortages. Therefore, I needed to interview women from a wide variety of countries. The Spirit of 45 celebration, held August 13, 2011 in San Jose, CA, gave me the opportunity to connect with an organization that would provide many of my future interviews.[5] The World War II War Brides Association had a booth at the event manned by the daughter of an Australian war bride. I realized that Peggy Pearce, a war bride, might be a member of the national group. The war baby (the name for children of war brides) told me that I could post my search for Peggy Pearce on the organizations web site and she invited me to attend their monthly lunch meeting. I have attended many of their lunches over the past years and three annual reunions. I am indebted to the association for providing the opportunity to meet and interview many of the members who generously shared their stories of living through years of rationing, deprivation, and austerity during World War II.

Methodology

This multi-method research project is qualitative in nature and based in grounded theory, a social science methodology that uses inductive analysis to build upon gathering and analyzing data (Bowen 2006, 1–2). The information collected is from in-depth interviews, surveys, diaries, historical references, period newspapers, and magazines. Over 50 interviews of women, and a few men, enrich the story of World War II scarcity and deprivation. Some interviews lasted up to two hours and were formally taped and transcribed. Other material came from notes taken during lunch meetings and national reunions of the War Brides Association. Diaries, newspapers, magazines, film clips, government resources, and in-depth content analysis of historical documents filled in interviewees' memories of life more than 70 years ago. These primary and secondary resources contribute to the authenticity of *Clothing Goes to War*.

Primary Resources—Interviews

Continuing my research, I elicited my parents' American, Austrian, British, and Japanese friends to tell me of their wartime experiences. Subsequently, colleagues put me in contact with women from Germany, Italy, Japan, the Netherlands, and the UK. I attended a breakfast at the Davis, California chapter of the Veterans of Foreign Wars where I met a French war bride who agreed to be interviewed. A notice in the local newspaper about the debut of a documentary about life in a Japanese American internment camp provided the opportunity to interview the filmmaker.

The research revealed that women from a cross section of social classes and nationalities experienced similar hardships and deprivation during the war, proving that money or position rarely resolved scarcity. All were forced to find creative solutions when stores were empty. Therefore, the comparison of creative methods used to deal with austerity and clothing shortages became the focus of the research. The results of some of the interviews are documented below. Others are entwined in the following chapters. The interviewees were asked if they preferred to reveal their identity or remain anonymous and their wishes have been taken into account.

United Kingdom

Ellen Miller Coile was born in 1930 in Ilford, UK, a small town twelve miles east of London. She moved to the USA with her American military officer husband, whom she met during an international folk dance session in London, soon after the war. Ellen and her sister, along with their entire school, had been evacuated from London during the war but unfortunately were sent to Ipswich, a port town in Suffolk on the East Coast, which became very dangerous when bombers started flying over from Germany. Her parents tried their best to get the authorities to move the children from this hazardous location, but it was nine months before they were successful in relocating them to a safer situation in Wales.

Ellen grew up in poverty. She described her childhood and meager wardrobe, "We lived in a working-class neighborhood (blue-collar in America). We were poor but proud, honest, hard-working, and clean (a patch or darn was nothing to be ashamed of, but a hole meant you were lazy)" (Coile 2017, 10). She described her

Sunday clothing as "mufti," a slang term referring to civilian clothing, or "civvies," worn by someone who had dressed in a uniform for a long period of time. Ellen spent the majority of her time dressed in her school uniform but changed when she got home so it would not get dirty or worn. It had to last. She explained that a child in her poverty-level socioeconomic class usually owned a minimal wardrobe composed of hand-me-downs from older siblings.

Ellen reported that the uniform and heavy shoes that she wore every day, except Sunday, simplified the restrictions of a limited wardrobe. However, the choice of unrestricted dressing on Sunday presented a challenge. Shoes were too scarce and took too many ration tickets to have an additional pair that you wore only one day a week. The only solution, she reported with some chagrin, was to wear her nonuniform dress on Sunday accompanied with the same heavy shoes worn every day.

Ellen described the clothing formula of the working class in the UK:

1 article of clothing being worn
1 article of clothing in case of emergency
1 article of clothing in the laundry
3 articles of clothing of each type[6]

Many women of average means only owned three shirts, three dresses, and three skirts and many men only owned the clothing they had on and one other "better" or Sunday outfit. Others owned less. Elizabeth, a child in the UK during the war, revealed how limited her family wardrobe was in the answer to a survey question about rationing:

> All clothing was strictly rationed. My mother was an ingenious dressmaker. I remember shorts made from my father's worn-out trousers, and an itchy dressing-gown she made for my birthday out of rough grey stuff which was all she could find. Shoes were very difficult and my brown lace-ups became painfully tight as I grew. It was a disaster when my sister's shoes were stolen at school. I have the impression my mother wore the same check tweed skirt for the duration of the war.[7]

Kath Eastlake, during my visit to Weston-super-Mare, was the first to mention the issue of underwear shortages. She reported that they had to make their own underclothes and, with elastic unavailable, ties were sewn on to keep their underdrawers up.[8]

Margaret, also a child in the UK, was eight years old when the war broke out. She was evacuated to Canada and did not see her family again for five years. On her return, she had developed a liking for wearing trousers, a habit her mother could never get used to and never approved of. She told me that she felt that she has never had a home since being evacuated from her family at such a young age and for such a long period of time.[9]

France

Natasha, a Russian woman who was born in Yugoslavia but raised in Strasbourg in Alsace-Lorraine, France after her family migrated, lived in Paris during the war. She was set up on a date with a major in the United States Army soon after the war ended. For her husband-to-be, it was love at first sight he told me when he saw his bride-to-be dressed in a print spring dress and stylish red and white shoes. The shoes, impossible to obtain in Paris during the war years, had been sent by a friend living in the USA. For their wedding a few months later, Natasha wore a white wedding dress given to her by a friend of her mother (Figure 0.3). Looking at a photo of the dress made of embroidered net and lace, fashioned in

FIGURE 0.3: *Natasha's wedding in Paris*, December 8, 1947. Courtesy Natasha.

a style popular in the 1920s or before, it is clear that it was probably from an earlier era. Her sister wore the same dress when she married Natasha's husband's brother ten years later in the USA. When I asked what had happened to the dress in hopes that I could see it, the answer was that it had fallen apart after the two weddings. This was additional proof that it was probably already an old dress when Natasha wore it in 1947.

Austria

Adina, who lived in Linz, Austria, told me that before the war, ready-made clothing was for the poor.[10] Her well-to-do family owned a fine cutlery store and employed a tailor and a dressmaker to make their clothing. When the Germans invaded, fabric for new clothing became very scarce and means had to be found to create new resources. The solution for the well-to-do who had larger wardrobes was to take apart dresses or suits that were no longer in style and to have the tailor make something new. A new custom-fit garment would be created from the outdated dress or suit. Adina's family seamstress spent a lot of time in their home sewing new clothing. The seamstress, whose sister was Adina's family's cook, was a fussy eater. This became a problem since food, as well as fabric, was scarce and difficult to acquire. One day the cook made her sister an omelet using some of the family's eggs. Adina's mother considered this a theft and immediately fired the seamstress. Scarcity of both fabric and food were serious issues; taking someone else's food, even two eggs, was considered stealing.

Italy

Carla, who was interviewed by her son for my research, lived on the outskirts of Rome during the war and would often drive a horse cart to town to sell produce to earn a little extra money for the family.[11] She later became a seamstress and ran a custom dress-making business in the family apartment in Rome. The war years were very difficult, and the family faced a great deal of scarcity of food and necessities. She recounted an example of re-purposing clothing to extend its use. Carla did not have the advantage that Adina had in Austria of using outdated clothing to make new styles. All her family's clothing was old and worn out. Therefore, a coat worn for so many years that the fabric was starting to wear out, would be carefully taken apart at the seams and put together again with the interior face of the fabric to the exterior. This example illustrates the wartime value of fabric.

Scarcity justified spending a considerable amount of time and work to remake old worn-out clothing to prolong its service life.

Germany

I interviewed two German women with very dissimilar backgrounds, Ursula Mahlendorf, a member of Hitler Youth, and Marion Blumenthal, a concentration camp survivor. Both women wrote autobiographies about their war experience, and although theoretically from opposite ends of the social spectrum, their stories illustrated the extreme deprivation and suffering nearly everyone experienced.

Ursula Mahlendorf's account of growing up in Germany, *The Shame of Survival: Working Through a Nazi Childhood* (2009), afforded me several insights into the economic and psychological factors related to the struggle to find adequate dress during an era of extreme hardship and vacillating social status. Ursula's life in Germany, since the age of ten an active participant in Hitler Youth, imploded when the lower Silesia region where the family lived was returned to Poland after World War II. Ursula and her family were forced to flee the Russian military and relocate to a refugee camp near Bremen, Germany. Her Hitler Youth uniform, which had solved the issues of clothing shortage and had been a symbol of honor and hope for a better future, became a source of shame when Germany was defeated (21).

Marion Blumenthal Lazan's biography, *Four Perfect Pebbles: A Holocaust Story* (1996), recounts the horrible experience of her Jewish family who missed the opportunity to flee Germany when their booked passage on an ocean liner from Holland to the USA was delayed (52). When Germany invaded the Netherlands, the family was trapped. They were first interned at a refugee camp in the Netherlands and later deported to Bergen-Belsen.[12] Marion's story includes details of the extreme difficulty of finding clothing for survival against the brutal elements and inhumane conditions in the camps. Her apparel was composed of just the few articles she wore all the time. At night she slept in all her clothes for warmth. In the morning, "All she had to do was to put her arms through the sleeves of the tattered coat that she had used as an extra covering under the coarse, thin blanket the camp provided" (3).

United States

The USA experienced the least amount of clothing scarcity and rationing. Some women I interviewed were not even aware of any rationing besides gasoline for automobiles. Although the least affected, the information obtained from interviewing

American women in personal interviews reinforced several themes of the research and led to further evaluation. Eileen, an American woman who grew up in Glendale, CA, was the first to mention underwear shortages in the USA, similar to what Kath Eastlake had reported in the UK. Eileen told me that she had to make her own underwear and, since elastic was unavailable, sew fabric ties at the waist.[13] Elastic shortages were due to Japan's occupation of natural rubber producing countries in 1941. Thereafter, all civilian use of rubber in the USA was restricted.

Additional stories of creative solutions to rationing and shortages of textiles and clothing are included in the following chapters.

Chapter 1—Rationale for Rationing: The Demanding War

Rationing was an inevitable consequence of shortages and scarcity in many countries (Hancock and Gowing 1949, 157). The imperative to outfit the troops forced governments to control distribution of essential products, clothing, and fabric. Consequently, the majority of sewing factories were turned over to military production (Summers 2016, 38). Remaining goods and services were thereafter parceled out to civilians in the most diplomatically possible fashion.

Chapter 2—Textiles Go to War: Military Uniforms Prioritized

The role of textiles in World War II includes a complex assortment of issues encompassing global shortages, embargos, creativity, and chemistry. Widespread reliance on natural fibers, which required specific climates to cultivate, predisposed the scarcity of apparel textiles. Cutoff from their suppliers by both embargos and the threat of attack by enemy warships cruising the oceans, creative solutions to relieve scarcity became essential.

Chapter 3—Gender Defined by Clothing: Women in Slacks

In the years prior to World War II, gender and culture strictly defined the clothing people wore. Women rarely dressed in slacks or trousers. Their role in society required a feminine appearance signaled by wearing a skirt or dress. The necessity for all people to fight, on the home front as well as the war front, brought immense changes to the cultural restrictions placed on women's appearance. World War II was a decisive moment in the expansion of women's freedom to choose comfort over appearance.

Chapter 4—Home Front Handicrafts: Creativity Inspired by Restrictions

"Making-do," marketed as an act of patriotism, required sewing, knitting, repurposing, and mending to save precious textile resources. Government propaganda and women's magazines urged homemakers to do their part to make the family wardrobe last for the duration, freeing workers to build equipment needed by the military (Summers 2020, 155). Nothing was thrown away as every treasured scrap of fabric was used to make clothing, quilts, patches, and eventually rags (Tarbell 1938, 155).

Chapter 5—Feed Sack Fashion: Nothing Was Wasted

Fabric scarcity and poverty forced women to look for other resources to make their family's clothing. Homemakers often used the cotton bags that animal feed, flour, sugar, rice, cornmeal, and a myriad of other products were shipped in to make clothing. The common cloth bag had actually replaced wooden barrels for shipping when wood became too expensive. Initially fabric bags were printed with product information but, as manufacturers realized the popularity of their sacks for other purposes, the printed labels were replaced with pretty colors and feminine prints as a marketing ploy.

Chapter 6—Wartime Weddings: Falling in Love During Wartime

Wartime wedding planning presented special problems for brides-to-be as rationing and scarcity increased the difficulty of finding clothing for the wedding party. Women improvised using curtains, sheets, mosquito netting, or any available textile to replace traditional silks and satins. The war intensified the strain of wedding planning as the majority of grooms in the service were beholden to their commanding officer and to the timetable of battle. Orders to ship out reduced preparation time to the minimum.

Chapter 7—Costumes Go to War: Clothing in Hollywood and British Film

Rationing and clothing scarcity became a topic in some wartime films. Women depicted sewing, mending, borrowing, and repurposing, as well as dialogue centered around the difficulty of obtaining coupons added authenticity to wartime scenarios. Characters in these films faced hardships similar to the audience and often served as inspirational models of survival, as well as figures of propaganda encouraging civilians to work together supporting the war effort.

Chapter 8—Clothing as Commerce: Hoarding, Bartering, and the Black Market

Alternative forms of commerce developed as a means to avoid government-enforced regulations and imposed scarcity. Hoarding, a means of stocking up before shortages depleted store's shelves, increased scarcity. Bartering, a common practice used between friends or acquaintances, allowed people to obtain necessary goods without using limited money or coupons, or when both became worthless. Black markets, on the other hand, although sometimes the only means of obtaining necessities, were illegal methods used to take advantage of shortages and make a profit for the dealer.

Chapter 9—Make-Do and Mend: Once Forgotten, Now Reborn

As generations followed in the 75 years since World War II, habits based on thrift learned during the 1930s and 1940s have been replaced with the mentality of a throwaway society. The practices of conservation, sewing, mending, repurposing, and an abhorrence of waste, second nature for our parents or grandparents, seem overly time-consuming and obsolete for contemporary busy lifestyles.

Fortunately, the 21st century has seen a renewed interest in do-it-yourself projects, crafting, and repairing that have many correlations to the creative practices inspired by the hardship and austerity of World War II. Much of the current revival is motivated by the goal of limiting fast fashion's negative effects on the environment. Stories of survival during wartime resonate in the 21st century for people looking for a way to reduce waste and live a more sustainable existence.

Chapter 10—Epilogue: Global Pandemic of 2020 Forces Revivals of 1940s Handicrafts

During the final months of writing this book, the world experienced a global pandemic caused by a novel (new) coronavirus. Shortages similar to those experienced during World War II forced people all over the world to turn to some of the creative practices used during the 1940s. Cloth masks became mandatory wear to control the spread of the virus. After many stores were ordered to close and fabric and elastic supplies were deleted, people turned to creative repurposing of old clothing, scarves, and bedsheets among other items to make masks.

Conclusion

A common thread runs through the experiences of people dealing with shortages and rationing during wartime. Creativity was the common skill needed to provide basic necessities for the family when all production was prioritized for the military. It did not seem to matter what side the person was on, Allied or Axis. Shortages and austerity were universal and motivated creative solutions. Therefore, the experiences of women dealing with scarcity are organized by commonality, not by country of origin.

NOTES

1. Emma (born 1925, Auckland, New Zealand) in discussion with the author at the Northern California Bay Area War Brides lunch, Campbell, CA, August 11, 2014.
2. Thom Cholowski in e-mail communication with the author, November 27, 2019.
3. For further information about the battalion, visit website: https://www.1270thengineer-combatbattalion.com.
4. Excerpt from the letter received by the author from the British family who befriended her father during World War II (Eastlake is a fictitious name), July 2010.
5. For more information about the Keep the Spirit of 1945 Alive! event, visit: http://www.spiritof45.org/home0.aspx.
6. Ellen Miller Coile (born 1930, Sunderland, County Durham; resident 1932–51 in Ilford, Essex, UK) in discussion with the author, Monterey, CA, May 2012.
7. Elizabeth (born prewar, UK), answer to the questionnaire circulated in the UK, 2017.
8. Kath (born 1927, Weston-super-Mare, UK) in discussion with the author, Weston-super-Mare, UK, June 11, 2010.
9. Margaret (born 1930, UK) in discussion with the author, 2011.
10. Adina (born 1929, Linz, Austria) in discussion with the author, Carmel, CA, 2016.
11. Carla (born 1929, Rome, Italy) in a recorded conversation with her son, 2014.
12. Westerbork is a Nazi transit camp for refugees in the northeast Netherlands. Bergen-Belsen is the camp where Ann Frank died of typhus, a disease spread by lice that was epidemic there.
13. Eileen (born 1927, USA) in discussion with the author, Davis, CA, June 2010.

1

Rationale for Rationing: The Demanding War

> Into this motley scene of trade in which merchants struggled with each other to please consumers rich and poor, young and old, chic and frumpish, with subtle mixtures of price, quality and style, came the war, the greatest consumer of all, like a giant tapeworm, exacting, changeable, insatiate.
>
> Henry Ewart Wadsworth, *Utility Cloth and Clothing Scheme*

Economic recovery after the Great Depression was just beginning and unemployment was still high in 1939 when Germany invaded Poland and set World War II into motion. The war was a massive consumer, needing,

> Labour, factory space, internal transport, domestically produced materials and fuel—indeed, resources of all kinds—must be diverted to the war effort, leaving only enough on civilian work to produce the "essential minimum" needed to maintain the population's strength and morale.
>
> (Reddaway 1951, 182)

The threat of attack on global shipping, embargoes on trade, and invading enemy forces pilfering supplies from occupied countries resulted in shortages that intensified civilian deprivation and suffering (Brinkley and Haskew 2004, 243). Rationing, defined as the "distribution of resources on the basis of equity or need or some criterion of priority," was inevitable in many countries as production of supplies for the military was prioritized, creating a scarcity of goods to fulfill the needs of private citizens (Lloyd 1942, 49). Sir William Beveridge, the British economist, addressed the issue of prioritizing the allocation of resources to the military in *The Times* saying, "It would be universally admitted that, in any danger of there not being enough for all, the fighting forces should have priority" (1939, 9).

The governments of Australia, Canada, France, Germany, Japan, New Zealand, Russia, the UK, and the USA implemented programs to ration consumer goods. Countries occupied by Germany and Japan were also subjected to rationing, often more intense and austere as the invaders pilfered supplies to send back home. Although rationing was "meant to be a token of mutual fairness and equality of sacrifice in wartime" (Lauterbach 1944, 209), it was sometimes just an "equality of misery" (Sladen 1995, 18).

Social class, occupation, and geographic location all played a part in the degree of hardship that rationing and restrictions inflicted on individuals. Upper class families, who already had large wardrobes, were better equipped to endure scarcity because they did not have to wear the same garment every day during the indeterminable length of the war (Summers 2016, 80). The lower classes who generally owned very limited wardrobes, especially after the economically challenging years of the 1930s, suffered the most (McDowell 1997, 39). Families with growing children experienced hardship as the young outgrew their clothing. Hand-me-downs, repurposing, and mending became universal solutions when new clothing was too expensive or not available due to war restrictions. After years of wearing the same patched and mended clothing daily, wardrobes became threadbare.

Rationing was a complicated issue, considered one's patriotic duty in some countries and the harsh order of the conquering enemy in others. The media in both the UK and the USA presented rationing as everyone's patriotic duty (Levine and Levine 2011, 437). Wearing sweaters with mended holes and clothing with patches were badges of honor for civilians who considered their fight on the home front as important as the soldiers on the war front (Summers 2016, 77). Julie Summers reported that "in war, the term 'battle-stained' [was] an honorable one" (2020, 161) and "to be badly dressed was to be considered patriotic" (2016, 77).

Implications of Rationing

Rationing was based on the principle that during times of austerity, government intervention and control ensured that each person would get their fair share of limited consumer products (Hancock and Gowing 1949, 157). By regulating production, pricing, wages, distribution, and even manpower, governments controlled consumers' ability to purchase food, fuel, and clothing. Efficiency and production increased as a result of regulations but also restricted workers' freedom (McDowell 1997, 178). For example, a "worker could be frozen in his job, transferred, or placed in a military training plan" depending on the government's needs (178).

FIGURE 1.1: Herbert Roese, *Rationing means a fair share for all of us*, 1943. Propaganda Poster. Alamy Images (2B9HMBX).

Food and fuel were always the first to be rationed. Clothing and shoe rationing followed as the demands of the military resulted in widespread scarcity (Mendes and Haye 1999; see also Reynolds 1999, 327). The military needed wool and cotton for uniforms, silk and nylon for parachutes, and leather and rubber for boots and shoes. The military's needs always took priority over civilians. Shops still selling pre-war stocks were soon depleted, leaving little to buy, even for those with money (Maines 1985, 39). As apparel workers and facilities previously employed in civilian production moved to war work, the scarcity of textile goods intensified (Summers 2016, 38–39).

The complexity and variety of apparel made clothing rationing much more difficult than simply rationing food items like butter or sugar which provided more leeway. With food items, consumers could easily take what they could get. If meat was not available, they could eat bread or potatoes. Clothing is not interchangeable in the same way. "A man who badly wants socks will not take kindly to a shirt or an overcoat as a substitute" (Lloyd 1942, 51). Walt Whitman Rostow, an American economist, weighed in: "Clothing is heterogeneous; it varies in quality; the demand for it varies with age, occupation, locale, and season; it is manufactured by numerous firms; and it is semi-durable. From these characteristics stem the major difficulties in any system of clothing rationing" (1942, 492).

Therefore, clothing rationing required a different system. Unlike food rationing, which offered consumers an equal share, the clothing system extended an equal opportunity to buy any commodity (Lloyd 1942, 49). Ration cards that provided a varied number of points for each category of clothing were issued in many countries (49). These cards worked as a form of alternative currency that limited consumers' ability to purchase more than their fair share. Even if they had the money to buy, they also needed to give the merchant the appropriate number of point coupons. Governments used the point system to control demand by regulating the amount of points required to purchase. For example, a higher point value could be offered for scarce or highly demanded products. If a particular fiber was scarcer than another, a high price could be placed on clothing made in that fiber (51). If an item was in demand, raw goods could be shifted to produce that item. For example, if the demand for socks increased, cotton or wool yarns could be shifted from a less needed item to sock production (51).

Problems existed in the rationing system because some people had more money than others and could therefore use their point allotment to buy superior quality clothing, yielding a higher profit for the manufacturer (Rostow 1942, 498). The danger was that if all manufacturers shifted production to high price clothing to increase their profits, fewer resources would be available for the less well-off. Rostow explained, "This is, however, a general characteristic of any system that permits unequal money incomes to express themselves in the market for consumption goods and, short of income rationing on an egalitarian basis, or total rationing of consumers' goods, it will tend to persist" (498).

Clothing rationing was not a perfect system. Shortages were common, leading to long lines at stores. A major part of a housewife's day during World War II was waiting in line for a chance to use her coupons to buy scarce necessities (Fussell 1989, 201). In many countries, at the end of the war when scarcity was extreme, neither money nor coupons could buy anything.

An array of negative opportunities, including hoarding, profiteering, price gouging, inflation, and discrimination between the haves and the have-nots resulted due to rationing. Even though the point system attempted to control or prevent these semi-legal activities, many civilians turned to alternative forms of commerce to acquire necessities no longer available. Nearly every person interviewed agreed that they had some experience with the black market. (For discussion of the black market, see Chapter 8).

Germany's Attempts at Rationing Fall Short

Lydia, a young woman of German/Chinese heritage who lived in Germany, spoke about hardship as the war broke out in Europe: "All the leather goods went to the army. All the good things went to the soldiers. To outfit them." Even after the war, shortages and deprivation of clothing continued for a while as Germany struggled to recover. Lydia recounted her feeling of shame when she realized that her grandmother had made her a dress from surplus military sheets:

> All clothing fabrics were rationed, people used towels, blankets to make coats or suits. My Oma had dirndls made out of bed sheets acquired at a swap meet for Sonja and me. They were linen, blue and white checkered, a good Bavarian color. One time, as my sister and I rode the streetcar, an ex-German soldier said to us, "We soldiers slept in these clothes." The sheets came from military surplus? That did it, no matter how tough the times, Oma could not get us to wear these dresses again.[1]

In spite of shortages caused by the military's needs, Germany was initially reluctant to introduce rationing because it had resulted in unrest during World War I. The government was hesitant to repeat their previous mistakes (Woolston 1941, 106). Hitler thought that the war would be quickly over and would have a negligible impact on the nation's economy (Milward 1965, 29). He even stated that he hated to restrict women's need to be beautiful and therefore did not want to impede cosmetics sales (Charman 1989, 135).

In 1939, in response to the German invasion of Poland, Great Britain and France imposed a blockade in the English Channel. The blockade closed the North Sea to all trade with Germany, thus cutting off essential shipments of war supplies (Doughty and Raugh 1991, 23). The formerly lucrative German textile industry, dependent on imported fabric, was now cut off from supplies of imported raw goods. Civilian clothing and shoe production declined severely. "In some regions all textile production was closed down and the floor space converted to other purposes" (Milward 1965, 108).

Despite Hitler's efforts to maintain an image of prosperity, the delusion of a quick victory did not last; even though civilian production maintained or even increased levels in some industries until 1941 (28). In November 1939, as textile shortages and scarcity intensified, clothing rationing cards were issued (Charman 1989, 49). Each person received 100 points to purchase apparel for one year

(Woolston 1941, 106). As scarcity increased during the following years, the allotment of points was reduced (Guenther 2004, 223).

The winter of 1941–42, as well as several following winters, were reported to be the coldest in Europe during the 20th century (Lejenäs 1989, 1). German soldiers, poorly equipped due to limited clothing, fuel, and food, suffered from the severe cold. Westbrook Pegler (1942), a popular US journalist, reported that Hitler "stripped most of the people of Europe to clothe his armies and civilians, [and] is now forced to strip his own people on the home front to remedy his blunder and with no prospect that he will be able to clothe these millions for next winter or the next" (B7). The article stated that Joseph Goebbels, Hitler's propaganda minister, ordered civilians to turn over "all overcoats, all shoes with warm linings, all heavy underwear and furs" to be sent to the Germans fighting in Russia (B7). On December 27, 1941, Hitler ordered the Sturmabteilung or Storm Detachment, known as the Brown Shirts, to enforce the collection of civilian clothing (Shirer 1960, 42). The Brown Shirts started a house-to-house collection of all warm clothing. Even "woolen bathing trunks for conversion into helmets for the troops" were demanded (Pegler 1942, B7). Try as they might, it was impossible for civilians to hide any remaining clothing because the rationing system kept records of who had purchased a winter coat, shoes, or long underwear. The Brown Shirts could come to reclaim them. Pegler surmised that "this is bound to suggest that Germany is beginning to run out of time, because a whole continent cannot go on indefinitely without winter clothing, and there is no apparent source of a new supply" (B7). The League of Nations report on rationing, published in 1942, called Hitler's efforts "negative rationing inasmuch as the population was obliged to give up heavy woolens, ski boots, blankets and furs already in their possession" (66). The report estimated, "32,000,000 pieces of woolen clothing and 533,000 fur coats were collected" (66). The consequence of any German citizen's attempt to resist was clearly stated, "Anyone who conceals or neglects to give up the requisitioned clothing and blankets will be subject to the usual penalties for sabotage and neighbor will spy on neighbor to enlarge the yield" (Pegler 1942, B7).

Finally, the Third Reich, desperate to relieve suffering, turned to raiding the countries it had conquered. Occupied nations, including Belgium, Denmark, France, Greece, Luxembourg, the Netherlands, Norway, Poland, and Yugoslavia, suffered intense rationing that was calculated to siphon off raw materials, products, and manpower to support Germany (Milward 1965, 30 and Charman 1989, 53). Citizens of invaded countries were forced to turn over all their warm clothing and blankets. Thereafter, only limited and heavily restricted supplies remained in stores. Unfortunately for Hitler, the occupants of the invaded countries were already severely impoverished and his tactic of raiding clothing only worked for so long.

It is difficult for current generations living in industrialized nations in the northern hemisphere, used to living with central heating, vehicles with heated seats and super insulated high-tech clothing, to understand the importance of warm clothing during the war. Grace Hodgson, an American woman recalling winters in the American Midwest during the 1930s Great Depression, wrote a poem called "Cold," that captures the essence of experiencing extreme winters.

"Cold"

You don't know cold,
Until you sink to your hips in fresh snow with each step, carrying a rifle.
Until you have followed your brother who has been following a pheasant for hours.
Until you watch the sinking sun and feel your sinking heart.
Until you trudge home in the fading light, empty handed and hungry.
Then you know cold.

You don't know cold,
Until all the beds are moved into the dining room near the wood burning stove.
Until your siblings are playing on the beds because the floor is too cold.
Until your mother goes to the kitchen in a wool coat, a knit cap and overshoes to make a milk soup for her family.
Then you know cold.

—Grace Hodgson (2016)

German clothing stores selling the last limited remains of pre-war stock struggled to survive the war. Allied bombings dealt a final blow, destroying any remaining retail outlets and ending any prospect of buying civilian goods (Guenther 2004, 260). Remscheid, a town in North Rhine-Westphalia, hit especially hard in a British bombing raid on July 31, 1943, lost 90% of their textile, hardware, and stationery stores (Ikle 1958, 152). Civilians bombed out of their homes, even with clothing ration coupons and money in their hand, had no means of replenishing their meager wardrobes (Guenther 2004, 226).

Hitler's war did not prove to be quick or easy, as originally predicted (Overy 1994, 311). The attempts to ration clothing to provide fair shares became a farce. There was no merchandise to buy, with or without ration tickets (Guenther 2004, 272). By the end of the war, when all resources had been depleted, clothing was so scarce that ration cards were suspended. Thereafter, new clothes could only be purchased by applying for a special permit and proving dire need (Charman 1989, 144).

Germany's attempt to maintain civilian morale and a sense of prosperity by delaying the onset of rationing resulted in both military and civilians suffering from the lack of food, clothing, and other basic commodities (Maines 1985, 40). Irene Guenther in her book *Nazi Chic* concluded that "once shortages reached crisis proportions and 'plenty' was only accessible to the well-connected few," the illusion of prosperity proved to be imaginary (2004, 19). Hitler's efforts to maintain a sense of prosperity in hopes of maintaining his popularity ultimately resulted in his demise. Germany had waited too long to implement rationing and the program was considered a failure.

United Kingdom

In the 1930s, Great Britain anticipated that war with Germany was again on the horizon. During World War I, 1914–18, when rationing was not enacted, civilians had suffered from shortages and scarcity. Therefore, even though various attempts were made to avoid rationing based on the previous negative experience, it was determined that government control of consumer products, including clothing and shoes, was inevitable (Hancock and Gowing 1949, 330). The UK declared war against Germany on September 3, 1939. Soon after, in January 1940, petrol and food rationing was initiated (Brinkley and Haskew 2004, 386).

The UK had initially tried to deal with shortages by asking civilians to voluntarily curtail buying new clothes but that attempt failed. The advent of rationing was kept secret until the day it was announced to avoid panic buying which would benefit the wealthy (Summers 2020, 160). When established, the government appealed to civilians' sense of patriotism by encouraging the public to view clothing rationing as their contribution to the war effort. Sacrifice and austerity became the central message of propaganda featured in posters, advertising, and newsreels. Any time a civilian could do without, they were freeing up production space and resources to provide for soldiers fighting the war.

Lynn, who was born in Southampton, UK in 1926, remembered several methods used to deal with hardship and shortages. She reported that when her shoes were worn through, she stuck an empty cigarette pack under her foot to cover the holes in the sole. To deal with the trauma of having her home bombed, she added, "When the bomb dropped on our house, my father said I could smoke a cigarette."[2]

Women's magazines helped deliver the message of patriotism and sacrifice in both their editorial content and advertising. Government ministers had realized that the best way "to influence [women's] thinking on food rationing, clothes, savings,

FIGURE 1.2: *So it's up to us chaps*, October 1942. Advertisement. Bairns-wear knitting wools. *Women and Home*, 6. St Peter's House Library, University of Brighton, UK.

spending, health, evacuation, education, hairstyles, stockings, entertainment—in fact anything and everything to do with a functioning society with a strong female workforce" was "to appeal to [them] through magazines that they trusted" (Summers 2020, 137). An especially touching ad for Bairns-wear Knitting Wools, featured a young boy (Figure 1.2). He declares, "So it's up to us chaps ... I heard Mummy saying how difficult it is to get Bairns-wear for knitting our woollies, so we'll have to be very careful—they've got to last a long time" ("So It Is up to Us Chaps" 1942, 6).

Christopher Sladen (1995), formerly a civil servant who lived through the war and had experienced clothing rationing, reported in his book *The Conscription of Fashion* that the majority of civilians accepted the reality of wartime austerity and "were prepared to face sacrifices of all kinds provided they thought the Government was making real efforts and the burden of restriction and shortages was seen to be fairly borne" (18, see also Barnett 1996, 171).

The Board of Trade (BoT), the government department concerned with commerce and industry, was selected to regulate civilian apparel distribution (Hancock and Gowing 1949, 51). The board devised two criteria to determine if a product needed to be rationed. There had to be either a shortage or a need to "release manpower, raw materials, and equipment for use in other industries" (Phillips 1945, 9). Clothing and textiles fulfilled both criteria since fabric, thread, needles, and sewing machines were in short supply and textile workers and factories needed to be shifted to war work. Clothing and shoe rationing, determined by the board to be "a consideration no less important than precautions against inflation and insistence upon efficiency in the processes of production and distribution," was inaugurated in June 1941 (Hancock and Gowing 1949, 50).

A point-based rationing system was instituted in which each article was given a value, regardless of the price. In this system, "the most costly gown from an exclusive West End salon calls for the same number of coupons as the cheapest frock from the most humble East End shop" ("Britain Orders" 1941, 5). Although their system was based on Germany's failed rationing technique, the UK pledged that all coupons would be honored. There would be no empty shelves as in Germany. This promise was kept and "there had never been serious 'coupon clumping,'" or consumers stuck with unusable coupons due to shortages (Hargreaves and Gowing 1952, 477).

On January 14, 1940, the *New York Times* reported, "With the army's size growing rapidly at each new conscription call there is such a heavy demand for uniforms and other garments that cloth manufacturers must meet government orders before attending to civilian demands" (MacDonald, E5). All fields of manufacturing, including civilian clothing, textile, and shoe factories, were mandated to produce for the military (Copeland 1945, 3). Some shops worked on both military and civilian goods but their time was precious and war work always took precedence. Civilian industries, deemed non-essential, were either shifted to military work or shut down, releasing their workers to take on wartime jobs.

In spite of government efforts to provide fair shares for all, initial attempts to conserve resources proved to have little success (Sladen 1995, 18). Even though the Price of Goods Act, initiated on November 16, 1939, prohibited raising prices above their August 21, 1936 level, manufactures "quickly switched production to lines plainly *not* subject to price control" (18). The Price of Goods Act carried no authority to control clothing consumption and as resources became limited, stores sold them at any price the market could bear. Prices of non-food consumer goods rose 75% above their pre-war level by May 1941 and affordable clothing was scarce (Earley and Lacy 1942, 171). With or without a ration ticket, clothing was hard to come by. Ultimately, a new solution was needed (Hancock and Gowing 1949, 336).

FIGURE 1.3: *Label for Utility System clothing.* The two letter C's were nicknamed "the double cheeses."

Utility System

Finally, the British government determined that the best way to deal with clothing scarcity was to take over manufacturing and produce specially designed garments meeting the requirements of rationing. To achieve this goal, the BoT devised the Utility Clothing Scheme in February 1942, created in hopes of making the distribution of limited clothing resources more democratic (Summers 2020, 186). To achieve this goal, the range of products was reduced to focus on a smaller and more practical assortment by limiting "the amount of material and labour used in the manufacture of civilian clothing" (186). Austerity regulations were enacted to conserve precious fabric by simplifying the design and reducing cost (Summers 2016, 95).

The Utility silhouette was slim and devoid of details and unnecessary trimmings. The Board of Trade standardized the size, weight, and weave of fabric, restricting yardage allowance to only 2¾ yards for a coat and 2 yards for a dress (Walford 2008, 49). Each garment then had to be clearly labeled with the Utility mark (Figure 1.3) (Hancock and Gowing 1949, 336–37). Many style features on men's and women's garments were prohibited including "the number of pleats, seams, buttons and buttonholes was limited and maximum widths fixed for sleeves, belts, hems and collars. Decorative additions such as embroidery, fur or leather on outerwear and ornamental stitching on underwear, were prohibited" (Sladen 1995, 22). The *New York Times* reported on March 4, 1942, "For women there will be shorter skirts, fewer styles and less choice of colors. Men will find their trousers without cuffs and their sleeves minus buttons, while double-breasted coats are destined to go" (Anderson, 11). Doreen, born 1931 in Ilford, a large town in East London, reported, "Hems of skirts etc. were no longer than 19 inches or just above the knee."[3]

The system was not immediately successful even though it was "cheaper and often of better quality than non-utility garments" (Summers 2020, 186). A brilliant marketing tactic was employed to improve the reception of Utility; the BoT

FIGURE 1.4: *A model poses on a Bloomsbury rooftop to show off her two-tone Atrima dress, costing 7 coupons*, 1943. Ministry of Information Second World War Official Collection. © IWM (D14837).

commissioned ten British fashion designers to create exclusive Utility collections. This group, called the Incorporated Society of London Fashion Designers, included Hardy Amies (Figure 1.5), Norman Hartnell, Peter Russell, The House of Worth, Bianca Mosca at Jacqmar, Angele Delanghe, Digby Morton, Victor Stiebel, Edward Molyneux, Charles Creed at Fortnum & Mason, and Michael Sherard (Sladen 1995, 41). These were some of the most well-known designers of the day in the UK. Styles were developed for both the domestic and the export markets, although revenue from exported garments supported the war effort and did not have to conform to restrictions. Women's magazines supported the effort by "telling readers that the woman on the street could now wear a dress designed by the couturiers for the wealthy but for a fraction of the cost" (Figure 1.4) (Summers 2020, 188).

The Utility System, in both political and economic terms, was a success (Maines 1985, 42). The method was also applied to "furniture, pottery, hollow ware,

FIGURE 1.5: *Incorporated Society of London Fashion Designers: A model wears a brown and beige all-wool-checked suit by fashion designer Hardy Amies.* London, UK, 1945. Suit designed by Hardy Amies (British, 1909–2003). Ministry of Information Second World War Official Collection. © IWM (D23782).

umbrellas, pencils, cutlery, suitcases and many other civilian articles" ("Britain Expanding Control of Goods" 1942, F2).

In 1944, Audrey Withers, editor of *British Vogue,* writing for the American version of *Vogue,* praised the rationing effort and coupon system. She claimed that both the Utility System and rationing improved style by simplifying it. She stated that austerity had served a valuable purpose:

> They save us from the plague of fussy detail which was so often used to take the eye from poor material, poor cut, poor workmanship. In this sense, austerity has done by law what *Vogue* has always advocated: stripped clothes of inessentials; made women conscious of dress fundamentals.
>
> ("Fashion: Fashion in England," October 1, 1944, 196)

British Vogue had attempted to train women before the war to "plan your wardrobe. Don't go in for thoughtless, spur-of-the moment shopping. Make each new purchase dovetail with the rest. The smaller your wardrobe, the more must each item be versatile, interchangeable and so on" (196). Withers called clothing coupons "the other great educator in dress sense" (196). Audrey praised the system for reinforcing *Vogue*'s message of "quality rather than quantity" and leaving "hats and accessory odds and ends unrationed as a loophole to let in light-heatedness in the way we have always advocated" (Summers 2020, 161).

Post-War Rationing

Civilians looked forward to relief from scarcity after the war. However, their suffering continued as rationing was extended for many years. Respite finally came on February 1, 1949, when Harold Wilson, President of the Board of Trade, announced that "the biggest relaxation [of rationing] since clothing rationing began in Britain nearly eight years ago will enable a man or woman to buy a new suit or dress from tomorrow on without coupons" ("Britain Relaxes Rationing" 1949, 10). Wilson reported that better production methods for wool had improved efficiency. However, cotton, still in short supply, resulted in men's shirts remaining on the ration system (10).

France

Attempting to relieve the strain on scarce raw materials, supplies, and new clothing, France initiated rationing six months after declaring war with Germany on March 1, 1940 (Hargrove 1940, 2). British foreign correspondent and soldier, Charles Hargrove (1940), who lived in France and whose native tongue was French, described the inception of restrictions by stating, "France definitely is entering a new economic phase—a regime of drastic restrictions on consumptions" (2).

The situation in France worsened quickly after Germany invaded on May 10, 1940. The French army was no match to the Germans and they were quickly defeated (Gluckstein 2012, 85; see also Shlaim 1974, 33). On June 22, 1940, France signed the Armistice which conceded northern and western France to German occupation (Christofferson and Christofferson 2006, 35-36).

A condition of the Armistice was that the majority of French production had to be shipped to Germany to support both civilians and the war effort (Veillon 2002, 39–40). Suffering from shortages of fuel, food, and clothing, Germany took advantage of the occupation of France to provide a source of desperately needed supplies as in World War I, when Germany had "requisitioned all the cloth, cotton, linen and silk" (Bass-Krueger 2019b, 271). Again during World War II, Germany imposed strict rationing which allowed barely enough to support life. "The burden was so heavy that French people were literally turned into slaves of the Third Reich, required to work for it, either directly or indirectly, for little or no recompense and forced to consume less and less each year due to its claims on French resources" (Christofferson and Christofferson 2006, 35). To further intensify clothing scarcity, Maréchal Pétain, the head of France's Vichy government, signed an order on September 1, 1940 that "limited the quantities of textiles manufactured to 30% of sales in 1938" (Veillon 2002, 40).

Rationing in France and rationing in the UK, "though the same in principle, differed profoundly in application. One was imposed by the enemy, the other had the consent of the people" (Baudin 1945, 326). In France where the fight had already been lost, the foreign invaders imposed rationing as an insult to civilians already living with barely enough to survive.

Lucie Aubrac, a member of the French Resistance, expressed the conflict and grief of the citizens of France, so proud of their country and anguished by defeat.

> Dans notre France si riche, il n'y a presque plus rien à manger. On nous donne des cartes de rationnement pour la nourriture, le charbon, les vêtements, les chaussures. On a souvent faim!
>
> (Aubrac 2000, 12)

> In our France so rich, there is almost nothing to eat. They give us ration cards for food, charcoal, clothing, shoes. We are often hungry.
>
> (translation author's own)

Germany claimed that rationing was necessary because of material and manpower shortages. However, the manpower shortage in France was not due to military enlistment but to the one million French soldiers sent off to Germany as prisoners of war or to work in factories (Christofferson and Christofferson 2006, 35). The deportation of Jewish apparel workers to German concentration camps devastated the French garment industry (Veillon 2002, 39; see also Mitchell 2008, 22). In spite of the deportation, the apparel industry still employed thousands in France and struggled to survive to provide the workers with livelihood.

System D

The clothing rationing system in France was called System D, the "D" stood for "débrouille," from the French verb "débrouillard," which means being resourceful, to manage, or get by (Le Maguet 2000, 11). First limited to shoes because of the shortage of leather, thread, and tanning material, the restrictions spawned the creation of shoes made of unrationed materials, including wooden soled clogs, plaited straw, cast magnesium, glass, lucite, cork, and old tires (Antelme 2016, 27–29).

Jeanne, born 1927 in Tours, France, remembered, "We wore shoes with platform soles made of wood. We called them 'Hollywood soles.' The top nailed to those soles were often canvas, fabric, seldom leather unless false leather" (Color Plates 2, 3, 4).[4]

Elizabeth Hoyt (1942), an American woman who lived outside of Paris during the war, described the footwear situation in France in a letter to her sister, published in the American edition of *Vogue*: "The only shoes readily obtainable have wooden soles, with little horseshoes of fiber nailed to the soles to deaden the clatter. The more expensive designs have hinges in the soles, which makes walking somewhat more comfortable, although with so much walking to be done and with the chilblains that everyone develops as soon as winter approaches, all walking is an ordeal" (65).

Adelaide, living in the Netherlands, worn similar wooden shoes. "I remember I had wooden soles they were made in sections so they moved. I even had dancing shoes made like that."[5]

Lydia in Germany also wore shoes with wooden soles.

> My sister and I were thrilled when we got our first wooden shoes. They were quite different from the well-known Dutch variety. Ours consisted with the upper part made of heavy, canvas type cloth, simulating leather and fashioned in the traditional Haferlschuh, [a Bavarian work shoe]. The lower part, had wooden slats, enabling the wearer to freely move the foot and Sonja and I had the biggest fun clattering around in our shoes; some styles had a thin rubber coating on the wood to cut down on the clattering noise or prevent slipping. In our excitement, we wrote to our father in France about it. The letter was returned to us, censured in red, because we indicated the war situation in Germany. Soon, no letter got to my father, nor did we receive any mail from him.

Rumors of impending clothing rationing circulated following shoe rationing ("Clothing Sale Halts" 1941, 8). Many women panicked and rushed to their custom tailors, intent on placing orders before restrictions were issued. Department stores as well experienced increased sales as the rumors spread. Finally on February 11, 1941, clothing rationing was announced (Veillon 2002, 55). The following week, all clothing sales stopped to await the distribution of ration tickets ("Clothing Sale Halts" 1941, 8). One week later, clothing could again be purchased but only by presenting ration tickets along with money.

Elizabeth Hoyt (1942) wrote to her sister once again, describing her reaction to clothing rationing:

> To a woman, clothing restrictions are quite as important as food restrictions and clothing rations are so meagre that it is impossible to dress comfortably—or even adequately—without recourse to "Black Markets" at enormous prices. [...] Fortunately, I have a pre-war wardrobe and have been gradually wearing this to shreds, resorting to all sorts of schemes to provide something new.
>
> (65)

Haute Couture

Germany envisioned moving the French couture, including the designers, the workers, and the Ecole Supérieure that trained future employees, to Berlin and Vienna. The move would end France's tyranny over fashion, which they argued was out of touch with what a woman of taste wanted to wear (Veillon 2002, 85). Designer Lucien Lelong spearheaded the movement to convince Hitler, who envisioned the move, that French fashion could only be created in its familiar surroundings in Paris (85–86). Lelong met with the authorities in Berlin and succeeded in convincing the German textile industry leaders to leave French fashion in Paris. Lelong continued to fight for the preservation of the Haute Couture, arguing that a maximum number of side businesses supplying specialty embroidery, accessories, jewelers, and footwear, benefited from the construction of clothing in France.

Keeping the industry alive and the workers on payroll proved to be a struggle, especially with the loss of the international clientele. Although the fashion houses benefited from special couture ration cards, allowing wealthy French women to buy from the Haute Couture houses, the end of nightlife due to the curfew eliminated most occasions to wear couture gowns (116). In spite of shortages of material and strict regulations imposed on the quantity and specifications of designs, even the denial of fashion shows, the industry struggled to continue working in the hopes of salvaging France's position as the world's fashion leader after the war (93).

Despite wartime shortages, Hans-George von Studnitz (1963), a German journalist who visited Paris in October 1943, noted that the French had not lost their style. He wrote in his autobiography:

> Parisian good taste is still triumphant, even in the fifth year of the war. Whether it be some luxury article or something of quite ordinary, everyday use, there is nothing here which is not beautiful to look at—a great contrast to our shops at home, in which one rarely sees anything that is not hideous. Many of the articles on show are made of substitute material. Shoes with wooden soles and ladies' handbags made of cloth are so beautifully finished, that no one bothers to buy the genuine article, which is still obtainable in the black market.
>
> (131)

By the end of World War II, French garment manufacturers were operating at only 25% of their pre-war capacity. Due to the extreme impact the German occupation had on the French economy, clothing rationing continued until 1949–50 (Chadeau 1993, 193).

Vogue (USA) reported on the first fashions from Paris in their October 15, 1944 issue, after four years of silence. The sketches shown were noted to be pre-war designs. *Vogue* explained that during the occupation the designers purposely created "to be deliberately fancy and exaggerated, in order to taunt the Germans" ("Paris Fashions: First Report" 1944, 100).

United States

One day after the attack on Pearl Harbor, the USA declared war against Japan. Two days later, on December 10, 1941, by declaring war against Germany, the USA officially entered World War II. Although rich with natural resources, the voracious requirement for war supplies and the responsibility of the lend-lease program with the UK resulted in civilian shortages and the need for rationing (Lauterbach 1944, 209). Lend-lease was a program where the USA leant war ships and other war material to the UK with the understanding that the equipment would be returned after the war. The program allowed the USA to maintain its neutrality while at the same time taking action to help defeat Hitler (Brinkley and Haskew 2004, 30).

Eventually rubber, gasoline, silk, nylon, shoes, and food were rationed. Economic scholar Albert Lauterbach (1944) defined the necessity for rationing during a time of prosperity and shortage as experienced in the USA: "Rationing is generally recognized as an indispensable complement to price control if the latter is to be effective in a period of rising money incomes and decreasing supply of consumers' goods" (209). In developing government controls on consumption, efforts were made to distribute limited resources fairly by equally weighing the needs of consumers against the needs for the war effort (Fairchild 1944, 17).

Rubber shortages created problems for both the military and civilians. Military needs, as always, were prioritized, leaving civilians who needed to buy tires, rubber boots, or work shoes out of luck after September 29, 1942, when restrictions were enacted. Rubber rationing was only the first step in the rationing program (Figure 1.6). The *New York Times* compared the USA austerity program with the UK,

> Rationing in this country is only a mild reflection of the program which has been in force in England since soon after the outbreak of the war. Only ten products have been ordered subject to rationing, as compared with a hundred or more in England.
>
> (Egan 1942, E7)

FIGURE 1.6: *America needs your Scrap Rubber*, 1942. Propaganda Poster by the War Production Board. Courtesy Boston Public Library, Print Department.

General Limitation Order L-85

Shoe rationing inevitably followed rubber rationing (Kolkman 2010, 3). As shoe industry workers joined up and leather resources became scarcer, government controls limited civilians to three new pairs a year (Shalett 1943, 1). The *Washington Post* reported, "Before the war we could get leather from South America if our own supply was inadequate; today we have more important uses for our merchant ships" ("Rationing Made Easy" 1943, B3). Not only was shipping hazardous due to the potential of attack, limited cargo space was prioritized for the military, restricting the importation of all products for civilians (Lauterbach 1944, 212).

People who needed more shoes than the ration allowed had to apply to the rationing board for special permission. The board's decision depended on the requesters' need. Work shoes not supplied by the employer might be permitted, but only if the shoes were not used for recreation or to maintain personal appearance (Kolkman 2010, 1). Applications for rubber boots or shoes required justification, especially if need was related to inessential work. Work essential to the war effort or protection of the nation's health and safety or to the maintenance of mines would more likely gain permission (3). Requests based on the need to follow fashion or to maintain appearance were never granted.

Shoe ration tickets were transferable among family members due to the difference between men's and women's buying habits ("Rationing Made Easy" 1943, B3). People often traded stamps with a relative who had less need or desire for a new pair of shoes. Coupons for shoes had no termination date so could be saved and used when needed (Kolkman 2010, 1).

Beth L., a teenager growing up in Davis, California during World War II, said, "I was hard on my shoes. I borrowed my father's ration stamps or wore non-rationed shoes."[6] Shoes made of unrationed cloth or rope with cork or wooden soles became the fashion in the USA, as they had in France when leather and rubber were restricted (Figure 1.7).

Rumors of clothing rationing followed the announcement of shoe rationing (Phillips 1945, 13). Consumers, motivated by fear, rushed to stores to buy new clothes before it was too late and stocked up. Unfortunately, their unnecessary hoarding only increased scarcity in the long run (13).

Eventually, the demands of outfitting the military stressed not only the available supply of raw materials but production capabilities as well. One example, a single order placed by the military for soldier's cotton underwear was predicted to deplete all available cotton cloth in the USA (Hagner 1942, B2). In view of these pending shortages, on Friday, April 10, 1942, the War Production Board (WPB) (Figure 1.8) initiated General Limitation Order L-85 to ration "Feminine Apparel for Outer Wear and Certain Other Garments" ("General Limitation Order L-85" 1942, 2722). The order stated, "the fulfillment of requirements for the defense of the USA has created a shortage in the supply of wool, silk, rayon, cotton, and linen for defense, for private account and for export; and the following order is deemed necessary and appropriate in the public interest and to promote the national defense" (2722).

The WPB hired Stanley Marcus, the oldest son of Herbert Marcus, the founder of the Neiman Marcus department store in Dallas, Texas, to help promote clothing rationing to manufacturers (Mower and Pedersen 2013, 40). Marcus joined the ranks of the dollar-a-year consultants who volunteered to leave lucrative jobs to come to Washington and apply their expertise to the war effort, receiving only $1.00 per year in pay. Marcus was assigned "to call together representatives of the

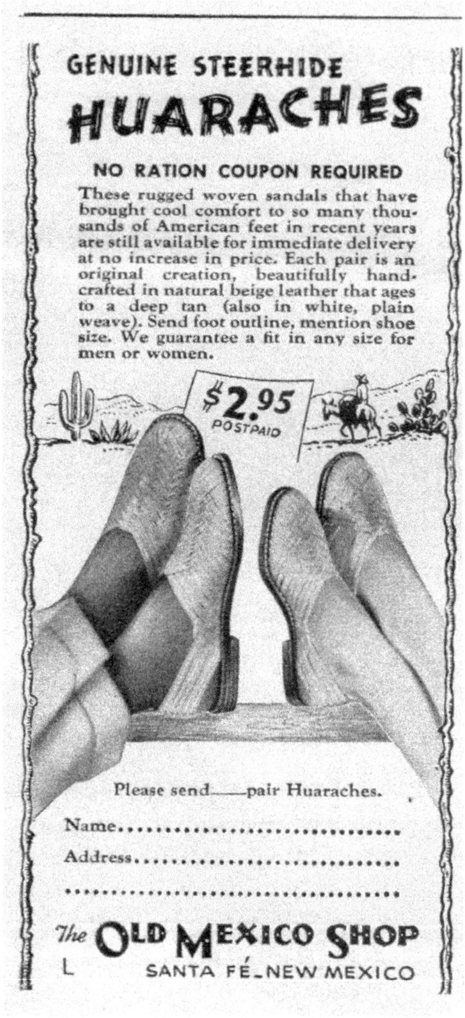

FIGURE 1.7: *Genuine Steerhide Huaraches, No Ration Coupon Required*, 1943. *Life*, April 19, 1943, 94.

various branches of the apparel industry to get their advice about steps which might be taken to conserve textiles, thereby saving not only yardage, but also the labor, which could be diverted to the war effort" (Marcus 1974, 112). He was also charged, "to devise orders (1) which would be self-enforcing and (2) which would virtually freeze fashion as it was in 1942, thus forestalling any radical change in fashion making existing clothes obsolete" (115). The idea behind freezing fashion was that if fashion no longer changed every season, as it traditionally had done, there would no longer be a need to buy clothing to keep up with fashion; new clothing would

FIGURE 1.8: *Insignia for the United States War Production Board*, World War II. Courtesy National Museum of the U.S. Navy, Public domain, via Wikimedia Commons.

only be necessary when it wore out. This fact, the "freezing" of fashion until the end of the war, made the effect of Dior's New Look, coming from Paris in 1947, more understandable as a symbol of peace and freedom after many years of sameness.

Specific rules of General Limitation Order L-85 regulated the lengths and measurements of garments to conserve resources. These regulations were primarily focused on manufacturers. Specifications were directed to "any person making feminine apparel for resale or on commission, including, but without limitation, the following: manufacturers to the trade, tailors, custom dressmakers, retailers and home dressmakers" ("General Limitation Order L-85" 1942, 2722). Garments and fabric measurements and weights were specified. Exceptions were made for garments put into work before the date of the enactment. The regulations did not apply to infants and toddlers clothing, bridal gowns, maternity dress, clothing for "persons who, because of abnormal height, size of physical deformities, require additional material," burial gowns, religious garments sold to religious sects or to the military (2722).

Style details regulated or eliminated to reduce fabric consumption included:

- French cuffs;
- Double layer material on yokes;
- Balloon, dolman, or leg-of-mutton sleeves;
- Fabrics which have been reduced from normal width or length by all over tucking, shirring, or pleating, except for minor trimmings;
- Inside pockets of wool cloth;

- Patch pockets of wool cloth on a lined wool cloth garment;
- Men's vests;
- Trouser pleats, cuffs;
- Suits with two pairs of pants;
- The number of metal pins used in packaged men's shirts;
- Interlinings containing any virgin or reprocessed wool. (2722).

Life (April 20, 1942) magazine explained the new restrictions on apparel,

> Uncle Sam, disguised as Stanley Marcus, of Dallas' Neiman-Marcus, [...] last week assumed the role of fashion designer. In a sweeping order affecting all women's and girls' outer wearing apparel, the WPB, of which Mr. Marcus is apparel consultant, decreed to what lengths and widths dresses, skirts, coats, suits, sleeves, belts, hems might go. Not as much as the flap of a pocket was overlooked in the order, aimed at 1) getting more garments out of materials available, and 2) preventing obsolescence of styles now current.
> ("Women Lose Pockets and Frills to Save Fabrics" 70-71)

The *Washington Post* assured civilians on November 16, 1942 that the WPB's efforts to simplify and standardize "threads, linings, and other materials, along the lines of the British utility cloth plan" ensured that minimal requirements would be available (Hagner, B2).

Donald M. Nelson, the War Production Chief, testified before the House Appropriations Committee on May 15, 1943, "We have even cut the [lining] fabrics out of women's hats in order to save fabric" ("Warns Wool Blending" 1942, 4).

Audrey Withers (1944) compared rationing in the USA to rationing in the UK in the American edition of *Vogue* titled "Fashion in England,"

> Another factor ranged against fashion is "austerity"—our name for the restrictions on design. Your L-85 regulations seem entirely framed to save material; ours are even more concerned to save labour—which is probably a still scarcer commodity in this country. Your rules, which lay down the sweep of skirt, the length of jacket and leave it at that, are far less cramping than ours, which lay down the precise number of seams, tucks, pleats, buttons, or pockets, which may be used; and put an absolute veto on the use of lace, embroidery and so on.
> (195)

Clothing manufacturers endured most of the responsibility for textile rationing, so it had little direct effect on consumers. Many American women interviewed had few memories of clothing shortage or rationing except for some comments about shoes.[7] Austerity and shortages, a part of life in the 1930s, had predisposed most people to accept the reality of getting by as much as possible without spending money. Manufacturers were proud of their contributions to the war and apologized to their consumers when civilian orders could not always be filled. For example, Talon, the zipper manufacturer, faced shortages of metal fasteners for consumers apparel. In a corset ad in *Good Housekeeping* magazine (Figure 1.9), the zipper manufacturer proudly explained the responsibilities their factories had undertaken for the US military in hopes that their customers would accept shortages and take the necessary steps to make her girdle last for the duration:

FIGURE 1.9: *Today, you've got to look ahead when you buy a corset!*, 1942. Advertisement. *Good Housekeeping*, April 1942, 131. Courtesy Talon Corporation.

Our Job in War Time

We are proud to have been given these responsibilities:

- To supply Talon fasteners for a wide variety of Army and Navy uses.
- To make precision ordnance parts and also precision gauges essential to the manufacture of munitions.
- To release metals needed by our Government and to use our research and engineering facilities for perfecting new materials (metals and non-metals) that are less important for war production.

In order to execute this all-important program, the production of Talon fasteners for commercial use cannot be maintained at the usual level (131, 1942).

Conclusion

War demands and consumes an enormous number of products, resulting in scarcity of civilian necessities. Goodin and Dryzek (1995), in *Justice Deferred: Wartime Rationing and Postwar Welfare Policy,* referred to government imposed rationing as "a corollary of modern total war" (49). Restrictions allowed governments to "redirect national economic resources toward the war effort" (49). Therefore, for many of the countries involved in World War II, restrictions and rationing of civilian consumption was an inevitability. The success of these programs varied, dependent on each countries' pre-war economic strength, available natural resources, and geographic location.

Before World War II, many countries without enough natural resources to fulfill domestic clothing needs relied on global shipping to obtain raw materials. With the advent of war, shipping became too dangerous because of the risk of enemy attack. Japan, and to a lesser extent Germany, attacked some of their own raw material suppliers, consequently reducing the availability of civilian goods. Countries retaliated by placing embargos which further disrupted international trade. Subsequently, civilian shortages were a universal issue.

Civilians in defeated countries suffered under rationing programs created to benefit residents of the occupying country. These countries were forced to send a large percentage of their production to provide for enemy troops and civilians, leaving extreme scarcity at home.

The poorest countries did not even have the benefit of rationing. Antonina B. Edillo, a young girl in the Philippines, reported that she wore the same dress throughout the war. When asked about any rationing system, she replied, "That I don't know. I don't think so. As long as you have money you could buy. But then even when you have money, there is nothing to buy."[8]

NOTES

1. Lydia (born 1929 in Sudan, German/Chinese, lived in Germany during the war) In discussion with author during the War Brides Association Reunion, San Diego, CA, October 9, 2019.
2. Lynn (born 1926, Southampton, UK) in discussion at the Northern California War Brides Association lunch, Campbell, CA, October 11, 2014.
3. Doreen (born 1931, UK), answer to questionnaire passed out at War Brides luncheon, Campbell, CA, March 12, 2012.
4. Jeanne (born 1927, Tours, France) in discussion with the author during the War Brides Association Reunion on the Queen Mary, Long Beach, CA, September 2015.
5. Adelaide (born 1927, Hague, the Netherlands) in discussion with the author, Davis, CA, November 20, 2014.
6. Beth L. (born 1935, Missouri) in conversation with the author, Davis, CA, April 2014.
7. This finding is also supported by Mower and Pedersen, "Pretty and Patriotic: Women's Consumption of Apparel During World War II," 39.
8. Antonina B. Edillo (born 1928, Manila, Philippines) in discussion with the author at the Northern California War Brides Association lunch, Campbell, CA, November 4, 2015.

2

Textiles Go to War: Military Uniforms Prioritized

> Being saturated and satiated with emotion and sensation, I went to bed and slept the sleep of the saved and thankful.
>
> Winston Churchill, *The Second World War: The Grand Alliance*

Prime Minister Winston Churchill expressed his relief, writing in his diary on the evening of December 7, 1941, after Japan's attack on Pearl Harbor. He knew that his long-awaited wish would be granted; the USA would join the UK in the battle against the Nazi aggressors (Beevor 2012, 247). Fearful of another war so soon after the end of World War I, the USA had taken an isolationist stance during the early years of war (Brinkley and Haskew 2004, 38–39; see also Heinrichs 1990, 6–7).

Obtaining essential resources to fuel the mechanics of war was a global problem. One natural resource, textiles, played a role in World War II that is often overlooked. This chapter will explore the role of textile fibers in World War II, especially how they related to women's clothing.

Dependence on Natural Fibers

At the end of the 1930s, textile production had not made the transition from using agriculture-based fibers to chemical-based fibers, as it would after the war (Handley 2000, 7–9). Natural fibers such as wool, cotton, rubber, silk, flax, and hemp were the principle sources of fabric for clothing. Countries lacking the proper climate to produce these natural fibers depended on foreign trade to supply raw materials for domestic clothing production. International shipping, endangered by the threat of attack, became too dangerous, intensifying shortages of already scarce food, fuel, and textiles (Klein 2014, 315).

Synthetic or manufactured fabrics were in the experimental stage before the 1930s and showed little probability of fulfilling the textile requirements of the military during World War II (Cook 1959, 193). By the late 1930s, only rayon and acetate had been successfully developed and marketed for use in clothing. Nylon, the first truly manufactured fiber, put on public sale on October 24, 1939 in the form of women's stockings, was a huge success and would play a major role in the war (E. I. du Pont de Nemours & Co. 1976). Polyester, the fiber that the majority of clothing is made of today, developed in the late 1930s, was not widely used for clothing until after the war (Brown and Reinhart 1971, 287). As supplies of wool, cotton, and other natural fibers dwindled due to the requirements of the military, the need to develop manufactured substitutes, a goal of scientists for decades, increased (Handley 2000, 8). *The Washington Post* reported on November 16, 1942 that the need for supplying the military was so great that "our enlarged Army naturally will press increasing numbers of cotton looms into Government services and civilians will play second fiddle" (Hagner 1942, B2). *The Washington Post* followed up on the situation on June 16, 1943, stating that in the USA,

> With the armed forces now absorbing 70 per cent of the output of the cotton textile industry, the remaining 30 per cent must take care of civilian demands for dresses, shirts, sheets, pillowcases, etc. With output declining, civilians obviously will have to get along with a very inadequate supply of cotton cloth for essential purposes, regardless of whether clothing made from cotton cloth is rationed or not.
>
> ("More Wool, Less Cotton" 16)

The Story of Rubber

Mobility and machine power, dependent on fossil fuel for gasoline and rubber for tires, determined success in World War II (Figure 2.1). Rubber was required for military tanks, trucks, jeeps, artillery, warships, and wire coating. Almost the entire source of natural rubber, produced from the sap of tropical *Hevea brasiliensis* trees, came from Ceylon (Sri Lanka), China, and Malaya (Malaysia) (Farrell-Beck 2011, 28). On December 7, 1941, a few hours before the bombing of Pearl Harbor, Japan invaded and quickly took control of Malaya (Beevor 2012, 252–53). The world's supply of rubber was now cutoff from the Western world, all exports stopped. With Japan controlling the global supply of rubber, the Allies were in a dire situation. Three days after the attacks, in a desperate move to conserve the stock on hand, the USA banned all sales of new rubber tires, followed with restrictions on all other rubber use (Adams 1942, SM6).

Rubber scarcity posed a problem for women, considered unladylike unless they wore a girdle or corset under their clothing in public (Brown 2010, 13). Prior to the 1920s, collective norms of modesty and propriety dictated that women's natural body shape should not be visible under their clothing (Ewing 1978, 135). Foundation

FIGURE 2.1: *Make Your Rubber Last*, 1942. Propaganda Poster. Courtesy History Nebraska, A.E. Sheldon, Lincoln, Lancaster, Nebraska (4541–695).

garments, whale-boned corsets, and later, rubber girdles, smoothed any distinguishable shape or improper movement (Cunningham 2003, 1). Fashion, ever fickle, historically dictated the often totally unnatural shape of the female body achieved by wearing these foundation garments. An "S" curve during the early 20th-century Gibson girl era, a boyish figure during the 1920s, and a narrow waistline in the 1940s (Fields 1999, 358, 378; see also Cunningham 2003, 15). Furthermore, girdles were marketed to women as necessary to maintain health and physical fitness and achieve societal prescribed ideals of youth and slimness (Brown 2010, 2). Women's standardized clothing sizes were based on measurements of the female body wearing a girdle. Therefore, clothing might not fit without the proper undergarment (Hackett and Rall 2018, 267).

Rubber had been used in clothing since the development of vulcanization in 1839. This chemical process improved the tensile strength and elasticity of the sap of the rubber tree, called latex, and allowed it to be used for clothing (Editors of Encyclopedia Britannica 2018). This new pliable rubber, along with fashion and social changes in the late 1920s, resulted in an evolution in women's undergarments as fashion relaxed and became more comfortable (Fields 1999, 355). In the 1930s, a new process of extruding rubber, or forcing it through a die to create a filament that could be knit or woven into fabric, was invented (Farrell-Beck 2013, 26). Girdles produced from these stretch fabrics were much more comfortable and lightweight than the restricting whale- or steel-boned corsets of previous decades (Cook 1959, 154). The traditional girdle, constructed with whale boning, steel, and lacing, was transformed into a more pliable and comfortable garment that used elastic rubber to support the body (Ewing 1978, 144). Thereafter, girdles became more of a "controller" than a "flattener" or a "bust-maker" (132).

The ban on civilian use of rubber halted girdle manufacturing (Klein 2014, 435). Women might have considered doing without girdles, but manufacturers were determined to keep them "straited-laced." Corset industry executives scrambled to find ways to stay in business in spite of the lack of rubber. Advertisements for the underpinnings industry marketed girdles made without rubber. For example, the girdle company, Artist Model, referring to rubber shortages in World War I, claimed, "We've been through all this before—and we've never lost the know-how" (Figure 2.2). Artist Model's girdle, "Laced to preserve precious rubber and to make a slimmer, trimmer you," solved the issue of rubber rationing.

Ever hopeful to keep their loyal customers, especially after the war when rubber would again be available, manufacturers promoted the health benefits of wearing girdles. Salespeople were instructed to use "innovative sales strategies and marketing techniques" to aggressively persuade customers that they could not function without wearing a girdle (Fields 2007, 15). Miss Mary Anderson, director of the Women's Bureau of the US Department of Labor, even "declared corsets to be essential to the performance of women's tasks in the war effort, pointing out that fatigue was the main reason why women frequently left their war jobs in the USA. To provide good corsets, which would reduce fatigue, was therefore necessary to the vigorous maintenance of the war effort" (Ewing 1978, 156).

Representatives of the Corset and Brassiere Association of America and the Associated Corset and Brassiere Manufacturers, faced with restrictions on the use of rubber and the consequential loss of profit, traveled to Washington, DC to visit the Office of Production Management, the precursor to the War Production Board. They pleaded their case for greater allotments of rubber by arguing for the importance of girdles for women. The association members argued that this was a matter of "maintaining civilian morale" ("Corset Industry Gets Jitters" 1942, 9). One of their claims was that girdles were worn by working women for health reasons, and not purely to improve their figures. The representatives backed their claims with letters from medical doctors proclaiming that women, now working for the war effort, would become fatigued more quickly if their flesh was not supported by girdles made of rubber (Brown 2010, 15).

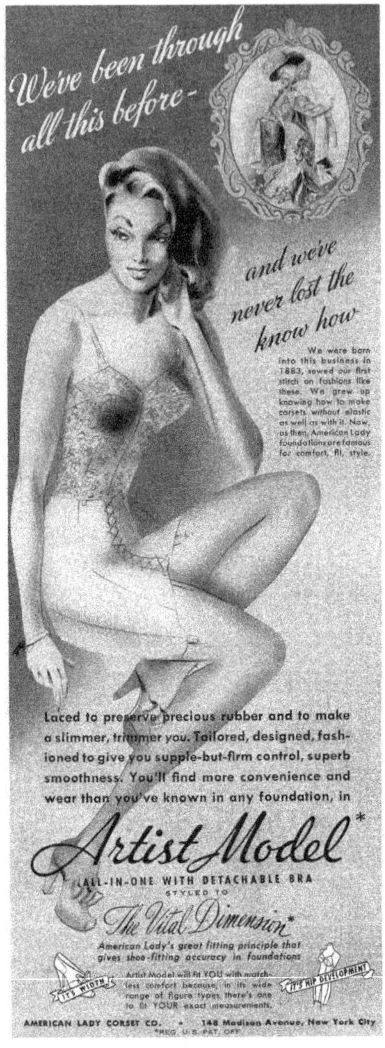

FIGURE 2.2: *We've been through all this before*, 1943. Advertisement. American Lady Foundations, Artist Model, American *Vogue*, March 1, 1943, 90.

Berlei, an Australian foundation manufacturer, ran an advertisement claiming that girdles were essential for "Woman-Power" (Color Plate 5). The ad proclaimed that not wearing proper support resulted in several problems, "Not only is physical energy reduced, but mental strain is increased, and morale is undoubtedly affected."

Girdle manufacturers published pamphlets and advertisements recommending the best way to care for girdles and other rubber-based garments. Many women owned only two girdles, and these had to last for the duration. Manufacturers

FIGURE 2.3: *Berlei Servicing Plan*, 1941. Advertisement, *British Vogue*, January 1941, 18. Courtesy Berlei Australasia.

advised women to wear each one on alternate days. Women who owned only one girdle "were encouraged to treat it with care, keep it clean and store it in a cool dark cupboard, not to overstretch it, to protect it from grease, perspiration and sunlight and where possible to wear it over a lightweight garment to give it a longer life" (Summers 2016, 123). Berlie even offered a cleaning and repair service. An advertisement in *British Vogue* (January 1941) announced that garments could be sent to Berlie for repair and even cleaned (Figure 2.3). The ad boasted:

> Our team of experts will get to work, doing everything necessary to make it almost as fresh as new. In addition to routine repairs (mending of tears, replacement of

> broken suspenders, shoulder straps, zips, etc.) the work will, where necessary, include laundering, the replacement of old lace, worn panels and any other part of the garment which can be so treated. You will find the charges for this service very moderate—Berlei are people who believe in service!
>
> (156)

Once prewar stocks of foundation garments were depleted, all clothing incorporating forms of rubber elastic became unavailable. Buying or even making underwear became difficult. Kath, who lived in Weston-super-Mare with her parents and sister during the war, remembers crouching in a wheat field with her mother as a German bomber, returning from dropping a payload on the nearby industrial town of Bristol, shot at civilians on the ground. Afterwards, the two sisters found silk parachutes, small ones used for incendiary bombs. They made underwear out of the fabric. The lack of elastic made it complicated. As a solution, the girls added fabric ties at the waist to keep them on. Kath remembered, "Well, there were a lot of droopy drawers going around."[1]

Girdles After the War

Postwar fashion, especially Christian Dior's New Look Collection of 1947 that featured wasp waists and voluminous skirts, was favorable for girdle manufacturers (Summers 2020, 304–5; see also McNeil 1993, 293). Girdles continued to be important for women to achieve the proper fashion silhouette throughout the 1950s. Fashion trends moved to a looser fit toward the late 1950s and 1960s; however, women were still expected to control their bodies by wearing foundation garments (Steele 2001, 160). New innovations such as the longline girdle, the panty girdle worn with trousers, wired strapless bras, and two-way stretch fabric promoted the continued sales of controlling undergarments (Farrell-Beck 2011, 35–36). Although most women, possibly motivated by the feminist movement, abandoned girdles in the 1960s. Judy, a colleague at the University of California, Davis, told me that even in the 1970s, when she was in college and participated in US Air Force basic training, the women in her group were told that they had to wear girdles under their uniforms. "Jiggling still not allowed."[2]

The Story of Silk

Before the war, "Japan was the source of 90 per cent of America's raw silk imports," used to knit women's stockings (Handley 2000, 35). When Japan invaded China in 1937, USA's sympathy turned against them and a consumer boycott of Japanese products was encouraged in the *New York Times* with the slogan: "Don't Buy Silk" ("Silk Boycott is Urged" 1937, 31). The silk boycott, especially of stockings, would be challenging since finding a substitute, "from the standpoint of price, style, appearance and wearing qualities would be difficult to develop" (31).

The *New York Times* later reported that the USA's ban on silk resulted in extreme panic buying, with estimates of sales increases of "200–500 per cent over the weekend" ("Women Stampede for Stockings" 1941, 21). Motivated by the fear of a ban on silk, "the belief that a shortage of 'sheers' was near due to government curbs caused customers to jam up for an all-day session of buying that resulted in some stores having to summon extra salesgirls, hire special guards and limit the number of pairs sold to each buyer" (21).

American women were encouraged to consider the deprivation of silk stockings and other silk garments as their contribution to the war effort. To encourage

FIGURE 2.4: *A woman donates her silk stockings so it could be repurposed as powder bags during the Second World War*. November 30, 1938. Alamy Images (HGB255).

them to accept the ban, the newspaper recommended that all, "Women's peace organizations, trade unions and all other groups desirous of preventing another world war are advised to cooperate in organizing a boycott until the Japanese are forced out of China" ("Silk Boycott Is Urged" 1937, 31). Civil groups held events to encourage people to support the boycott. These events included a fashion show held by the Washington League of Women Voters. The show, "Life without Silk," promoted the boycott and made "the average person much more conscious of his or her inevitable participation" in indirectly supporting a "war of flagrant aggression" if they continued to buy silk ("Life Without Silk" 1938, 8).

Vassar College students, attending the annual convention of the American Student Union, protested Japan's aggression against China by removing their silk stockings, shirts, and ties and burning them in a bonfire. They chanted "Make lisle the style," suggesting that wearing stockings made from an American grown fiber would help the war effort ("Life on the American Newsfront" 1938, 18). Lisle is a fine cotton thread that can be knit into stockings, but is much heavier than silk and not sheer. The boycott was truly an act of patriotism for women who were dependent on silk for stockings.

Finally, when the USA entered World War II, all commerce with Japan ended. Reserves of raw silk yarn and quantities of silk stockings already produced allowed for sales to continue for approximately two to four months, although the *New York Times* suggested that the military would most likely seize the reserves ("Dependence of U.S. On Silk Continues" 1941, 30). The American edition of *Vogue* (February 1, 1942) promoted cotton for stockings because "buying it defies no priorities tabu. Cotton

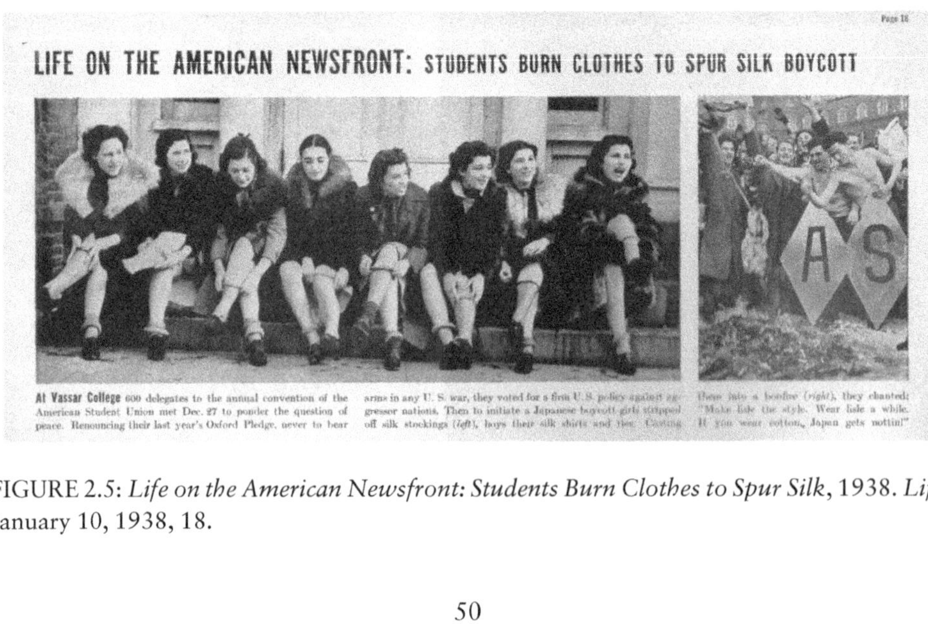
LIFE ON THE AMERICAN NEWSFRONT: STUDENTS BURN CLOTHES TO SPUR SILK BOYCOTT

At Vassar College 600 delegates to the annual convention of the American Student Union met Dec. 27 to ponder the question of peace. Renouncing their last year's Oxford Pledge, never to bear arms in any U. S. war, they voted for a firm U.S. policy against aggressor nations. Then to initiate a Japanese boycott girls stripped off silk stockings (*left*), boys their silk shirts and ties. Casting them into a bonfire (*right*), they chanted: "Make lisle the style. Wear lisle a while. If you wear cotton, Japan gets nottin!"

FIGURE 2.5: *Life on the American Newsfront: Students Burn Clothes to Spur Silk*, 1938. *Life*, January 10, 1938, 18.

is 'not on the list'—it is one product which, apparently, will be plentiful enough to buy with a relaxed conscience, but—need it be said?—not to buy or use wastefully" ("Fashion: America's Own-Cotton," 89). *Vogue* (December 1, 1943) suggested that lisle stockings, "For the young girls with nice, long, slim legs [...] are fine and fun in the country. Once more Necessity is a Mother" ("Fashion: Veils For Legs," 105).

Due to the shortage, silk stockings became very special possessions. My relative, Leila, who grew up on a farm outside of Emporia, Kansas, told me that her sorority sisters shared two pairs of stockings among all the girls that were only used for special date nights.[3] Ilene reported that her college dorm "had about 4 good pairs of hose shared by 34 women for only very special occasions or serious 'dates.'"[4] Anne recounted that her mother had to borrow a pair of stockings for her wedding because she did not have a single pair and buying any was impossible.[5]

The UK also prohibited silk sales. *The Times* announced the ban because silk was needed for "the manufacture of barrage balloons, parachutes, and other essentials of the day" ("Farewell to Silk Stockings" 1940, 2). Jean, a British woman born in Welwyn Garden City, UK in 1927, remembered the value of silk stockings, "You knew in the beginning of the war that people still had silk stockings. I don't think I did because I was young at the beginning of the war, but silk stockings were prized possessions."[6] Artificial silk or rayon stockings were suggested as a good substitution for real silk stockings, which in fact many women were already wearing. Silk stockings were more expensive and a luxury, often saved for special occasions. The same article in *The Times* quoted a woman who stated that "pure silk is nicer," but rayon was "bearable" (2). The article went on to suggest that "thousands of women have already given up stockings, silk or artificial silk. Many, usually those employed in the civil defense services have taken to the regular wearing of 'slacks'" (2). (For discussion of women wearing slacks, see Chapter 3.)

The Story of Rayon

Rayon was developed in the earlier years of the 20th century from reprocessed cellulose produced from wood pulp (Hollen et al. 1979, 82). Decades of experimentation on viscose and acetate were carried out in countries including Germany, France, Italy, the UK, and the USA before the American Viscose Company in Marcus Hook, Pennsylvania produced "artificial silk" on December 19, 1910 (E. I. du Pont de Nemours & Co., 1976). In 1924, the USA textile industry christened their newly developed fiber "rayon." The name was "a generic term coined from 'ray' (for the sheen of the fiber) and 'on' (to suggest a fiber, as the 'on' in cotton)" (E. I. du Pont de Nemours & Co. 1976; see also

Handley 2000, 37). The new fiber, marketed as "artificial silk," proved to be an acceptable and less expensive alternative filament for stockings, although it exhibited many negative qualities (Handley 2000, 35; see also Blanc 2016, 111). Rayon stockings were criticized as being "too lustrous, too inelastic and insufficiently sheer" and lacked many qualities of their silk predecessor ("$10,000,000 Plant to Make" 1938, 1). Rayons bagged at the knee since the fiber lacked good recovery. They were "shiny, thick and clumsily shaped, consisting of a tube of knitting made on circular machines and failing to cling to the leg" (Ewing 1978, 140).

FIGURE 2.6: *This is my Duration Dress*, 1943. Tubize Corporation advertisement. *Life*, April 19, 1943, 14.

The Story of Nylon

Nylon stockings were introduced to the public at the 1939 World's Fair, held in Flushing Meadows Park, Queens, New York. Nylon stockings were widely distributed to stores in the USA and were available for purchase on May 15, 1940 ("Sales Begin Today" 1940, 31). The *New York Times* (October 25, 1939) reported that the initial shipment of 4,000 pairs was sold out in Wilmington, Delaware, the location of the DuPont Company's lab, by 1 p.m. in the afternoon. Customers had "lined three deep at the counters most of the day" ("First Offering of Nylon Hosiery Sold Out," 38). Nylon stockings became so popular in the two years after their introduction that the disappearance of silk did not seem to be so terribly drastic.

Unfortunately for women, nylon was also a valid replacement for silk in military parachutes, as well as "glider tow ropes, aircraft fuel tanks, flak jackets, shoelaces, mosquito netting and hammocks" (Cutlip 2015). The military considered the new fiber so valuable for the war effort that in March 1942 they requisitioned DuPont's total production. Nylon stockings disappeared from stores ("Plan to Divert All" 1940, 39). Thereafter, until the end of the war, women could only purchase old stocks of nylons. The black market was the only other resource to buy nylon stockings at exorbitant prices. (For discussion of the black market, see Chapter 8).

The hosiery industry was hard pressed to ensure their customers would return to buying and wearing stockings after the war. Earl Constantine, president of the National Association of Hosiery Manufacturers, reassured the hosiery industry, "He saw little chance for a bare-leg vogue and expressed the belief that many people would find themselves allergic to leg-painting" ("Hosiery Industry Through with Silk" 1942, 36).

The lack of silk and nylon was a serious concern for women. Silk for stockings was essential to their wardrobes as not only social mores but also corporate and school dress codes required stockings (Howell 2012, 149). The option to cover ones' legs by wearing trousers, except for manual labor on a farm, or for sports, was not acceptable at the start of the war (Summers 2016, 68, 177). Lingerie and undergarment stores were quickly depleted of prewar stock of hosiery. Thereafter, women had to make do with what they had for the duration.

Women were forced to find creative ways to make their legs look like they were wearing stockings. Face makeup was a good resource to create the look of appropriate leg coverings.

Jean remembered painting her legs with "gravy browning" in Welwyn Garden City, UK.

Ilene recounted, "Products appeared to paint legs 'tan,' and this actually became kind of chic. I had 'painted' legs for my wartime wedding."

FIGURE 2.7: *We Borrowed Their "Nylons" to Make Tires for the Navy*, 1943. Courtesy B. F. Goodrich.

Doris, an art student at the Cleveland Institute of Arts during the war, described using leg makeup. "I did use leg makeup. You had to be clean shaven or hair would show. I used the standard stuff. Buy it in a screw top jar. Put it on with hands. Wear

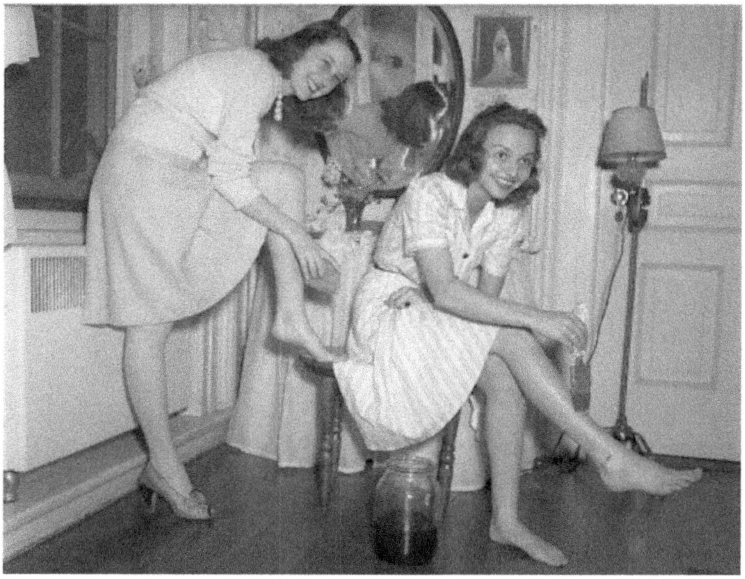

FIGURE 2.8: *Two students in Alpha Delta Pi paint their legs so it appears they are wearing stockings.* The Wallace Richter Album (Image 197). Courtesy Hargrett Rare Book and Manuscript Library/University of Georgia Libraries.

with sandals." She also related the drawbacks to wearing face makeup on legs, "You could leave the makeup on a man's clothes. Worse than lipstick on his collar."[7]

Stockings during the 1940s were not made on tubular machines as they are today and had to be stitched up the back of the leg after they were knit. The seam created a visible line up the back of the leg. To replicate the look, many women drew the line with an eyebrow pencil to simulate the seam. I remember my mother talking about her sorority sisters helping each other to draw the line on their legs to mimic the look of a well-dressed leg. Jeanne, who lived in France during the war, said, "We dyed our legs and drew a seam with eye liner sometimes."[8] Lynn in Southampton, UK also remembered, "No hose, we drew a line on our leg to simulate hose."[9] Ilene added, "Service men [in the USA] had access to hosiery through PX stores; huge treat when a gal received a pair via the boyfriend."

The shortage of nylon stockings even inspired a popular song: "When the Nylons Bloom Again," written by George Marion Jr. and Thomas Fat's Waller (Handley 2000, 48). The lyrics tell the story of a woman's lament about the absence of nylon stockings and her desire for the war to end. The final stanza references Mr. Henry A. Wallace, who was the 33rd Vice President of the USA, serving with Franklin Delano Roosevelt. Wallace was a man who dreamed of, "a better world—a world of peace, freedom, and abundance" (Schmidt 1960, 313).

"When the Nylons Bloom Again"

Gone are the days when I'd answer the bell
Find a salesmen with stockings to sell
Gleam in his eye and measuring tape in his hand
I get the urge to go splurging on hose
Nylons a dozen of those
Now poor or rich we're enduring instead
Woolens which itch
Rayons that spread

I'll be happy when the nylons bloom again
Cotton is monotonous to men
Only way to keep affection fresh
Get some mesh for your flesh

I'll be happy when the nylons bloom again
Ain't no need to blow no sirens then
When the frozen hosen again appear
Man that means all clear

Working women of the USA and Britan
Humble dowager or lowly debutant
We'll be happy as puppy or a kitten
Stepping back into their nylons of DuPont

Keep on smiling to the nylons bloom again
And the WACS come back to join their men
In a world that Mr. Wallace planned
Strolling hand in hand

—George Marion Jr. and Thomas Fat's Waller (1943)[10]

Caring for Stockings to Last for the Duration

Stockings needed to last for the length of the war, just like girdles did. Early forms of rayon, unstable when wet, made it difficult to care for. It might shrink or stretch, or both, especially when washed. An ad for Lux soap powder in the November 1942 issue of *Good Housekeeping* magazine recommended to, "Cut down runs in

FIGURE 2.9: "*You can help your Rayons last longer—if you coddle 'em when you wash 'em!*" 1943. Cannon Hosiery. *Life*, April 19, 1943, 12. Courtesy Iconix Brand Group, Inc.

your new RAYONS—LUX them nightly" ("Cut Down Runs," 96). Lux suggested that after the stockings were washed and rolled in a towel to remove excess water, to "hang [...] over a smooth towel bar, distributing the weight evenly. Dry thoroughly—24 to 48 hours. Rayon is temporarily weak when wet."

The Spool Cotton Company, in their 1942 publication *Make and Mend for Victory*, advised additional precautions to increase the life of rayon stockings. The advice also illustrates rayon stockings' drawbacks:

> a. Buy cotton reinforced toes or reinforce [yourself] on wrong side with cotton darning thread, weaving back and forth with small running stitches.

FIGURE 2.10: *Cut down runs in your new rayons— Lux Them Nightly*, 1942. Lux advertisement, *Good Housekeeping*, November 1942, 96. Courtesy Unilever.

b. Buy feet extra-long—they are likely to shrink.
c. Buy leg length about 2″ shorter than silk or nylon—they are apt to stretch (5).

These care guidelines point out the issues involved with rayon stockings; they could shrink or stretch or both when washed.

Tubize, a rayon manufacturer, placed an advertisement in the October 1942 issue of *Good Housekeeping*, instructing women how to make their rayon lingerie last (Figure 2.10):

> Lingerie that will help you in your war-time duty to make everything you wear last as long as possible. To save and serve in every detail of our daily lives is the order of the day. Here are simple ways to make your lingerie last longer, and save your time, energy and money:

FIGURE 2.11: *Lingerie for your war-time budget*, 1942. Tubize Corporation advertisement. *Good Housekeeping*, October 1942, 121.

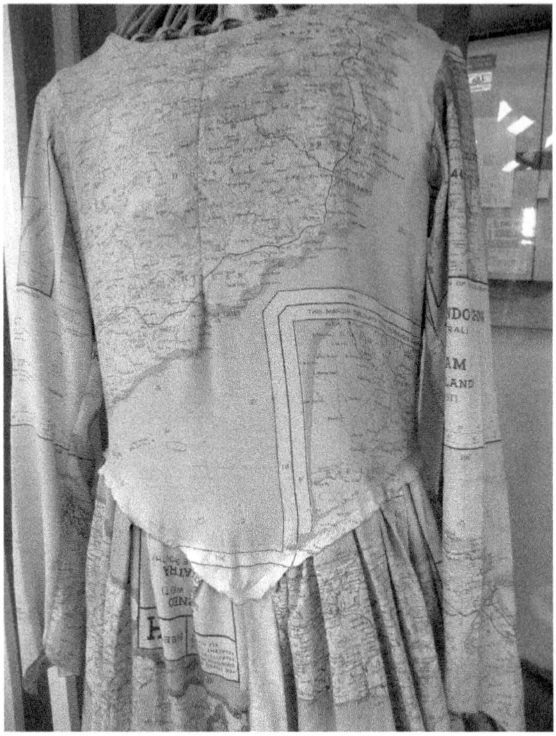

FIGURE 2.12: *Wedding dress made from silk escape map*. Tangmere Military Aviation Museum, Chichester, West Sussex, UK. Photo courtesy Gillian Collins. https://paisleypedlar.wordpress.com/2012/07/31/spitfires-hurricanes-and-soe/.

When Buying

- Don't buy hurriedly—take time to seek the qualities that stand for durability.

When Washing

- Wash after each wear—gently and quickly in rich suds of mild soap and lukewarm water.

When Mending

- Keep a well stocked mending kit—replete with fine needles and threads—ribbons and tapes.

("Lingerie for Your War-Time," 121)

Domestic Commerce: A Weekly Bulletin, a publication of the USA government, commended Tubize for aiding the war effort by educating women about how to conserve, "In advertisements it warns the women of the land that waste of textile materials is sabotage. Major copy space is devoted to instructions on how to make garments last longer through proper selection, care and cleaning" (1942, 8).

Conclusion

Textiles, including rubber, silk, rayon, and nylon, went to war by providing clothing, tires, automobile, and airplane parts for the troops. Natural rubber, sourced from Southeast Asia, was essential for tires, lifeboats, gas masks, covering for military wire, and many other uses. "Sherman tanks were made with half a ton of rubber and some battleships contained 20,000 rubber parts" ("The History of Rubber").

Silk was not only used for parachutes but also for powder bags for guns and canons to hold the powder charge ("Devise Powder Bags with Silk Substitute" 1941, 31). Silk escape maps were issued to British pilots to use in case they were shot down and needed to know their surroundings. A silk map, unlike paper, could survive a crash landing in the sea and still be useable. The USA copied these maps and issued them to pilots and intelligence personnel. The maps were also produced in cotton and rayon acetate ("WWII Escape Maps"). These silk maps became another resource for women to make clothing. Museums hold examples of wedding dresses made out of silk maps like this image of a dress displayed at the Tangmere Military Aviation Museum, Chichester, West Sussex, UK (Figure 2.12).

Textile shortages during World War II were predisposed by not only the need to outfit and equip the military but also due to widespread reliance on natural fibers that required specific climates to cultivate and, therefore, had to be imported to support domestic apparel industries.

During the war, global commerce, obstructed by embargos and warfare, made textiles scarce. Manufactured fibers would eventually relieve dependence on natural fibers but were in early development before the war. Therefore, when textiles were prioritized for the war effort, civilians had to struggle to make the clothing they already owned last for the duration.

Textile scarcity during World War I had served as a dress rehearsal for World War II. Scientists were well aware of the effects of textile shortage and raced to develop chemically produced fibers. Unfortunately, they had not yet experienced much success before 1939.

Women eagerly accepted the new nylon stockings, especially since silk from Japan and China for stockings was embargoed. Nylon fiber proved to be so useful for the war effort as a replacement fiber for silk parachutes and other products that the military took over the entire production, depriving women of their preferred leg covering for the duration of the war.

Women were encouraged to accept shortages during the war as their patriotic duty. As scarcity became more severe and women could no longer always dress in proscribed stockings and girdles. *Woman's Day* magazine (December 1942), quoted a woman who declared that wearing stockings with runs was "a service stripe" (17).

> I have a run in my stocking. Not a fresh, impromptu snag, but a wide, shameless bull run up the whole fatted calf. Am I embarrassed? Self-conscious? Not at all. Nonchalance is the word for me, since I can blame my genteel shabbiness on the ever-reliable war. [...] A run is practically a service stripe.
>
> (Fishback, 17)

NOTES

1. Kath (born 1924, Weston-super-Mare, UK) in discussion with the author, Weston-super-Mare, UK, June 11, 2010.
2. Judy (born 1954, CA) in discussion with the author, Davis, CA, February 2011.
3. Leila Ruddick (born 1926, Emporia, KA) in discussion with the author, Wichita, KS, May 2010.
4. Ilene (born 1924, Salinas, CA) in e-mail communication with the author, January 15, 2020.
5. Ann (American) in discussion with the author at the Costume Society of American Symposium, Seattle, WA, April 20, 2019.
6. Jean (born 1927, Welwyn Garden City, UK) in discussion with the author, San Jose, CA, November 24, 2014.
7. Doris (born 1925, Cleveland, OH) in telephone conversation with the author, July 23, 2014.
8. Jeanne (born 1927, Tours, France) in discussion with the author during the War Brides Association Reunion on the Queen Mary, Long Beach, CA, September 2015.
9. Lynn (born 1927, Southampton, UK), answer to questionnaire passed out at the War Brides luncheon, Campbell, CA, March 12, 2012.
10. "When the Nylons Bloom Again"
    Written by Thomas Fat's Waller and George Marion.
    Published by Redwood Music Ltd
    All rights administered by Round Hill Carlin, LLC, London.

3

Gender Defined by Clothing: Women in Slacks

Patricia Ford, born in 1927 in Emporia, Kansas, was fifteen when the USA entered World War II in 1941. Pat stands with her three aunts and stepmother in an early 1940s' family photo taken in Great Bend, Kansas (Figure 3.1). Her uncles and father are in the back row. The photo illustrates the binary divide between men's and women's clothing before the war. Women wore skirts and men wore trousers. Women rarely wore pants, or slacks as they were called, before the war (Farrell-Beck 2011, 25). Pants for women were considered appropriate for very limited and specific occasions—shorts for tennis, jodhpurs for hiking or horseback riding, or jeans to work on the farm. The traditional mores

FIGURE 3.1: *Gendered dress in the 1940s, women in skirts, men in trousers*, 1944. Great Bend, Kansas. Courtesy Turner family.

of society embodied in the binary rules of gendered dress were challenged during World War II, which served as a springboard, giving women a greater choice of comfortable dress.

Before World War II, gendered clothing defined and reinforced the distinct separation between the sexes (Goodman, Knotts, and Jackson 2007, 104). For centuries women's prescribed dress indicated their position in society, often defined by their husband's wealth and social class (Fields 1999, 357; see also DeLong, Salusso-Deonier and Larntz 1983, 327; Roberts 1977, 566). Restrictive or binding clothing that inhibited movement indicated a woman had married well and did not need to work outside the home (564).

During the early part of the 20th century, women's clothing started to be less restrictive and the hemline raised, allowing more movement. As bicycling and tennis gained in popularity, designers created less confining styles that allowed women to participate in active pastimes and sports (Lurie 1981, 224-25). The loose-fitting flapper silhouette, developed in the 1920s, worn with less restricting underpinning, allowed women the freedom of movement to dance the Charleston (Dirix 2016, 75).

The Traditional Family Structure

Before the war, the middle-class family structure reinforced the binary gender opposition. Husbands, the established breadwinners, worked outside the home to financially support the family. Wives were homemakers, responsible for housekeeping and child rearing (Gluck 1987, 4–7). During the 1920s, many young unmarried women experienced new freedoms by taking jobs outside the home. Working-class women had always worked to earn money. Unfortunately, during the economic depression of the 1930s, high unemployment forced many women out of their jobs and back into the home. During the decade of economic hardship, married women who wished or needed to work were often criticized. Men had priority of employment as it was their duty to provide financial support for their family (Davis 1984, 405). Only women unfortunate enough to not have found a husband were considered to have the right to work. Some people even believed that laws should be passed to prohibit married women from seeking employment (Gluck 1987, 8; see also Bixler 1945, 369–70).

The term "homemaker" came into parlance during the 1930s. An early example of the definition of the term was illustrated in an ad for *Ladies Home Journal* magazine in a 1930 issue of *The Saturday Evening Post* (Color Plate 6). The ad defined "homemaker" as "a bigger job than housekeeping" and "a bigger job than that of any man in any business." The ad suggested that women's role in the effort to end the Great Depression was to carefully and creatively manage the meager allotments of food and supplies that the family could afford, "as well as leaving public sector employment to men, that could ensure an end to the Depression" (140).

High Fashion Trousers

Trousers slowly started to appear on high fashion runways as a new option for women's dress throughout the 1920s and 1930s. Designers challenged the binary definition of gender by introducing evening pajamas, beach lounging ensembles, or even overalls on the runway (Hall, Orzada, and Lopez-Gydosh 2015, 237). The June 1938 issue of the American edition of *Vogue* featured an article titled "Foreign Shores," with fashions showing trousers suitable for beachwear (Figure 3.2). The Molyneux[1] designed outfit on the left, described as a "pair of overalls like [those worn by] a steel-worker's—blue linen, hand-stitched in white, with no shirt—only a proletarian red bandanna looped carelessly about the neck," clearly shows the influence of men's workwear. Designer's attempts to elevate trousers to high fashion had little influence on the clothing of the average women who continued to wear traditional skirts and dresses (Summers 2016, 24).

Pants Signify Power

During World War II, the image of women evolved from that of a housewife taking care of the home and family to a slacks-wearing war worker (Rupp 1978, 165). Historians have earmarked the 1940s as the decade in which women used pants as a "bridge to shift the hegemony of men holding greater economic power" (Buckland 2000, 141). The transition to slacks-wearing women was not free of trepidation. People feared that women might take on the qualities of men by dressing like them (Lant 1991, 69).

Women's magazines featured articles explaining how and when to wear pants in an attempt to assuage fears that wearing slacks would make them lose their femininity. Similarly, during World War I, women who replaced men in factory jobs dressed in men's clothing as "female overalls had not yet been designed" (Brucker 2019, 238). In France, some of these women were even accused of "'interfering' with gender norms when they donned work-issued outfits and coveralls" (Bass-Krueger 2019a, 43). Fashion magazines during World War I featured women wearing men's overalls for work but styled the models to emphasize their femininity "and even sexualized the work overall," reassuring both men and women that the traditional feminine identity would not be lost (Brucker 2019, 238).

Good Housekeeping magazine's April 1942 issue carried a four-page article titled "The Men at Good Housekeeping Say—If You Must Wear Slacks." One

FIGURE 3.2: *Foreign Shores*, 1938. American *Vogue*, June 1938, 59. Courtesy *Vogue*.

of the men's most watchful comments: "Do consider the occasion. Wear utility slacks for utility jobs; dark faille or jersey slacks for evening comfort—if your family approves" (50).

Defining the Appropriateness of Slacks

The American edition of *Vogue* (April 1, 1942), acting as an arbitrator in the dialogue about the appropriateness of slacks for women, emphasized their practicality. The article concluded that three occasions "practically demand" the wearing of slacks: "When you're in the country. When you are on war service duty, and they're prescribed wear. When you're busy, at good hard work" (75). *Vogue* advised: "If you're sure they're right, do wear them. If you're at all in doubt, *don't*. A skirt is *never* wrong" ("Fashion: A Primer on Pants," 75).

When Americans were asked to turn down their thermostats to 65 degrees to conserve fuel during the winter of 1942, *Vogue* (October 15) suggested that wearing slacks was the perfect practical and patriotic method to keep warm. "The most spectacular anti-freeze costume of the season," gray fur slacks, designed by Traina-Norell,[2] were suggested to wear in "a frigid country home, or a fuel rationed flat in town" ("Fashion: A New Heating Plan," 56-57). *Vogue* concluded,

> And, of course, remember that the best personal heating system of all is your own circulation system [...] Your war work is the most nearly perfect way there is of keeping warm... whether it's direct war work or any work on the home front. The reason it is so effective... it helps to keep you nice and warm outside *and* inside. (57)

Vogue's endorsement of slacks for women for specific occasions reinforced the belief that women's duty on the home front was as important as men's duty on the war front.

Women Take to Wearing Slacks

Women from a range of countries, born between 1920 and 1933, were interviewed about when and for what occasions they started to wear pants or slacks. These women had grown up in Australia (3), Austria (1), Belgium (1), France (4), Germany (3), Italy (1), Japan (3), New Zealand (1), Philippines (1), the UK (10), and the USA (19). The results presented a surprising range of answers. Many reported that they did not wear slacks until after World War II and some not until well into the 1970s and 1980s. Their recollections revealed a wide disparity in the acceptance of trousers.

Adina, who lived in Linz, Austria during the war, reported: "I can't remember when I started wearing pants, but never during World War II. Only women in the military wore pants. We didn't even have pants available to buy. In winter, we did wear pants for skiing. For skating we wore short skirts. No shorts. I never saw a woman wearing shorts."[3]

Hazel, who lived in Australia, said, "Trousers no, that's for men. No way. That would be a disgrace."[4]

Exceptions to the rigid female dress code were only for specific casual occasions requiring ease and movability, like a play day at school or helping on the farm. Vivian, who lived in Iowa, remembered, "I did not wear pants. Only at my aunt's farm, only jeans."[5]

Laney, a young American girl in Missouri, described her introduction to pants:

> In 8th grade (1946) in my sewing class we made pedal pushers. Yes, that is what they were called. That was my first pair of pants [...] that I can remember. We had dress codes at school. Then several of us decided to wear the pants to school and got called in the office, but our teacher excused us because they were a school project.[6]

Margot attended school in Germany during the war. She was sometimes ordered to work on Sundays, filling in at a bullet factory. She told me that her job was "replacing a mother who had children at home. To give her a day off. We had no men, so we helped out when they asked: 'Would you mind helping out?' It was not really a question, but an order. 'No, you will, you will report.'" Margot said that she wore a dress to work in the factory. When asked if she ever wore pants, she replied:

> That was not pants time yet. We hadn't quite made it yet. The pants time came in the winter of 1944–45. That was when we finally decided to put our training, our training suits, the training pants under our skirts. He (the instructor) just made us take them off, so that we would look like girls again in school. When we went home, we would put them back on so we wouldn't be so cold. And that was the beginning of women wearing pants. And even my mother would later, for comfort and ease, wear pants, and I remember getting her some at the PX (Post Exchange). I got her some nylon pants after the war.[7]

Gwen, who lived in Kansas, received her first pair of pants in 1935 when her mother placed an order with the Montgomery Ward's catalogue. "I loved them. Something I hadn't had! I thought they were just wonderful, and my mother could hardly get me out of them. We wore them to school, on special days, when we were going to do something at recess."[8]

The opposite point of view was presented by Nancy, born in 1921 in Texas, who basically never wore pants. She said, "I started wearing pants only in old age. I never felt comfortable in them."[9] She was in fact dressed in a skirt at the time of the interview.

Marianne provided a photo of her mother, Gennie, who wore pants in the 1920s while visiting a farm, near her Fort Scott, Kansas hometown (Figure 3.3). Denim overalls were very unusual but must have seemed appropriate for the visit.[10]

FIGURE 3.3: *Marianne's parents visiting a farm*, Fort Scott, Kansas. Courtesy Marianne.

Ilene offered a 1939 photo of her family who lived on a ranch in Salinas, California (Figure 3.4). She said that since there were no boys in the family to do the farm work, the four sisters all wore slacks. "We all wore pants except Mom. Also, living on a ranch, we rode horses, so that required chinos or Levi's." Ilene added about her mother: "She never had even one pair." She suggested that her mother might have been influenced by her husband's sisters:

> Two aunts (Dad's sisters—very powerful family figures) considered themselves the arbiters of all that was "proper" in adult women's fashion and they made no secret of the fact that they believed only women of loose morals wore *pants*!! However,

FIGURE 3.4: *Ilene's family posing on their ranch*, Salinas, California, 1939. Courtesy Ilene.

> I think my Mom didn't take to the fashion [...] or maybe she wanted to "keep peace in the family." (Nurses somehow were at the top of my aunts' list of loose women.)

Ilene added, "I have no idea how the opinion was formed! But [...] according to the aunts, these nurses were often spotted having a drink when off duty at the Jeffery Hotel Bar on Main Street!"[11] Lucy Adlington (2019) shed some light on the issue of nurse's reputation in *Women's Lives and Clothes in WW2*. "The drunken slattern nurse was a familiar caricature in Victorian literature, only tempered by images from the other end of the spectrum—holy ministering angels, who healed by generic goodness" (229).

Doris reported that she regularly wore pants. "I always liked them. Easy to live in and get around. It made you feel that you could walk more, a little more masculine."[12] She described herself and her fellow female students all dressed in the same style of men's jeans, a necessity in the paint and clay covered art studio environment where they spent most of their time. "Women's jeans just did not exist," she said.

In Cleveland during World War II, women's Levi's were not available. According to Tracey Panek, Levi Strauss & Co.'s historian:

> Levi Strauss & Co. introduced "Lady Levi's® jeans"—the world's first jeans made exclusively for women in the Fall of 1934. The line was developed for Western

> women who started wearing men's jeans on ranches and farms, and for those women vacationing at the au courant vacation destination at the time—dude ranches.[13]

Panek's statement may explain why Gennie, Marianne's mother, wore denim overalls to visit the farm in Kansas in the 1930s. They were "in."

Doris recollected another story about wearing trousers that illustrated the ambiguity people felt about gender roles defined by dress. "I remember meeting a friend for dinner who went to Chouinard Art School. They kept giving me the bill. My friend said they think you are the 'top girl' between the two of us and that was why they were giving me the bill. I wondered if that was because I was wearing pants."

When asked if she wore pants during the war, Emma, born in 1929 in Auckland, New Zealand, replied:

> Very seldom. I did after we were married. I made up a pair, a little outfit in fact. I went on the train to visit with my sister in Paremata, and everybody was looking at this woman in pants. Well, it was after the war. So, that did not mean anything because the girls wore pants in the war. But, very seldom actually. [...] I was horrified years later when I was living over here and the girls in Saratoga, California could wear slacks to high school. I thought that was terrible. I do not know why? I was just so used to dressing. We did wear shorts in the summertime. But we certainly did not travel in them like they do today.[14]

Joy Beebe, a war bride who left the UK after the war, recollected: "In 1968, when I visited my mother in England, she saw me coming down the road from her window and said, 'I never thought I'd see you wear trousers!'"[15] Joy's memoir, *Snapshot of a War Bride's Life* (2015), tells the story of her life during World War II, sleeping in an Anderson shelter, watching London burn, marrying American soldier Carl, and leaving the UK behind.

Women in Military Uniforms

Both men and women donned uniforms as they joined up to fight the enemy, each in their prescribed gendered role. Military divisions formed corresponding women's divisions. The UK formed the Women's Royal Naval Service (WRENS), Auxiliary Territorial Service (ATS), the Women's Auxiliary Air Force (WAAF), and the Women's Land Army (WLA). The USA female services, Women's Army Corps (WACs), the Women Accepted for Voluntary Emergency Service (WAVES), the Marine Corps Women's Reserve (Reserve), and the Coast Guard Women's Reserve (SPARS), enlisted women to serve in noncombat roles. Women in the military, framed in the cultural definition of that era, served to support the male soldiers

(Hall, Orzada, and Lopez-Gydosh 2015, 234). Women's duties in the military generally involved taking over office duties and other traditional female work to free male soldiers who would have more self-respect serving their country by fighting the enemy on the front (Campbell 1984, 43). Enlisted men did not initially react favorably to women in uniform—possibly because they were viewed as a threat to their masculinity (Patnode 2012, 236). Some husbands and boyfriends expressed fear that the military, especially the masculine dress of women in service, would change their sweethearts. Therefore, the military needed to develop special strategies to encourage women to join up in spite of their resistance to the uniform and hostility they faced from enlisted men.

Author Leila Rupp (1978) reported: "Magazine illustrations and advertisements pictured women in uniform to an extent out of all proportion to their actual numbers. The woman in uniform was, of course, a new and exciting phenomenon, and military recruitment relied greatly on the supposed glamour of service with the armed forces" (143). Propaganda recruitment posters reinforced the glamorous aspect of women's roles in the military by picturing "beautifully groomed women as nurses, potential volunteers, or factory workers" in order to encourage enlistment (Hall, Orzada, and Lopez-Gydosh 2015, 236). The military advised potential female recruits that the benefits of service comprised better understanding their husband's war experience, including the language and terms of the military, as well as the ability to help in their returning hero's readjustment to civilian life (Campbell 1984, 43).

Women received little consideration of their own need for help in adjusting to the hostile environment of the military, let alone readjusting to civilian life and their role as a wife and mother after the war (43). Despite women's commitment to military service and wartime jobs, society still believed they were best equipped to stay at home as wives and mothers (Hall, Orzada, and Lopez-Gydosh 2015, 232).

Many women's branches of the military issued trousers as part of the uniform. British Land Girls were issued long pants so that they would not be hampered by skirts while working in the fields (Figure 3.5). The Land Girls uniforms included "fawn corduroy (or occasionally gabardine) breeches, and fawn knee-length socks" worn with Wellington boots (Edwards 2010, 19). Female pilots, who ferried planes from location to location, wore flight uniforms. Women working in factories wore coveralls for protection and safety (Patnode 2012, 233). Nurses on the battle front wore pants for protection and mobility.

The ideal that women were only proper when dressed in a skirt persisted in the military, sometimes even in situations where slacks would have been much safer and more comfortable. May Buelow Alm (Figure 3.6), a nurse in the military who attended the *Spirit of 45*[16] celebration in San Jose, California, in 2014 ("Remembering Our Veterans" 2014), recounted that she was still angry with her senior officer for the way her unit was treated when they landed on Omaha Beach, July

11, 1944, 35 days after D-Day. The commanding officer insisted that the women change into their nursing dresses worn over their long underwear before climbing over the side of the Landing Craft Infantry transport ship that had carried them across the English Channel. She wanted them to look like proper ladies when they waded through the waves to the beach and then marched across the battlefield.[16] The commanding officer's action represented the continued uneasiness and the minimal acceptance of women in trousers during World War II.

FIGURE 3.5: Dennis Wile, *Three Land Girls*, 1944. UK.Courtesy Dennis Wile.

FIGURE 3.6: *May Buelow Alm, a military nurse.* Courtesy Marie Alm.

Women and Society

Women's identity and success in the 1940s was based on their feminine appearance (Hall, Orzada, and Lopez-Gydosh 2015, 236). Society dictated that women should look attractive to men as "beautiful objects worth fighting for" (236). Therefore, women were advised not to wear their uniforms in the evening because soldiers wanted to see females dressed as women (Hartmann 1978, 229). Men, however, were considered handsome in their uniforms, and they wore them even to social occasions, including weddings and dances.

Political Satire

Tillie the Toiler, a political cartoon drawn by Russ Westover, weighed in on the topic of women in trousers. Tillie, a young single woman, worked as a secretary in an office (Turner 1977, 31). During the war, she joined the WACs and started to dress in slacks (Figure 3.7).

Westover, interviewed in *The San Antonio Light*, expressed his dislike for women in pants. "Slacks designed for all hours of the day are available now, but as a uniform to replace skirts in public, they are affected and in bad taste" ("Women Everywhere Taking to Slacks" 2012). Westover continued his negative appraisal of women in trousers by stating, "Most women to whom slacks now occur as revolutionary garb for everyday wear, will probably have to go through the novice coyness about them, or they think they will. One group will get too mannish and look like fools; the other will go too far in the opposite direction" (Figure 3.8).

FIGURE 3.7: Russ Westover, *Tillie the Toiler—What kind of trousers shall I wear and when?*, 1942. Cartoon. Courtesy Tillie The Toiler © King Features Syndicate.

FIGURE 3.8: Russ Westover, *Tillie the Toiler—The opinion is mutual*, 1942. Cartoon. Courtesy Tillie The Toiler © King Features Syndicate.

As a final point, Westover revealed that he was not totally against women in trousers, "Tillie the Toiler is no slacker when it comes to slacks. You shouldn't be either, if by wearing them you can do your war-time job better." Westover reinforced the idea that successfully doing one's part to win the war was top priority.

Women Working in Factories

When the war broke out, industries realized they needed replacements for the men going off to fight (Figure 3.9). They found the solution by hiring "those who would not normally be employed at all, women, older men, Negroes, and those handicapped by physical defects" (Campbell 1984, 108). Many women who answered the call to work in factories, doing what had been considered "men's work," wore traditionally male protective garments, such as pants, overalls, and coveralls for safety (124).

Both men and women expressed fear of the effect that working in a factory and wearing trousers would have on females and their relationship with men (Patnode 2012, 234). Some men were fearful that their slacks-wearing, factory-working women would no longer cater to their needs, maintain their comfortable home life, clean, cook, wash, and iron. Wartime propaganda posters asked men to give up some comforts of home to allow females to do their part for the war effort and reassured them that the slight discomfort would be only for the duration of the war (Figure 3.10). Men might "even pitch in and help a bit with the housework, temporarily, of course" (Rupp 1978, 153).

Women who worked in factories were called Rosie the Riveters (152). The name may have come from a popular tune written by Redd Evans and John Jacob Loeb and sung by Kay Kyser in 1942 (Kimble and Olson 2006, 535). Rosie is commended in the lyrics for taking a wartime job and contributing to the war effort, but no mention is made of her iconic clothing style (Figure 3.11).

"Rosie the Riveter"

While other girls attend their fav'rite cocktail bar
Sipping Martinis, munching caviar
There's a girl who's really putting them to shame
Rosie is her name

All the day long whether rain or shine
She's a part of the assembly line
She's making history, working for victory
Rosie the Riveter

Keeps a sharp lookout for sabotage
Sitting up there on the fuselage
That little frail can do more than a male will do
Rosie the Riveter

Rosie's got a boyfriend, Charlie
Charlie, he's a Marine

Rosie is protecting Charlie
Working overtime on the riveting machine
When they gave her a production "E"
She was as proud as a girl could be
There's something true about
Red, white, and blue about
Rosie the Riveter

Everyone stops to admire the scene
Rosie at work on the B-Nineteen
She's never twittery, nervous or jittery
Rosie the Riveter

What if she's smeared full of oil and grease
Doing her bit for the old Lendlease
She keeps the gang around
They love to hang around
Rosie the Riveter

Rosie buys a lot of war bonds
That girl really has sense
Wishes she could purchase more bonds
Putting all her cash into national defense
Senator Jones who is "in the know"
Shouted these words on the radio
Berlin will hear about
Moscow will cheer about
Rosie the Riveter!

—Redd Evans and John Jacob Loeb (1942)[17]

FIGURE 3.9: Spencer Beebe, *Line up of Some of Women Welders Including The Women's Welding Champion of Ingalls (Shipbuilding Corp. Pascagoula, MS)*, 1943. U.S. National Archives' Local Identifier: 86-WWT-85-35.

The image of Rosie dressed in coveralls with a bandana around her head is often mistakenly credited to J. Howard Miller's poster (Color Plate 7) produced for Westinghouse Electric and Manufacturing Company in 1943 (Kimble and Olson 2006, 535). The woman in the poster wears blue coveralls and a polka dot scarf tied on her head to protect her hair from moving machine parts. The blue coveralls are reminiscent of Molyneux's 1938 design for beachwear shown in the June 1938 American edition of *Vogue* (see designer Molyneux's overalls, Figure 3.3). Miller's image of Rosie, only displayed at the Westinghouse factory from February 15–28, 1943, had little exposure to the general public during World War II.

Although Miller's image is very well known today, Norman Rockwell's cover art on the May 29, 1943 issue of *Saturday Evening Post* had much greater circulation and actually popularized the image of Rosie dressed in men's work clothing. Rockwell's Rosie, inspired by Michelangelo's painting of the prophet Isaiah on the ceiling of the Sistine Chapel, appears more muscular and powerful than Miller's. The name Rosie, printed on her lunch pail and surrounded by imagery, speaks to her commitment to the war effort. Rockwell symbolized her

FIGURE 3.10: *Women At Work—For Their Uncle Sam*, 1942. *Good Housekeeping*, March 1942, 135.

patriotism by placing Hitler's autobiography *Mein Kampf*[18] under her foot, and "V for Victory" and "Red Cross medallions" pinned to her bib overalls (Kimble and Olson 2006, 541). Mary Doyle Keefe, a telephone operator who lived near Rockwell, served as his model. Rockwell telephoned Mary, who was thinner than the image on the cover, to apologize for depicting her with a larger and more muscular build (Roberts 2015, D8). The powerful build of Rockwell's Rosie did not fit the fashionable silhouette of a slim woman of the time and therefore required an apology from Rockwell to Mary.

Hollywood's Influence

Parisian designers dictated fashion styles for decades before the war. Women all over the world looked to the twice-yearly French fashion shows to see what style, skirt length, silhouette, and color they should wear. Fashion lost its direction, and women lost their traditional fashion guide, when Germany occupied Paris and cut it off from the Allied world (Rantisi 2004, 96).

The American movie industry, which had a huge influence on clothing trends and style and had started to rival Paris even before the war, moved into the fashion void left by the absence of Parisian influence (98). Hollywood costume designers had picked up the slacks trend decades before trousers were widely accepted for day wear (Hannon 2012, 73). Film stars Marlene Dietrich, Katherine Hepburn, and Greta Garbo, early adopters of slacks, probably influenced women more than high fashion designers. Movie studios mass-marketed film inspired fashions and profited from the actresses' star quality, which influenced audiences to adopt new looks not yet in their wardrobes (Balio 1995, 171). Movie stars dressed in trousers took on a glamorized appeal when seen in films. They probably increased women's acceptance to wear slacks a few years later when they filled the factory jobs left by men off fighting the war.

Ellen, a young American woman who worked as a bookkeeper during the war, said "The movie industry was very glamorous for people to see, the movie stars and the men. We were very aware of them."[19] Women looked up to Amelia Earhart, Marlene Dietrich, and Katherine Hepburn, celebrities and movie stars often photographed in slacks who made them look both elegant and feminine. Women, eager to look like the stars, became more receptive to slacks.

Amelia Earhart, the American aviator who was only the 16th woman awarded a pilot's license in the USA, embodied the modern women of the 1920s and 1930s through her profession and her appearance. She wore aviator garb, helmet, leather jacket, and jodhpurs. Although tragically lost at sea in 1930, her image and accomplishments continued to influence modern women. She helped women accept the possibility to remain feminine while dressing comfortably in slacks.

Marlene Dietrich, credited by several women interviewed as an early influencer for women to adopt wearing trousers, was featured in her battle fatigues in the American edition of *Vogue*, May 1944 ("Fashion: G. I. Siren for USO," 109). Ellen reminisced, "Marlene Dietrich photographed wearing pants probably started the trend. As I recall, she had pictures taken sitting in a bar and I think that had some influence on women wearing pants."

When Dietrich entertained troops during World War II, she not only packed revealing sequin dresses but also a "handsomely tailored jacket of her official Camp Show uniform; officer's shirt and tie; and what she claims are her first pair of slacks" (109). Miss Dietrich, quoted in the American edition of *Vogue*, said, "I always wear men's pants" (109).

Siren Suit

The siren suit, a one-piece coverall, came equipped with plenty of pockets to store flashlights and other necessities for sleeping in a bomb shelter (Color Plate 8). Winston Churchill, often photographed in his siren suit, helped to popularize the garment. Many women adopted the practical suit since it was easy to put on quickly and convenient during a nighttime bomb raid. *The Times* (1939) reported that "Women have now invented or accepted the siren suit, a one-piece suit, complete with zipp-fastener and pockets for torch, face-powder, and cigarettes, with a special pocket for the identity card—a whole suit of clothing that can be slipped on in the once more fashionable 'arf a mo'"[20] ("What Suits the Sirens Wore," 9). *Vogue Paris* turned the siren suit into fashion with a sketch of what the most style-conscious women wore in the bomb shelter at the Hotel Ritz (Figure 3.12).

Nella Last, a housewife who lived in Barrow-in-Furness, England, kept a diary for the Mass Observation Project during World War II. She wrote about her siren suit, a gift from her son, on September 12, 1940 (Figure 3.13).

> It's a *"syren suit"*!! It's navy stockinette, with a zip front to the "blouse" and to make ankles snug; "roomy enough and easy-fitting enough to slip on or wear anything extra underneath." It's the maddest, most amusing thing a sedate matron of fifty-one ever possessed! I often wonder what I look like in that one's eyes, and I've a great thankfulness he has not a lot of money to spend, for his taste in hats etc. is not mine, and I know he would buy me some queer and unsuitable ones
>
> (Broad & Fleming 1981, 73).

Kath and Sophie, the British sisters who befriended my father in 1944 while he was stationed in Weston-super-Mare with the 1270th Engineer Combat Battalion, told me about the "siren suits" their mother had made for them to wear. They slept in the suits in their stone basement air shelter during the eighteen months or two years that the town was subjected to nightly bombings.[21] They

FIGURE 3.11: Redd Evans and John Jacob Loeb, *Rosie the Riveter Sheet Music, 1942*. Courtesy National Museum of American History, Smithsonian Institution.

hated wearing the suits probably almost as much as they hated the war, the bombings, and having to sleep in the basement. The sisters remembered the first night of bombing:

> Sophie: "I remember the first night we had a raid, we were in our bedroom which is where the kitchen is now and then mother and father rushing in."
> Kath: "Quick, quick! Up you get, Get your siren suits on."
> Sophie: "What's happening?"
> Kath: "There is an air raid!"

FIGURE 3.12: Eric, *La Cave-Abri du Ritz, Pyjamas de Molyneux et de Robert Piguet*, 1939. *Paris Vogue*, December 1939, 22. Courtesy *Paris Vogue*.

Sophie: "And we could see all the glow from Weston out the bedroom window. Remember that Kath?"
Nan: "What was the glow from? From a bomb?"
Sophie: "Well, fires, all over Weston. From incendiary bombs."

Protective Clothing

Protection during the war was vital for women. Some chose to wear men's clothing and trousers to hide their gender identity. Ursula Mahlendorf (2009), remembering her childhood in Germany, said she dressed in men's clothing and shoes on her long walks to school (220; see also Beevor 2002). She was fearful of being stopped by occupying soldiers. At one point during the war, her English teacher noticed that her boots were split at the seams and suggested she visit the American mission to get a new pair.

FIGURE 3.13: *Marshall & Snelgrove: Specialists in Siren Wear*, 1939. Advertisement. *The Times*, September 25, 1939, 12.

The woman who assisted Ursula at the mission tried to persuade her to take a pair of gender-appropriate shoes. She was only allowed one pair, and remembered:

> A friendly elderly lady in heavy makeup and a pink suit took me into a room full of shoes, both new and used. Pointing to the women's section, she selected a pair of high-heeled lady's pumps.

> "No, thank you, they would not last me a week." I said as I motioned to the other side of the room. "These are what I need." I chose a pair of men's shoes with heavy rubber soles.
>
> The pink lady looked at me doubtfully. "But you can't wear those. They are men's."
>
> "I walk at least two hours a day to go to school. None of the women's shoes, even those with flat heels, have the kind of soles that can withstand walking in rain and snow." I tried to explain[...]
>
> I would not budge. I could see her frustration with me, her look even of suspicion at my lack of femininity. I did not want to offend her, but I held on to the men's shoes. They lasted me a year.
>
> (301-302)

Adelaide, a young woman living in Holland during the war, spoke about the problem that wearing skirts during the war created: "We didn't wear pants. We had very cold legs. There was very little electricity and no gas. We got chilblains. An awful condition where your fingers and toe get red and swollen."[22]

Men Dressed as Women

Women could dress in men's clothes for occasions requiring safety, movement, protection, and/or athletic freedom, especially if the clothing helped them do work supporting the war effort. Men did not have the option to wear women's clothing. Their traditional clothing already provided safety, protection, movement, and athletic freedom. There was no logical reason for men to dress in anything else. On the extremely rare occasions when men wore women's clothing, it was only for humor or for the stage (Vickers and Jackson 2017, 41). Among my father's World War II photos is one of a soldier dressed as a woman (Figure 3.14). He was actually only wearing a woman's wig with long braids, but his appearance, especially the long-braided wig, needed some type of justification. Therefore, on the back of the photo is a handwritten note describing the man's appearance as "part of a costume for a show." Authors Emma Vickers and Emma Jackson reported that men dressed in women's clothing to entertain the troops. Their performances provided "welcome respite from the tedium and destruction of daily life" (42). This kind of entertainment, however, was only "temporary behavior, behavior that was bound to a stage and limited to a specific context and time frame" (49). According to Corinne Sawyer (1987), a man dressed in women's clothing is always considered humorous. She posits that:

> If our laughter comes easily, automatically, thoughtlessly-perhaps we could be a little bit ashamed of our assumptions: that the woman who dresses like a man is just being sensible, but the man who dresses like a woman is either insane, or he is intended

FIGURE 3.14: Photo by Joseph Earl Turner, *Soldier wearing a woman's wig: Part of a show costume*, 1942. Fort Ord, California. Courtesy Turner family.

> to be comic, because there is no reason so compelling that a man in his right mind would willingly accept such a demotion in status!
>
> (14)

Post-War Fashion

After the war, society reinforced the idea that women would return to their proper and natural role in the home, wearing a dress, and taking care of the family (Rupp 1978, 151–65). Women's war work was framed as temporary to discourage them from attempting to continue working after the war was over (Chafe 1990, 21). Rupp (1978) reported: "Women were essentially housewives and mothers, and workers only 'for the duration'" (155). The traditional family, considered a basic element of culture and society, "was regarded as a key link in the nation's defenses and women were deemed essential to the family's survival and stability" (Mitchell 1987, 154).

Lucy described what happened to her job after the war: "I was a riveter in a factory in England. When the war was over, our jobs just went away. There was just no need for riveters."[23] Nurseries and after-school programs for children that enabled women with families to work during the war closed immediately after Victory over Japan Day, August 15, 1945 (154). Child daycare, just like wartime jobs for women, had been a wartime convenience and was not permanent.

Returning veterans needed jobs more than women. The long-standing "marriage bar," the belief that a married woman should not work, ensured there would be jobs for men (Goldin 1988, 2–5; see also Chafe 1990, 24). As mentioned earlier, society expected men to be the "breadwinners of the family." The ability to support one's wife and family was a sign that a man had successfully reached middle-class status (Chafe 1990, 23).

Barbara worked in a bank on Wall Street in New York City during World War II. After she married and had children in the 1950s, she asked her husband if he thought she should go back to work. He replied, "No, I am the breadwinner in this family."[24] Barbara did not go back to work until after she had raised her children.

Conclusion

The war necessitated civilian populations to participate in home front military operations. Wearing trousers or overalls traditionally defined as men's clothing allowed women the freedom of movement and protection to do a man's job. This brought immense disruption to the previous culturally defined roles for men and women's responsibilities and employment. The war provided a turning point that empowered women to seek greater opportunities for equal rights with men, including the right to vote, work outside the home, equal pay, health, and education (Lowe 2017, 122–29). Unfortunately, according to historian Keith Lowe, "In many parts of the world the dream of equal rights and equal opportunity seems just as far away as ever" (128–29).

In peacetime, almost as an artifice to ensure that the traditional divide of gendered fashion would return, Christian Dior's influential "New Look" collection of 1947 confined women once again to traditional female dress. The tight girdles and excessive yards of fabric of Dior's midcalf length skirts correlated with the restricted movement of women who were either willingly or forcefully returned to their traditional role in the home. (For further information about Dior's "New Look," see Chapter 9).

My mother, Pat, pictured with her relatives on the first page of this chapter, continued to wear skirts throughout the war. A review of her high school and college yearbooks reveals photos of her only in skirts and dresses. The earliest photo I could find of her wearing pants was probably taken in 1945 or 1946. Dressed in pleat front pants and saddle shoes, she clowns with her father in the front yard

FIGURE 3.15: *Pat Ford wearing slacks. Posing with her father, Fred Ford*, 1943. Emporia, Kansas. Courtesy Turner family.

FIGURE 3.16: *Pat Ford Turner wearing slacks with daughter, Nan*, 1955. Monterey, California. Courtesy Turner family.

of their Emporia, Kansas home (Figure 3.15). This was obviously the casual dress of a teenager. The next earliest photo, one of my favorites, taken on Christmas 1955, shows my mother sitting on the floor, wearing capri pants, supporting me, 13 months old and just barely standing on chubby wobbly legs (Figure 3.16).

Women have now gained the right to wear pants whenever they want to. Until the 1970s, skirts and dresses were dictated as proper attire for business, school, formal occasions, and church. Some women who attempted to disrupt the status quo and wear trousers to work were sent home from their jobs to change, even into the 1970s. Even when teenage girls were finally allowed to wear slacks to school, jeans were still forbidden for many years. For example, when Leslie, a young woman starting her career in a retail job in San Francisco in 1976, dressed up in a red pants suit, she thought she looked very stylish.[25] Unfortunately, she was sent home to change. It was still not yet "pants time." Women today wear pants more often than skirts. Comfort, rather than status or tradition, is the deciding factor now in women's dress.

NOTES

1. For more information about Molyneux: Caroline Rennolds Milbank, *Couture: The Great Designers* (New York: Stewart, Tabori & Chang, Inc. Publishers), 144–9.
2. Traina-Norell was the partnership of manufacturer Teal Traina and designer Norman Norell, (1941–1959). See also: Eric Wilson. 2002. "Teal Traina, SA Legend, Dies at 85," *WWD.com* (New York City), April 15. https://wwd.com/fashion-news/fashion-features/article-1168823/.
3. Adina (born 1929, Linz, Austria) in discussion with the author, Monterey, CA, May 18, 2019.
4. Hazel (born 1924, Queensland, Australia) in discussion with the author during the *War Brides Association* Reunion of the Queen Mary, Long Beach, CA, September 2015.
5. Vivian (born 1928, Iowa) in telephone conversation with the author, Los Gatos, CA, August 7, 2014.
6. Laney (born 1933, Missouri) in personal conversation with the author, Monterey, CA, July 31, 2014.
7. Margot (born 1929, Osterwieck/Harz, Germany) in discussion with the author, Vallejo, CA, November 9, 2014.
8. Gwen (born 1924, Kansas) in telephone conversation with the author, Monterey, CA, July 23, 2014.
9. Nancy (born 1921, Nacogdoches, TX) in discussion with the author, Pacific Grove, CA, June 1, 2014.
10. Marianne (born 1934, Fort Scott, KS) in telephone conversation with the author, Monterey, CA, July 29, 2014.

11. Ilene (born 1924, Salinas, CA) in e-mail communication with the author, Pebble Beach, CA, January 15, 2020.
12. Doris (born 1925, Cleveland, OH) in telephone conversation with the author, Monterey, CA, July 23, 2014.
13. Tracey Panek in telephone conversation with the author, August 16, 2014.
14. Emma (born 1925, Auckland, New Zealand) in discussion with the author at the Northern California Bay Area War Brides lunch, August 11, 2014.
15. Joy A. Beebe (born 1925, London, UK) in telephone conversation with the author, Portland, OR, June 13, 2018.
16. May Alm (born 1916, Alberta, Canada) in discussion with the author at the *Spirit of '45 Weekend*, History Park at Kelley Park, San Jose, CA, August 13, 2011 and Marie Alm, daughter of May Alm, in e-mail conversation with the author, September 15, 2020. May Alm tells her war time story on Morlin, Bill, 2017. "Voices of War: May Alm." YouTube Video, 2:13. Accessed April 13, 2021. https://www.youtube.com/watch?v=LJVXlH2SKsg.
17. "Rosie The Riveter" Words and Music by John Jacob Loeb and Redd Evans Copyright © 1942, 1970, 1998 Fred Ahlert Music Group and Music Sales Corporation Copyright Renewed. All Rights for Fred Ahlert Music Group Administered by BMG Rights Management (US) LLC. All Rights Reserved Used by Permission *Reprinted by Permission of Hal Leonard LLC.*
18. Adolf Hitler wrote his autobiographical manifesto, *Mein Kampf*, in 1925.
19. Ellen (born 1923, Kansas, USA) in discussion with the author, Sacramento, CA, July 22, 2015.
20. "Arf a mo," refers to a political cartoon of a soldier lighting his pipe and asking the Kaiser for "half a moment," to take a pause in the war for a smoke.
21. Kath and Sophie (born 1924 and 1925, Weston-super-Mare, UK) in discussion with the author, Weston-super-Mare, UK, June 30, 2011.
22. Adelaide (born 1927, The Hague, the Netherlands) in discussion with the author, Davis, CA, November 20, 2014. Chilblains is an uncomfortable skin condition, found usually on the hands and toes, caused by cold weather and poor circulation. People who have poor nutrition, like the French suffering under Nazi occupation, are especially susceptible.
23. Lucy (born 1924, UK) in discussion with the author at the Northern California Chapter of the WWII War Brides Association lunch, Campbell, CA, March 13, 2017.
24. Barbara (born 1928, Detroit, MI) in discussion with the author, Oakland, CA, July 6, 2014.
25. Judy (born 1954, Inglewood, CA) in discussion with the author, San Francisco, CA, September 2016.

4

Home Front Handicrafts: Creativity Inspired by Restrictions

> You never sat idle, you knitted everywhere. The elevator operator would be knitting. I knitted all my first baby clothes.
>
> Australian War Bride[1]

During World War II, "making do" was an act of patriotism. Every scrap saved, every garment patched and patched again, freed a factory worker to build something essential for the military. The acts of sewing, mending, remaking clothing, and going without were all doing one's part by saving precious resources for the war effort. Every leftover piece of fabric was saved, made into clothing, patched into quilts, laundered and reused, and eventually used as rags until they ultimately disintegrated (Maginnis 1992, 60). All income levels saved scraps as their "noble sacrifice" (60).

The National Cotton Council, in a pamphlet titled *A Bag of Tricks for Home Sewing* (1945), published in the USA, advised, "The War has taught us that it isn't *how much* we have that counts but *how well we use what we have*." The information ended with a rallying cry for the home sewer, "A Yard Saved is a Yard Gained, for Victory!" (1).

The Great Depression of the 1930s had hit hard around the world, engraining habits of thrift to last a lifetime. Many women (and men) lost their jobs and no longer had the money to buy store-bought goods (Hall, Orzada, and Lopez-Gydosh 2015, 232). Therefore, thrift was already a part of most people's lives when the war started. Money was scarce and alternative means were needed to get by. I remember my Aunt Leila, who lived on a farm outside Emporia, exclaiming in her Kansas twang, "That costs money!"[2] It was not until I started to research the habits of women in the 1930s and 1940s, that I came to understand that her statement did not mean it costs a lot of money, but actually that an item would cost any money at all. During the Great Depression, especially on farms and in small communities, money was a "scarce commodity" (Chesky 2010, 25). Bartering chickens, eggs, or farm products for clothing or other items was accepted at the local store in place of money.

During World War I,

> Domestic skills, especially of sewing and knitting, became deeply integrated with cultural ideas about how all women could contribute to the waging of modern, total war. [...] the militarization of women's domestic labor in France, Great Britain, and America—especially sewing and knitting—became one of the more ubiquitous and significant ways in which women contributed to the war and by which the war came home.
>
> (Grayzel 2019, 135)

Making over old clothing, restyling, and repurposing material helped stretch the family budget (Gordon 2009, 37–38). Clothing that did not fit or was worn out was remade or given to someone who could use it. Virginia, who was born in 1922 in Pasadena, California, told me that her mother shortened a skirt that had become too small and used the fabric cut from the hem as a side panel insert to increase the size and make it wearable again.[3] Susie, a French woman born in 1924, told me that still today, she gives away clothing she is not using because she is concerned that someone else might need it.[4]

Consumers, especially women, responded to the deprivation of goods and clothing by using ingenuity and creativity to "make-do." This chapter will explore creative handicraft inspired by rationing, scarcity, and shortages.

Sewing

Sewing was not a hobby as it sometimes is today but a necessary skill and part of the homemaker's job. Most women during the war and earlier were skilled at sewing and commonly made some, if not all the clothing for their families (Taplin 1997, 91). Fashion historians Elizabeth Wilson and Lou Taylor (1989) reported, "Home-made clothes lacked the status of the ready-made, and many women probably made their own (and/or their children's) out of economic necessity rather than the love of it" (95).

Several women interviewed reported that their mothers made their clothing. French war bride, Jeanne, reported that, "My parents never bought clothes from the store because it was more expensive to buy them already made and they were not well made, and you could not do very much to alter them. The homemade outfit, you could always repair it since you had a little bit left over, you could do something, you could let out the hem, make them better."[5]

Joy Beebe recollected that her mother in the UK sewed most of her clothes, including her school uniform, "My mother handmade my school uniform—it lasted for 6 years of school 1936–41. We had to change out of our school uniform right when we got home so it would last."[6] Joy elaborated in her memoir, *Snapshots of a War Bride's Life* (2015),

> Ma was shocked at the price [of the uniform] and was finally able to purchase the correct fabric and make my [school] clothes herself; she was good at tailoring and was pleased with the results. [...] My mother had to design the pattern for this whole outfit as it was exclusive to our school; they didn't print patterns as they expected everything to be bought ready-made. This was a major project for Ma but she was clever with the needle and really did all she could to have me going to school looking like all the other girls. We wore lisle stockings, black shoes, a black velour hat with the school hatband and a dark coat and carried our gym clothes in a drawstring bag. In the summer we wore checked cotton dresses (choice of pink, green or blue and white) with white collars and cuffs and a Panama straw hat with a ribbon band of the school colors [...] Owing to the war and clothes rationing, my father's illness and death and my mother's expert care and alterations—that outfit lasted me the five years I went to the school!
>
> (80–82)

Governments promoted home sewing in an effort to ensure that both materials and labor would be prioritized for the military. Consequently, sewing classes reemerged and became popular with women representing all social classes (Reynolds 1999, 337). Celia Wiggins' domestic-science class in the school she attended in the village of Shafton, South Yorkshire, UK, included a "remake project" (Held and Sanderson 2020, 47). For her project, Celia bought a fur collar at a large outdoor market and turned it into warm gauntlet gloves to wear while waiting for the bus (47).

Wealthy women, who formerly employed dressmakers to make their clothing, were encouraged to take sewing classes so that their prewar seamstresses could be free to seek employment in military work (Reynolds 1999, 328). The Imperial War Museum's World War II collection includes images of women who learned to sew in a dressmaking class in Brixton, a district of South London. The photo shows the "fashion parade" held to show the clothing the women had learned to make in the class. Mrs. Hill, the second woman in the image, wore the skirt she made out of a pair of postman's trousers (Figure 4.1) Using men's clothes to make new was a common method of getting around fabric scarcity and rationing during the war.

The French women's magazine, *Mode de Jour,* ran an advertisement in their March 20, 1941 issue for a sewing course at l'Académie de la Femme de France.

FIGURE 4.1: *Pupils of a London County Council dressmaking class in Brixton, London, hold a fashion parade to show their friends and family what they have learnt*, 1943. Courtesy Imperial War Museum, 1943© IWM (D 12897).

The ad declared, "Apprenez à faire vous même vos robes et chapeaux." *Mode de Jour*'s readers were offered the opportunity to learn to make their own dresses and hats (translation author's own) (Figure 4.2). Once France was occupied by the Germans, these skills would become even more essential.

Propaganda films, shown before the regular movie feature in theaters, encouraged people to turn their old clothing into new. The short British film, *Make Do and Mend,* opens with a family seated around a table (Figure 4.3). "We haven't got enough coupons!" exclaims the daughter! "And I've got to have a few for towels and things for the house," replies her mother. A knock is heard coming from inside the family clothing wardrobe. Then the clothes, including a wedding dress, fly out and have the following conversation with the family:

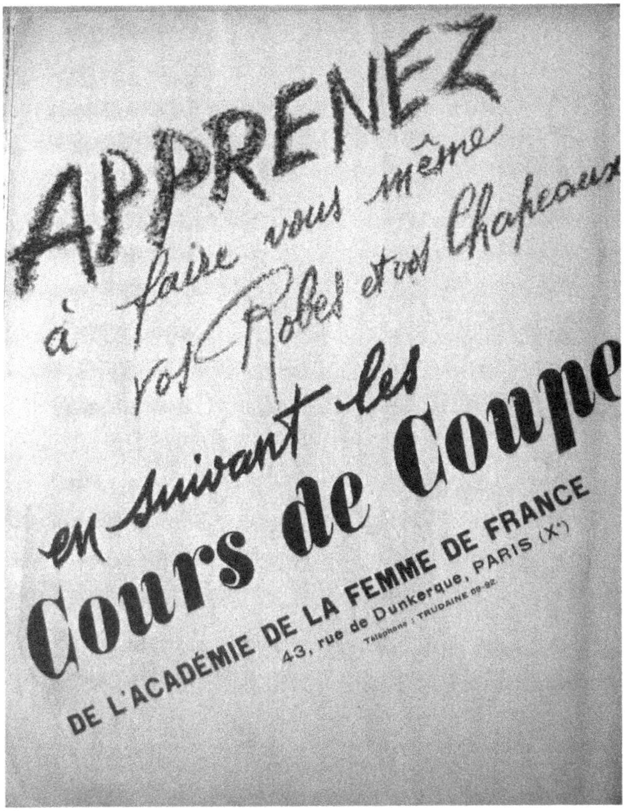

FIGURE 4.2: *Apprenez à faire vous vêtements*, 1941. *Mode de Jour*, 1009, March 20, 1941, 32. Palais Galliera Library, Paris.

> "Perhaps we can help you?"
> The wife exclaims, "My wedding dress!"
> The wedding dress answers, "I'd like to be a night shirt and panties!"
> A pair of men's trousers suggests, "Well, if the youngster wants some shorts, I don't mind being cut down!"
> The wife reacted, "That's all well to do but I have never turned a pair of trousers into a skirt in my life!"
> The suit answers, "Never mind, it is quite easy to do. Ask at your Technical Institute. There is probably a local *Make Do and Mend* class where you can learn."
> ("Ministry of Information" 1943)

The film ends with a woman in a sewing class suggesting, "Or why not get together with your friends and form a *Make Do and Mend* group. Then you can all help each other."

FIGURE 4.3: *Make Do and Mend,* 1943. British Ministry of Information © Imperial War Museum (NPB 13037). https://www.iwm.org.uk/collections/item/object/1060034062.

Nella Last, a housewife in Barrow-in-Furness, Lancashire, UK, kept a diary of her wartime activities for the Mass Observation Project which started in 1939 and "invited members of the public to record their day-to-day lives in the form of a diary" (Sheridan 1991, 1). The organization celebrated its seventy fifth anniversary in 2014 with a conference in Brighton, UK attended by the author.

Nella, a skilled seamstress, created children's nightgowns, cloth dolls, and bandages that she made out of salvaged garments and fabrics. The need to stretch the limited clothing resources of her family was a constant theme in her diary and she often mentioned how she felt about creating something from nothing. "There's a great satisfaction in seeing a thing take shape and form under one's hands, especially if they are made from oddments into something worthwhile," she wrote (Malcolmson and Malcolmson 2008, 34). She considered her handsewn hospital donations one of her many contributions to the war effort. "You are the Salvage Queen, I believe," exclaimed the nun who received Nella's package at the hospital (Broad and Fleming, eds. 1981, 88). Being a "salvage queen" was a badge of honor during the war when scarcity and outfitting the military affected all aspects of life and "creating something from nothing" was an important skill.

Lydia, born in 1929, had spent her early years traveling internationally with her parents, who were entertainers, and her sister. Her father, from China, performed

FIGURE 4.4: *You Could Be Shot for Wasting Paper*, 1943. Advertisement. U.S. Government, *New York Sun*. Courtesy Duke University Library. https://idn.duke.edu/ark:/87924/r4154f812

what she called "ancient acts," including juggling, jumping through hoops and other things. Her mother, from Munich, was a dancer. When the girls were old enough to go to school, right before the war started, they returned to Germany and their parents went to Paris for an engagement. War broke out soon after and Lydia's mother was interned immediately. Lydia's father offered himself as a replacement for his wife so she could return to her children. Although he was eventually freed, Lydia's father could never rejoin his family in Germany.

Lydia reported that in Germany, she, her sister, and her mother learned to scrounge and use everything that could be found. She reminisced that discharged bullets made good sewing thimbles for her small fingers, "So, they got the cartridges for bullets. That makes a perfect thing for thimbles. For a sewing kit. The whole family went out scrounging. Whatever you could find, we used."[7]

Valerie Maier, the young German woman mentioned earlier who made red dresses for herself and her sister from flags, continued to be resourceful in finding ways to obtain materials to make clothing. Military service was mandatory for women her age in Germany and she was assigned to work as a weather forecaster at the airport. She grew tired of this work and came up with a scheme. She invented a malady, a parasitic infection that landed her in the hospital. Since her infection did not make her that sick, she was still required to work while in the hospital. Her job was rolling cotton bandages. She saved short ends of bandages that would have ended up in the trash. Putting all the ends together, she was able that to make bathing suits for herself and her younger sister, Ingrid. The fabric, Ingrid reported, was stretchy and perfect for the tap pants and bra type bathing suits she made.[8]

Paper Shortages

Among the extensive list of scarce products, paper shortages caused unexpected difficulties for home sewers (Figure 4.4). Conserving paper was patriotic and not a scrap could be wasted. Even sewing patterns had to do double duty or more.

FIGURE 4.5: *Patron pour 5 Manteaux*, 1941. *Mode du Jour*, November 20, 1941, 18–19. Palais Galliera Library, Paris.

Fashion magazines helped by featuring articles showing ways to use a pattern to create many different looks, thereby conserving tissue paper. For example, *Mode du Jour* (1941), a French magazine, featured a pattern for a coat in their November 20, 1941 issue that could be styled in five different ways, “1 Patron Pour 5 Manteaux,” one pattern for five coats, (translation author’s own) (Figure 4.5). Each coat looked very different from the others, but was created with only a few simple variations, including color blocking and collar and pocket variations. Therefore, the pattern consumed much less paper.

FIGURE 4.6: *Our Special “Three-Way Saving” Pattern*, 1942. *Woman and Home*, October, 1942, 31. St Peter’s House Library, University of Brighton, UK.

Like the article in *Mode Du Jour*, which showed variations on one coat pattern, *Women and Home*, a British magazine, illustrated a way to make three dresses from one pattern, "Our Special 'Three-Way Saving' Pattern." (October 1942) (Figure 4.6) The article states,

> However firm your resolve to save, there comes a moment when you have "simply nothing to wear," and a new frock becomes a necessity, either for the office or a "leave-time" celebration. You will have an easier conscience if you know that, by choosing a frock as economically planned as our Special Pattern and making it yourself, you are saving material, money and the country's labour.
>
> (31)

Version B of the three dresses was made with contrasting fabrics, which offered "further scope for saving on short lengths and remnants." Remnants are pieces of fabric left over at the end of the bolt, too short to make anything. Consequently, coupons were not required to purchase remnants, although a little creativity was needed to make an attractive garment using them (31).

Non-Rationed Materials

Many kinds of non-rationed fabrics were valued and used to make clothing. Prewar fabric stocks, black-out cloth, remnants, fabric scraps, butter muslin (a mesh cotton fabric like cheesecloth), parachutes, carpet, mending yarn, and home furnishing fabrics were all turned into clothing (Summers 2016, 137; see also Norman 2007, 8).

Kath and Sophie Eastlake, the sisters mentioned in the introduction who befriended my father in Weston-super-Mare, UK, both rode horses during the war. Sophie told me that she wanted a new shirt to wear horseback riding, but fabric was not available. She found an old tablecloth in "a nice brown color" that she asked her dressmaker to turn into a new shirt.[9] She was able to have the new garment she wanted without using any precious coupons (Figure 4.7).

Karin Yount, born 1923 in Yalta, Crimea, also wore a dress made from a tablecloth (Figure 4.8). "My mother made [it] from a tablecloth we found in a bombed-out apartment." Karin's mother also made a blouse out of a white silk parachute, which the two women shared. She noted, "I do not know if it was a German or American parachute."[10]

Helen, who was born in 1926 and spent her entire life in Davis, CA, was a teenager when the war broke out.[11] Her brother served in the Navy and had an extra parachute that he gave to his family. Helen did not know why the lightweight silk

FIGURE 4.7: *Kath riding with Dan Law, an American soldier stationed in Weston-super-Mare,* 1944. Courtesy Kath Eastlake and Norman and Carol Law Stanley.

FIGURE 4.8: *Karin Trenina Yount and Burton Yount. Karin is wearing the dress her mother made from a tablecloth.* 1945. Courtesy Yount Family.

parachute was no longer needed. However, I suspect that nylon parachutes had replaced the old silk ones. Helen's mother used the parachute to make her daughter a prom dress (Figure 4.9). The entire circumference of the skirt at the hem measures seventeen yards. Helen's mother saved time by using the finished hem of the parachute, sewn in black thread, as the bottom edge of the dress, instead of

FIGURE 4.9: *Helen wearing her parachute silk prom dress*, 1944. Courtesy Helen.

hemming it all herself. The name of the factory that made the parachute, Baldwin New York, is visible along the dress hemline. Constructed with boning inside the bodice, the dress closes in the back with tiny loops and buttons. The black ruffle on the neckline picks up the color of the hem stitching. The exceptionally fine silk fabric is still in excellent condition.

Carla, the teenager in Rome mentioned in the introduction, only owned one good dress to wear to church. During the war, she wore out her dress. Since no dress fabric was available, her mother used a roll of cotton percale, a high thread count fabric most commonly used for sheets, left over from her own wedding trousseau (Cohen and Johnson 2010, 266). The fabric, intended to be used to make sheets, had not been touched since her parent's wedding day. Carla's husband explained that when women got married in Italy in the 1920s, they were expected to bring a trousseau of hand-embroidered sheets, towels, and tablecloths, enough to last their entire life. Girls learned at an early age to embroider and started sewing

FIGURE 4.10: *Soldiers dressed in greens and pinks*. Courtesy U.S. Army Medical Department Office of Medical History.

in childhood to fill their trousseau. Carla's mother dyed the fabric and gave it to their dressmaker to sew the dresses. After the war, Carla started a sewing business, but it was still difficult to find fabric:

> The Americans were selling blankets. We used to make coats with the blankets. We bought parachutes and made blouses, underwear, skirts, shorts, everything. It was nice silk material. I don't know who was selling the parachutes, but we could buy one in the black market.[12]

Celia Wiggins, a British woman born in Shafton, South Yorkshire in 1921, started her first teaching job during World War II, but lacked appropriate clothing. Her husband, serving in the Royal Air Force, was able to bring home a set of wool curtains from the officer's mess that were being replaced. Celia, a skilled seamstress, turned the curtains into a dress to wear to her new job. Her daughter and granddaughter reported in *PieceWork* magazine that she also made "underwear and nightgowns from parachute silk," some of which was still in her fabric stash when she died (Held and Sanderson 2020, 47).

Vera, who was born in 1930 and lived in London with her parents, was evacuated to Somerset, UK with her sister when the bombing started in 1942. She related, "I was the youngest of three girls so during the war I always had hand-me-downs. Of course there were no new clothes though a few things were available with clothing coupons. My skirts always had hem line creases where they had been lowered." She reported that buying underwear was almost impossible. "We were able to get a parachute now and then and made underwear—'French' panties, loose at the bottom [...] We washed ours every night and drying was a problem, with no central heat." The girls also took advantage of other non-rationed fabrics, "My sister could sew, and she bought drapery material and made a skirt and jacket for me."[13]

Jeanne, the French woman mentioned in Chapter 1, told a story about a coat her mother made from a blanket after World War I. During World War II, the coat, already over 20 years old, was remade into a coat for Jeanne.

> My mother had a coat in her wardrobe which had become too small for her and was not exactly fashionable. It was made out of an old American blanket that my grandmother had got at the end of the First World War [in France] from a store selling American army surplus. At that time in 1919, she had a dressmaker turn it into a coat for my mother after having it dyed. It was a khaki blanket and she had it dyed dark grey. It probably was intended to be black but did not turn out to be coal black. So that was the kind of coat she had which was very heavy, nice, woolen fabric, not really nice but very sturdy and warm, and that was made into a coat for me by a dressmaker.

Repurposing Men's Uniforms

Men's old clothes or uniforms, left in the closet while a husband or brother was off fighting, became a ready resource for clever women to make new clothing. Adelaide, living in The Hague, Netherlands, sadly reported that her father had cancer during the war and looked terrible. Unfortunately, he did not realize that he was sick because everyone looked awful and had lost weight. When his illness was discovered, he had surgery and was given extra coupons for food. Unfortunately, it was too late, and he died. Adelaide reported that "he had several good suits and then it was common to have suits custom made. The tailor who made the suits [originally for her father] remade them into woman's suits. They were very nice."[14]

Jean, the British woman mentioned in Chapter 2, who was born in 1929 and grew up in Welwyn Garden City, met and married an American military officer while he was stationed in the UK. She reported that she used her husband's excess uniform fabric, purchased at the Post Exchange (PX) to have clothing made for herself.[15] "I had one beautiful suit and coat that was made from some fabric my husband brought to his uniform tailor and there was enough left over. I had a suit and a coat made. The suit was army dark green and the coat was a paler fabric they called 'pinks' (Figure 4.10) They used the 'pink' fabric for the military pants."[16] The "pinks" and "greens" that Jean referred to were described in the *New York Times* (May 5, 2019) as the name that, "The troops who beat the Axis powers in the 1940s gave the service uniform, with its slightly rose-hued trousers or skirt and distinctive belted olive coat, an affectionate nickname, 'pinks and greens'" (Phillips 2019).This iconic uniform has recently been reissued for service people in the US Army, renamed as Army Greens.

Karin Yount was forced to flee Eastern Prussia with her mother by foot during the freezing winter of 1945. Arriving finally in Bavaria, Germany, they lived in refugee camps for many months. Karin wrote, "We possessed practically nothing and the only items we could buy were from the black market." Karin spoke three languages and was able to find employment with the American military where she met her future husband, Burton Yount. When she moved to the USA to join her husband-to-be, Karin carried the only suit she owned in a cardboard suitcase.[17] Her mother had made the suit out of two pairs of her husband-to-be's "pinks fabric" military trousers. Karin described the process of turning men's trousers into a woman's suit:

> If you are familiar with sewing, you can imagine man's trousers are cut from many different pieces of material. Those officer's trousers were worn with an Eisenhower Jacket and were made from fine quality gray gabardine, they were called "pinks." It was an intrigued work to piece all this together creating a design for a tight-fitting jacket and a skirt. But as a proverb says—poverty creates inventions.

Karin spoke very proudly of her suit and the suitcase she carried when she arrived in the USA, which are now housed in the National Museum of American History, Division of Cultural and Community Life of the Smithsonian Museum, as a tribute to the ingenuity required to survive World War II.

Lydia also used old coats to make new: "Because of rationing and scarceness, we had to use anything to make clothes, sheets, towels, blankets, etc. We found German military coats of real wool and dyed them black, ripped them apart and turned them into nice, warm coats for us!"

Twice-Turned Garments

Aus Alten Sachen Neues Machen (Making New Things Out of Old Things), a German women's magazine, offered several ways to use men's clothing to make "new" for women or children (1943-45?). Examples include,

- A tuxedo, no longer needed, found a new life as a woman's suit (Figure 4.11).
- A man's wool suit became a growing boy's jacket and short pants (Figure 4.12).
- A Chesterfield topcoat turned into a sleek woman's coat with hood (Figure 4.13).

The topcoat instructions suggested "der gewendet wird," or to turn the fabric to the interior, unworn side. The practice of taking apart a garment and remaking it with the interior side of the fabric turned to the outside was a widespread practice common in many countries when scarcity inspired ingenuity and hard work.

FIGURE 4.11: *Aus Alten Sachen Neues Machen suggests turning a man's tuxedo into a woman's suit.* 1943-45?, 3.

FIGURE 4.12: *Aus Alten Sachen Neues Machen suggests turning a man's suit into a boy's suit.* 1943-45?, 6.

FIGURE 4.13: *Aus Alten Sachen Neues Machen suggests turning a man's topcoat into a women's coat.* 1943-45?, 7.

Kathryn Squitieri, a fashion historian and textile conservator based in New York City, explained the concept of twice-turned garments:

> Twice-turned means that you wore out the wrong side too and have turned the fabric back to the original right side. Thrice turned means that you've once again turned the right side of the fabric inside. I've seen this used more often in the 18th rather than the 19th century, but it was still done if either the wrong side of the fabric was just as nice as the right side, or if you were terribly poor.[18]

Luise Van Dyne, who was born in 1930 and lived with her Estonian father and Japanese mother in Tokyo, had a hard time finding clothes while growing up in Japan during the war.[19] "You could not go to a department store. They had beautiful stores, but they were empty. No merchandise. It was all toward the military." Luise outgrew her clothing so her father offered to have the dressmaker make her a coat out of one of his old ones. Luise reported:

> Here [in the USA] we have a hairdresser. In Japan, we had a dressmaker. My mother took my father's coat to the dressmaker and asked: "Can you make anything out of this for Luise's coat?" The dressmaker took the lining out of it and inside found that it was a beautiful brown. So, she turned it inside out and made me a beautiful brown coat.

Luise's dressmaker had to unpick all the seams of the coat and carefully lay the pattern pieces for a girl's coat out on the interior face of the old man's coat. After re-stitching and finishing, Luise's new coat looked brand new since the wrong side of the fabric had not become worn. Luise shared another experience she had trying to get shoes in Tokyo during the war:

> My feet were growing and eventually I had to get another pair of shoes. We went to the custom shoemaker and he said, "I cannot give you anything in leather because it all had to go to the military. I do have whale skin that I can make shoes out of." My mother said, "I guess you do have to because my daughter's feet are growing." So he did make a pair for me and I wore them. They were so ugly, black, no shine. When they got wet they just fell apart. I can't remember what I wore after that, they were the one pair of shoes I owned.

Carla, in Rome, also used the technique to turn garments. She said that poor people, "Had to mend. They had to patch. They had to reverse coats and suits and pants. Everything! If the material was worn on the right side, we used to reverse the material to show it looked better inside."

Taking a coat apart to remake it with the wrong side of the fabric as the face, requiring careful ripping out of many seams, was not an easy job. Traditional tailored garments are underlined with a separate fabric for support and shaping. Tiny "feather stitches" mold the exterior fabric to the interlining (Baker 2009, 6). This method does insignificant damage to the fabric since the stitches are exceptionally fine. Removing the stitches takes some time to cut and unpick the threads but would be a project easy enough for a child to do. Jean reported that picking out the stitches was her job because she was a teenager and did not know how to sew.

Adelaide, who was born in 1927 in The Hague, Netherlands, reported that under the German occupation, "You made do with things." She said, "So often a man's shirt would wear down on the collar, there was a way that you could turn it upside down, so the frayed area didn't show. Also, edges of sleeve cuffs that frayed could be turned so the worn edge was hidden."

Even sheets were turned. When they became a little worn and thin in the middle, a sheet could be cut in half and resewn with the unworn selvages seamed in the center. *Cassell's Household Guide*, published in 1869, directed homemakers to "salvage edges of worn sheets to use for babies cribs and even to turn pillow cases. The same method of turning pillow-cases may be observed. The cases thus repaired answer very well for family use. To be profitable, they should be turned before the threads break into holes" (299).

Mending

Easy Ways to Sew and Save (1941), a pamphlet distributed by an American thread manufacturer, suggesting methods to make clothing last longer, recommended:

> Cultivate the habit of mending, repairing, and altering. A small investment in time will return substantial dividends in comfort and good grooming, to say nothing of the actual money savings effected by this lengthened life of garments and accessories.
>
> (44)

The British Board of Trade's 1943 booklet, *Make Do and Mend* recommended:

> Mend clothes before washing them or sending them to the laundry, or the hole or tear may become unmanageable. [...] Keep a look out for loose buttons and other fastenings, frayed buttonholes and split seams, and mend them at once.
>
> (2–3)

In the 1930s and 1940s, clothing was more expensive relative to income than today (Summers 2016, 26). Fine quality material and classic styling, that would last for a long time, was valued (Palmsköld 2015, 35). Mending allowed the garment to serve a longer life, be passed down to a family member, or remade into children's clothing. An economic necessity, mending was a widespread practice until about the mid-1970s (31, 35).

Even runs in stockings were mended using a tiny crochet hook called a latch ladder mender (Figure 4.14). The process involved inserting a tiny crochet hook at the bottom of the run, then picking up each dropped stitch, traveling up the "ladder" or "run." A talented seamstress could make a pair of stockings look new. Ilene, who grew up in Salinas, California, reported that stocking mending "spawned small home businesses with signs in windows 'Silk Hosiery Mending Here.'"[20] Lucy remembered, "My mother [in Nottingham, UK] had her silk stockings mended. There were little tables in department stores where a lady sat and mended."[21]

Jean told me about her sister's talent repairing silk stockings:

> My sister used a very fine crochet needle and she could pick up the runs. If you got a run, she would pick that up and it would be as good as new. You know it was quite clever of her. I don't think I could have done it. She got so good at it that people would just beg her to fix their nylons. They would pay her, a pittance I am sure, but they would give her something for having made nylons as good as new.

FIGURE 4.14: *Latched ladder mender.* Courtesy Eirlys Penn.

Kath and Sophie, the sisters in Weston-super-Mare, along with their sister-in-law Sarah, remembered issues with the heavy black stockings they wore in the winter that sometimes got holes:

> Sophie, "If we had a hole in them, of course, we filled it in with ink."
> Sarah, "It did not show then. Until we got home and could do something about it."

The women were filling in the hole with black ink on their skin, a clever way to temporarily look well dressed.

Vincent Schoenstein, serving in the US Army in Europe, had a traumatic experience while pressing his Eisenhower jacket in preparation for his wedding in July 1946. Fortunately, his US-issued sewing kit and his mending skills saved him from embarrassment (Color Plate 9) (Figure 4.15).

> All my clothing was stuffed in a duffel bag wrinkled and badly in need of sprucing up. I acquired a very old, cast iron flat iron that had to be heated over the potbelly stove in our barracks. I would moisten one of my undershirts and then iron over my footlocker covered with my army blanket. This worked very well for my trousers and shirt but when it came to the jacket it was much more difficult. The pockets, pleats and sleeves were very tedious and when I got to the lapels, I became careless. The iron was made hot on the stove. I was concerned about burning my hand and forgot to place my moistened civvies shirt over the lapel. The moment I placed the iron on the jacket I knew I had made a stupid mistake. The odor of burnt wool told the story.

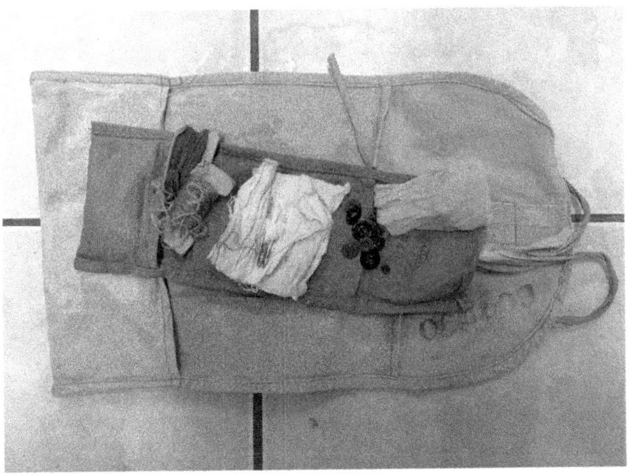

FIGURE 4.15: *World War II issued US Army sewing kit.* Photo by Nan Turner.

> I had been brought up being handy with a needle and thread, so I decided to make an attempt to rectify my mistake. The jacket was useless as it was, and I thought I could salvage it if I could replace the burnt right lapel. The first problem, where could I find the same material? My olive drab (O.D.) overseas cap was the same material, so back to the supply sergeant to see if I could get another. He gave me a used one, but the color was not the same. I decided I would wear the used cap and disassemble my own cap that matched the jacket. With a "Gem" single edge razor blade, I took the burnt lapel apart and saved as much of the thread as possible. Much to my dismay, the material from the cap was not large enough to replace the burnt lapel. By this time I was determined that I was going to complete this project even if I had to make a seam in it. Using the burnt lapel as a pattern, I cut out the new lapel from the seamed cap material, using the small manicure scissors I had carried all during the war. The thread I had removed I now used again making the smallest stitches I was capable of, just inside the fold of the lapel. The outer visible area around the perimeter of the lapel I folded and tucked, basting it in place with white thread in large stitches. I carefully ironed and pressed it.
>
> We had German POWs (prisoners of war) that we used as an overhead attachment, meaning that they did our menial work. They were our barrack orderlies and kitchen cooks. They also had a foot treadle sewing machine. For a pack of cigarettes, a German "schneider master"—a tailor—sewed the outer edge and pressed the whole jacket. Good as new, two days later, I left for England [for my wedding].[22]

Vince still wears the jacket, although he did use his sewing skills again recently to let out just a little along the side seams. At over 94 years old, he needed just a little more room (Color Plate 10).

Today mending has become nearly a forgotten art (Palmsköld 2015, 36). Many people discard clothing just because they have not worn it in some time, and buy something new (36). Today, clothing costs very little in relation to income and therefore often lacks the value to make it worth mending (36). The fabrics worn today, the majority cotton knits, are generally of poor quality, reducing the motivation to take the time to mend.

Rags and Patches

During the war, rags were valued for their many household uses (Strasser 1999, 81). Keith Ayling (1942) discussed the value of rags, clean or dirty:

> Rags are riches today. If Hitler had only a small percentage of the old clothes and rags that are hidden in American homes, every German soldier in Russia could

> have warm clothing and two changes of winter underwear. Rags make uniforms, blankets, rugs, roof coverings and packaging-case linings for delicate instruments. In Europe, science has achieved miracles with rags; so bring yours out even if they are dirty. In dispatching them separate the oily from the dry, but send them all.
>
> (188)

Excess rags were not thrown away, but donated to the "ragman" or the "rag-and-bone man," who in many countries went door to door in working class neighborhoods of large cities, picking up valuable scraps of fabric and other discarded material (Strasser 1999, 46, 118). He in turn peddled them to manufacturers to make paper or recycled fabric (13). Rags were shredded to make shoddy or rag-wool, an inferior quality fabric or yarn. Shoddy was used to make recycled yarn or fabric possibly to make woven blankets and carpets.

Women's magazines suggested getting into the ragbag and using old swatches to make a patched garment. The British magazine, *Woman and Home's Good Needlework* (December 1941), ran an article for the Board of Trade called "Patriotic Patches," which suggested,

> A neatly patched garment is something to be proud of nowadays. To discard clothes that are not completely worn out is as unpatriotic as to waste good food. Every yard of wool, rayon, cotton or other fabric that you buy unnecessarily deprives the war effort of vital material.
>
> (6)

Woman and Home (October 1942) offered suggestions to make a child's patchwork apron out of old scraps of fabric (Figure 4.16).

During the Great Depression, patched garments had been a sign of poverty. However, during the war, they became a mark of pride. Gail, born in 1922, was a teenager in Ferndale, Michigan during the war. She described the clothing she wore, and the effort made to get the most wear out of them, by proudly stating, "We wore patches on our patches."[23] Some times patches even became a fashion trend. For example, decorative elbow patches on jacket sleeves "became quite fashionable," even though it might be covering up a worn area (Norman 2007, 11).

Children's clothing, handed down to younger siblings, cousins, or neighbors, consequently saw a great deal of wear (Figure 4.17). The British Board of Trade advised women to reinforce the elbows, knees, and seats of children's clothing with old fabric scraps. This would ensure that several children would get extended use of the garment.

FIGURE 4.16: *Two Ingenious Aprons*, 1942. *Woman and Home*, October 1942, 10. St Peter's House Library, University of Brighton, UK.

Knitting

Relief knitting was an excellent way to do one's part for the war effort, as important as service on the warfront (Color Plate 11 & 12) (Ayling 1942, 1). Women and men were seen knitting all the time, in the underground, at movies, or during any spare moment; their needles and yarn were ready. Queen Elizabeth, various movie

FIGURE 4.17: *Reinforce Children's Clothes: They will last twice as long*. Issued by the Board of Trade. Courtesy Imperial War Museum © (PSR 8294).

stars, and the young princesses, Elizabeth and Margaret, were all photographed knitting. Eleanor Roosevelt, who "kicked off the United State's war knitting effort for World War II," was called the "First Knitter of the Land" (Colopy 2009, 19).

Wool yarn was needed for military uniforms and it was as scarce as fabric and clothing. Therefore, stretched-out or out-of-styles sweaters were frequently unraveled and reknit. Jeanne remembered in France,

> Unraveling sweaters that were too small or too large and worn in places, washing the wool which had been wound in skeins, then dying the wool, dried and wound into balls to be knitted in a new garment. We had to be more careful with clothes - washing by hand (but we had little soap). Sweaters were very precious, washed carefully, rolled in towels to extract the water, spread out to dry on other towels.

The same story was repeated in the UK. Joy Beebe said, "I remember unravelling woolen knitted jumpers (sweaters), washing the wool, and using it for another jumper."

Yarn manufacturers, hoping that their business would return after the war, issued instruction booklets that encouraged women to continue knitting, even when yarn was hard to come by (Macdonald 1988, 289). The USA thread company, Spool Cotton, published *Knit for Defense* (1941) and *Knit for Victory: Warm Wools for the Long Watch* (1943) (Figure 4.18). The booklets were illustrated with drawings of servicemen relaxing by reading letters from home and opening care packages containing hand knit sweaters to inspire civilians to knit. *Knit for Defense*, issued before the USA entered the war, started with a patriotic declaration of encouragment:

> The National Defense Program isn't all tanks, airplanes and battleships. It's people, too—you and I and 130,000,000 others. North, South, East and West women are taking up the behind-the-scene tasks of an Unlimited National Emergency. You, too, can play a leading role in this greatest defense program of all history by anticipating the needs of our boys in training.
>
> (2)

Service men appreciated the handmade knits they received in care packages because their uniforms, although serviceable, were not always "comfortable or

FIGURE 4.18: *Knit for Defense*, 1941. H-9002 C-8, 3rd edition, *Knit for Victory: Warm Wools for the Long Watch*, 1943. Spool Cotton Company, USA.

well-fitting" (Summers 2016, 41–42; see also Howell 2012, 125). Called "comforts" or "home comforts," handknit scarves, sweaters, and balaclavas, a head covering that incorporates a neck band, were very popular with service men.

Ellen Miller Coile, even as a child in London, worked hard for the war effort. She and her classmates knit socks, gloves, sweaters, and balaclava helmets for the British Red Cross to send to prisoners of war. They also knit sea boot stockings, using yarn made from unwashed sheep fleece, for Merchant Marines (Figure 4.19). The lanolin in the fiber made the socks naturally waterproof. Ellen remembered knitting so much that her hands bled.[24] Ellen's first knitting project at age nine years was a cover for her gas mask case.

Elsewhere in England, Doreen also had to knit in school; it was mandatory. She knit for the Chinese Merchant sailors.[25]

Joy Beebe's mother taught her to knit when she was four years old. During the war, she had to always carry a gas mask. She recollected in her memoir, "It was quite fashionable to knit or sew an outer cover for [the gas mask] to match my coat. We would have 15-minute sessions of wearing the masks in class. They smelled awful and steamed up so one could not see" (2015, 85).

FIGURE 4.19: *Ellen Miller Coile's knitting group during World War II in England.* Courtesy Jennifer Coile.

Executive Order 9066

Knitting sometimes became a survival skill. The following recollections of two young women who learned to knit, one while in wartime prison and the second while hiding from the enemy, illustrate the value of knitting.

Marian Kanemoto, a young Japanese American who lived with her family in Seattle in the early 1940s, learned to knit in an internment camp. After Pearl Harbor, fear of an eminent attack gripped the population of the West Coast of the USA ("Sheean Sees Jap Invasion" 1942, A1). All people of Japanese descent, even natural born citizens, were suspected of collaborating with the enemy and treated with anger and apprehension. On February 19, 1942, ten weeks after the Pearl Harbor attack, US President Franklin D. Roosevelt signed Executive Order 9066, "empowering the U.S. Army to designate areas from which 'any or all persons may be excluded'" (Burton et al. 2002, 25). The order sought to prevent any dangerous sabotage by Japanese loyalists. All Japanese Americans on the West Coast, citizens born in the USA or immigrants, were relocated to spartan camps far from the coast (Conrat and Conrat 1972, 21–22). Given so little warning, many families had to sell their businesses at a loss.

Marian Kanemoto and her family were moved to the Minidoka War Relocation Center in Idaho ("Minidoka National Historic Site").[28] The quickly built structures at the camps were "inadequate in size, sanitation, and protection from the elements for even minimum standards of human comfort" (Conrat and Conrat 1972, 22). Marian's family, unprepared for the freezing weather since they were not told where they were going, arrived at the camp with only the possessions they could carry. Locked in the camp, the sole resources for supplies were Sears Roebuck's or Montgomery Ward's mail order catalogues. The meager income that some internees received from jobs within the camps, from $8.00 to $16.00 a month depending on their skill level, barely provided enough for a few necessities (Chapman et al. 2019).

Marian learned to knit in a class organized by the internees. When she ordered yarn to knit a sweater, economizing was essential. She could only afford to order two skeins or 14 oz. of yarn. The sweater had to be made slightly shorter since the yarn ordered was insufficient. No money was left to buy buttons, so Marian knit them from a small amount of scrap yarn. The sweater is now housed at the California Museum in Sacramento, California and was displayed in the exhibit, *The Art of Gaman*, March 5, 2010–January 30, 2011 (Color Plate 13). It is a testament to wartime creativity, motivated by both deprivation and imprisonment.

Mary McKay Maynard, an American child who lived with her family in the Philippines, learned to knit while hiding from the invading Japanese army. Her family fled when the Japanese attacked in 1942 and spent the next years hiding in the jungle. Mary did not have any yarn, so she used twine left over from the mining industry where her father was employed before the war. She wrote in her memoir that she knit, "On fat knitting needles my father made for me [out of old tire spokes], I made washcloths from string meant to tie up the sacks of gold concentrate" (Maynard 2002, 133).

Conclusion

During World War II every scrap of fabric had value. Old clothing was used to make new apparel when store shelves were bare, or ration coupons had run out. Old sweaters were unraveled and reknit. It was important to take care of clothing already owned, so it would last for the duration (Howell 2012, 124). Most women practiced careful laundering, mending, and, if necessary, repurposing. They wore pinafores and aprons over their day dresses to keep them clean. Civilian's efforts to creatively conserve limited resources was considered as important as working in a bomb factory, serving in the military, or spotting an airplane (Ayling 1942, 154). "You didn't throw away anything, *ever* [...] It was unheard of" (Cline 2012, 21).

NOTES

1. Discussion at the Northern California War Brides Association lunch, Campbell, CA, October 11, 2014.
2. Leila (born 1926, Emporia, KS) in discussion with the author, Emporia, KS, May 22, 2015.
3. Virginia (born 1922, Pasadena, CA) in discussion with the author, Monterey, CA, 2010.
4. Susie (born 1924, France) in discussion with the author, Paris, France, July 2018.
5. Jeanne (born 1927, Tours, France) in discussion with the author during the War Brides Association Reunion on the Queen Mary, Long Beach, CA, September 2015.
6. Joy A. Beebe (born 1925, Sidcup, London, UK) in discussion with the author during the War Brides Association Reunion on the Queen Mary, Long Beach, CA, November 2015.
7. Lydia (born 1929 in Sudan, German/Chinese, lived in Germany during the war) in discussion with the author during the War Brides Association Reunion, San Diego, CA, October 9, 2019.
8. Ingrid (born 1926, Fürstenfeldbruck, Bavaria, Germany) in discussion with the author during the War Brides Association Reunion. Las Vegas, NV, October 2017 and San Diego, CA, October 2019.
9. Sophie (born 1922, Weston-super-Mare, UK) in discussion with the author, Weston-super-Mare, UK, June 2011.

10. Karin Yount (born 1923, Yalta, Crimea), answer to the questionnaire passed out at War Brides Reunion on the Queen Mary, Long Beach, CA, November 4, 2015.
11. Helen (born 1926, Davis, CA) in discussion with the author, Davis, CA, October 2014.
12. Carla (born 1930, Rome, Italy) in a recorded discussion with her son, 2014.
13. Vera (born 1929, London) in e-mail communication with the author, March 8, 2012.
14. Adelaide (born 1927, The Hague, The Netherlands) in discussion with the author, Davis, CA, November 20, 2014.
15. PX stands for Post Exchange—the military store for enlisted men and their families.
16. Jean (born 1927, Welwyn Garden City, UK) in discussion with the author, San Jose, CA, November 24, 2014.
17. Karin Yount (born 1923, Yalta, Crimea) memoir written for the War Brides Association.
18. Kathryn Squitieri (fashion historian and textile conservator, NYC) in e-mail communication with the author, 2016.
19. Luise Van Dyne (born 1930, Tokyo, Japan) in discussion with the author, Sacramento, CA, August 17, 2017.
20. Ilene (born 1924, Salinas, CA, USA) in e-mail communication with the author, January 15, 2020.
21. Lucy (born 1930, Nottingham, UK) in discussion with the author at the Northern California War Brides Association lunch, Campbell, CA, November 11, 2017.
22. Vince Schoenstein, *End of the War in Europe*, 2019a. Unpublished.
23. Gail (born 1922, Michigan, USA) in discussion with the author, Monterey, CA, May 2011.
24. Ellen Miller Coile (born 1930, London, UK) in discussion with the author, Monterey, CA, May 2012.
25. Doreen (born 1929, UK), answer to the questionnaire passed out at the War Brides luncheon, Campbell, CA, March 12, 2012.
26. For more information about Minidoka National Historic Site, please visit: https://www.nps.gov/miin/planysit/index.htm. To listen to Marian tell the story of her family's internment: https://www.youtube.com/watch?time_continue=17&v=lAPYCJUvMfE&feature=emb_logo.

Color Plates

COLOR PLATE 1: *World War Two Memorial Ceremony*, June 26, 2011. The Cenotaph Memorial, London. Photo by Nan Turner.

COLOR PLATE 2: Olivier Rahard, *Women's sandal in heavy khaki color canvas mounted on a wooden wedge sole,* 1940s.
COLOR PLATE 3: Olivier Rahard, *Woman's shoe in hemp with red leather reinforcements,* 1940s. Courtesy Musée des Métiers de la Chaussure, Saint-André-de-la-Marche. France.

COLOR PLATE 4: Olivier Rahard, *Trio of shoes for women, in leather with wooden soles*, 1940s. Courtesy Musée des Métiers de la Chaussure, Saint-André-de-la-Marche, France.

COLOR PLATE 5: *An Essential Aid to "Women Power,"* 1942. Advertisement. *Woman Magazine*, November 2, 1942. Courtesy Berlei Australasia.

COLOR PLATE 6: *Homemaker*, 1930. *Ladies' Home Journal* advertisement. *Saturday Evening Post*, June 21, 1930, 142. Courtesy Meredith Publications.

COLOR PLATE 7: J. Howard Miller, *We Can Do It!*, 1943. Poster for Westinghouse Electric. Courtesy of the National Museum of American History, Smithsonian Institution (1985.0851.05).

COLOR PLATE 8: *Two-Way Siren Suit*, 1940. Weldons So-Easy 19. https://vintagepatterns.fandom.com/wiki/Weldons_19.

COLOR PLATE 9: *A Stitch in Time Saves Coupons*. World War II. Poster. Courtesy Imperial War Museum © IWM (PST 14931).

COLOR PLATE 10: *Vince wearing his mended US Army Eisenhower jacket and hat*, November 11, 2016. San Jose, California. Courtesy Vince Schoenstein.

COLOR PLATE 11: Christian Bérard, *Cover Image*, 1939. *Vogue Paris*, December 1939. Courtesy *Vogue Paris*.

COLOR PLATE 12: *Remember Pearl Harbor/Purl Harder*, 1942. New York City Works Progress Administration War Service. Courtesy Division of Political and Military History, National Museum of American History, Smithsonian Institution.

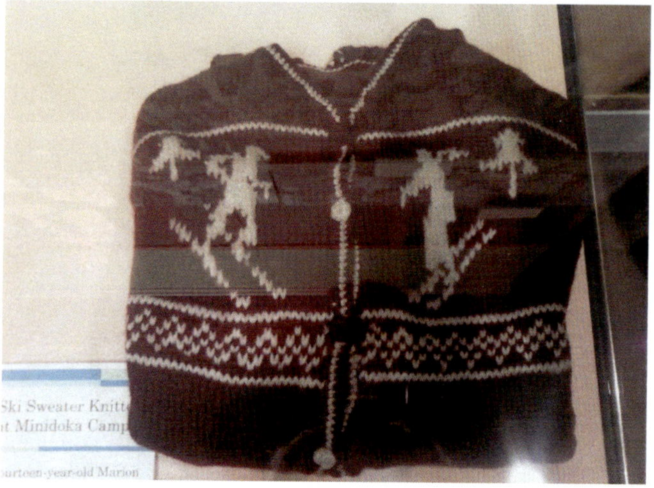

COLOR PLATE 13: Marian Kanemoto, *Hand Knit Sweater*, 1944. Displayed at the California Museum, Sacramento, CA. Photo by Nan Turner.

COLOR PLATE 14: *Quilt top made from feed sack print fabrics*. Gift of Lois Breida. Photo by Nan Turner.

COLOR PLATE 15: *Francesca Stewart's Wedding*, July 7, 1945. Napoli, Italy. Courtesy Francesca Stewart.

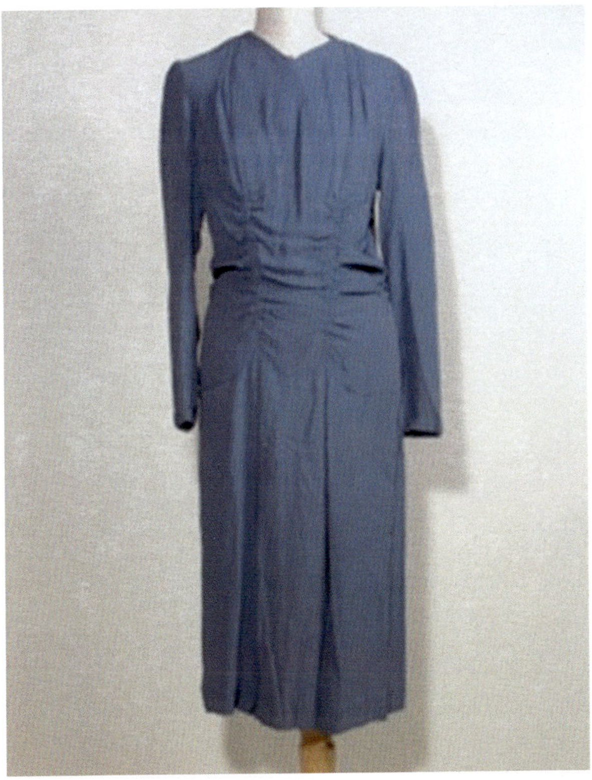

COLOR PLATE 16: *A Romney CC41 model*, June 1943. Killerton Museum Wedding Dress Image Reference 808375 Utility. Courtesy Killerton Museum. Photo by Sophia Farley & Renée Harvey.

COLOR PLATE 17: *Dorothy wearing her mosquito netting veil*, 1943. Brisbane, Australia. Courtesy Dorothy E. Pence Berry.

COLOR PLATE 18: *Vincent and Moira Schoenstein – wearing her future sister-in-law's dress*. June 27, 1946. Wallasey, UK. Courtesy Vincent Schoenstein.

COLOR PLATE 19: *Andriani Chalkiadakis's wedding dress knit from parachute cords*, 1941. Courtesy Maritime Museum of Crete, Chania, Greece.

COLOR PLATE 20: *Costume for Dorothy (Judy Garland)*, 1939. *The Wizard of Oz*. Costume designer Adrian. Courtesy ITV/Shutterstock.

COLOR PLATE 21: *Millions Like Us*, 1943. Film Poster. Gainsborough Pictures, UK. Courtesy ITV/Shutterstock.

COLOR PLATE 22: *You Are Wanted Too! Join the ATS*. Propaganda poster. Featured in the film *Millions Like Us*. Courtesy Imperial War Museum © IWM PST (14548).

COLOR PLATE 23: *The Gentle Sex*, 1943.
Film Poster. Two Cities Films, UK.
Courtesy ITV/Shutterstock.

COLOR PLATE 24: *HRH Princess Elizabeth in the Auxiliary Territorial Service*, April 1945.
Courtesy Imperial War Museum © Art. IWM TR 2832.

COLOR PLATE 25: *Stamp Out Black Markets... With Your Ration Stamps*, 1943. Propaganda poster. U.S. Government Printing Office.

COLOR PLATE 26: *I Pay No More Than Top Legal Prices, Housewife Pledge*, 1940s. Decal. Courtesy Nebraska State Historical Society, 10019-9-(2).

COLOR PLATE 27 (left): *Advance Pattern 2427*, c. 1940. View 1 - Afternoon Dress with higher neck and short sleeves. View 2 – Dress with lower neck and longer ¾ sleeve. https://vintagepatterns.fandom.com/wiki/Advance_2427.

COLOR PLATE 28 (right): *Advance Pattern 2552*, c. 1940. Softly Tailored Dress. https://vintagepatterns.fandom.com/wiki/Advance_2552.

COLOR PLATE 29: *A Woven Basket Made From Old T-shirts.* Craft School of Oz. Copyright Ruth Woods 2020. https://craft-school-oz.teachable.com/p/textile-coiled-baskets.

COLOR PLATE 30: Mae Krier, one of the original Rosie the Riveters, makes coronavirus masks using the iconic red and white polka-dot Rosie bandana fabric to help her country. Mae spoke at the Rosie the Riveter Trust in Richmond, California on December 1, 2021 on her way to Hawaii for the 80th anniversary Commemoration of Pearl Harbor. Courtesy Mae Krier.

5

Feed Sack Fashion: Nothing Was Wasted

During World War II, when yardage was either unavailable or unaffordable, many people used recycled fabric from feed sack bags to make clothing. The history of feed sacks, and their use as fabric for clothing and home accessories, is an interesting perspective into the years of scarcity, poverty, and deprivation that motivated creativity during the 1920s, 1930s, and 1940s.

Before the 1910s, produce was shipped in wooden barrels. However, when wood became scarce in the early 1900s, farm and home products, including sugar, flour, and livestock feed, were packaged and shipped in cloth bags. A memory of the wooden barrels still remained as the size of cotton bags was directly related to the size of the formerly used wooden barrels (Connolly 1992, 19). The Bemis Bag Company, located in St. Louis, Missouri, was one of the first to make cloth bags to replace wooden barrels (22). Empty sacks were especially plentiful for rural farm families who purchased large quantities of livestock and chicken feed. Aprons, dresses, underwear, men's shirts, and children's clothing were often made from the empty feed sack fabric.

The Stigma of Feed Sack Clothing

According to Lu Ann Jones and Sunae Park in *From Feed Bags to Fashion* (1993), during the 1930s, "Clothing made from cotton bags became an emblem of the depression—simultaneously a sign of poverty, a badge of pride, and a testament to ingenuity" (93). In rural America, "use of these sacks for clothing was a mark of poverty" and much effort was made to hide the fact that family members were clothed in feed sacks (Brandes 2009, 4). Several people interviewed recalled the embarrassment and stigma of wearing underclothing with the feed sack company name still printed on them. One woman recalled her feeling of shame when her school mates caught a glimpse of the feed sack label, still evident on her underwear when playing in the playground, the mark of austerity and shame of coming from a family who could not afford store bought clothing. Even when the feed companies started selling their products in pretty floral printed cotton fabrics to increase sales, the memory of wearing the garments their mothers had made out of sacks was humiliating.

Leila, my relative who grew up on a farm outside of Emporia, Kansas, reported that her mother made all her clothes, sometimes even using fabrics from empty cloth feed sacks that the family bought to feed the chickens they raised.[1] Leila was embarrassed to wear these dresses, even though she knew that no one could tell where the fabric came from. *She knew,* and that was enough. Anne Chesky (2010), in the *North Carolina Folklore Journal*, interviewed women who reported they felt no shame wearing feed sack clothing because most people in their communities wore them (31). For Leila however, clothing made by her mother from feed sacks represented the Great Depression era shame of having to "get by" (Maginnis 1992, 60). Leila dreamed of going into a store and buying ready-made clothes. However, it was not until she got her first store-bought dress, purchased with money she saved from her job working during college, that she realized how nice her mother's homemade dresses actually were. Her mother's sewing skills and custom fit were much better than store bought.

Loris Connolly (1992), in the journal entry, "Recycling Feed Sacks and Flour Bags: Thrifty Housewives or Marketing Success Story?" reported that "an obvious flour company trademark on clothing or a household textile was an unmistakable 'trademark' of poverty, or at least of an inability to afford store-bought goods" (19). The association between poverty and wearing clothing made out of flour sacks is evident in a *New York Times* article on November 4, 1931, titled "Miners' Children Face Starvation" (30). A total of 25,000 children of unemployed mine workers in West Virginia and Kentucky were reported to be dressed in clothes made by their mothers out of flour sacks. The mothers seeking charity were reported as stating that "if they could only have one change [of clothing] they could keep them clean and in school" (30). This article represents and reinforces the stigma of wearing feed sack clothing and furthermore, draws the glaring connection with poverty and starvation.

The main problem with using feed sack cotton for clothing was the printed label, which was often very difficult to remove. The Textile Bag Manufacturers Association, in a pamphlet titled *Sewing with Cotton Bags*, published in 1935(?), advised:

> The ease with which printing ink may be removed from cotton bags depends on the kind of ink that has been used. Under ordinary circumstances, it is sufficient to cover the inked places with lard or soak them in kerosene overnight.
>
> (2)

Evidently, this supposedly easy process was not always successful. The pamphlet continues with the following adage: "If only a faint, barely discernible marking may still be seen, it is safe to assume a few washings will remove the remaining traces" (2).

Marketing Feed Sacks for Clothing

Fortunately for home sewers, the cotton bag industry realized the value of marketing feed bags as dress yardage and changed their method of printing the bags labels. By 1945 instructions on how to remove the ink were much simpler. *A Bag of Tricks for Home Sewing* (1945), a pamphlet published in the USA by the National Cotton Council, helped housewives conserve cotton resources by illustrating the many uses of fabric feed sacks. The pamphlet described the following steps to remove the printed label:

> Soak the bag overnight in heavy soap suds, squeezing suds through the fabric. The following day, wash thoroughly in warm suds, gently rubbing the parts covered by the ink. If all traces of ink are not then removed, boil in soap suds [in a pot on top of the stove] for at least ten minutes.
>
> (3)

The pamphlet is full of suggestions on how to use the empty feed sacks for women's and children's clothing, underwear, stuffed animals, and pajamas. Bags could be used for home decorations, table covers, luncheon sets, and cushions, as well as projects to sell at charity bazaars.

When mills developed inks that would truly come out in the wash, the stigma of wearing feed sack clothing lessened (Connolly 1992, 21). "Soaking off logos, dying fabrics, and adding embellishments of ribbon, rickrack, embroidery, and decorative buttons helped make the feed sack dress or shirt less distinguishable from 'store bought' garments" (Brandes 2009, 4). The Bemis Bag Company ultimately solved the problem of removing the stamped on label in 1944 by developing a paper label that would clearly advertise the manufacturer and be easily removable since it was attached with water-soluble paste (Connolly 1992, 26).

Before the cotton bag manufacturers realized the marketing potential of selling sacks as dress goods, farmwives used color dyes to make the plain cloth fabric more attractive. Synthetic dyes for home use had come onto the market during World War I. The most well-known company, RIT, which is still in business today, started selling dye for home use around 1917 with the slogan, "*Never Say 'Dye'… Say Rit!*"[2] The boxes of dye sold in a wide range of colors for 10 cents and came in either cake or flake form.

In addition to dyeing the bags, store-bought trims such as colored rick rack or premade bias binding were often added to improve the look and help to "pass" as store-bought clothing. Since home sewing was very popular, stores that carried sewing notions carried a wide range of trims.

Printed Feed Sacks

Pretty calico florals printed on feed bags came into use when the manufacturers and suppliers realized the marketing opportunity. "Although there is conflicting evidence about when textile manufacturers began turning out colored and printed bags, they clearly had taken their place beside plain cotton bags by the 1940s" (Jones and Park 1993, 94). The result, even if the printed bags were slightly more expensive, was that cheery floral prints or fashionable solids sold better than those in the original natural color. The idea was not only a method to increase sales in general but also a defense technique against competition from feed and food packaged in the newer and cheaper paper bags.

The Textile Bag Manufacturers Association was not a newcomer to marketing techniques to boost sales. During the Great Depression, farmers tried to economize by returning old cotton bags to be refilled at the mill. Foreseeing a loss of revenue, the association deployed a campaign to denigrate used bags as unsanitary and at the same time promote the idea of utilizing printed flour bags for dress fabric. Bakeries were encouraged to sell their used bags to customers as a tactic discouraging their desire to return the bags to the mill to be refilled. To promote this idea, the pamphlet, *Sewing with Cotton Bags* (1935?), informed readers that bakers were glad to sell bags "for a few cents apiece, and the bags are generally of the larger sizes that cut to excellent advantage" (4). This tactic would later be used by the paper bag manufacturers, positing that cotton bags were unsanitary; and ultimately winning by the late 1960s when cotton bags were phased out.

During World War II, the use of cloth bags for clothing was promoted as an act of patriotism, as cotton and other fibers were needed for the war effort (Connolly 1992, 24). Jute, a strong fiber also used for feed bags because it was sturdier and less expensive than cotton, was needed by the military, and by 1942 became totally unavailable for civilian use. Thereafter, even more products were shipped in cotton bags, increasing the source of dress yardage (Jones and Park 1993, 94).

As World War II prolonged, the demand for cotton cloth to be used by the troops became so severe that the government promoted a drive asking civilians to turn in their cloth bags for the war effort (Connolly 1992, 20).

After the war, rural housewives continued to prize the printed feed sacks for use in household items. Cotton bag sewing projects were a regular feature in Home Economics courses. The *Chicago Tribune* (1954) reported that cotton bag sewing contests at county fairs even crowned an "International Sewing Bag Queen" from among the winners of local contestants in the USA and Canada ("Putting on the Feed Bag," F42).

The National Cotton Council sponsored a contest in the USA using cotton bags to make household products. Some of the prize products and winners photographed in the 1945 edition of *A Bag of Tricks for Home Sewing* may appear odd to viewers today. One in particular resembles a mini skirt with two ruffles at the bottom edge and is called a broom skirt (a skirt for a broom to wear). The purpose of this useful contraption is to contain the dust swept up by using the broom. In 1946, the council held an exhibition of garments that "illustrated use of natural, dyed, and print bag fabric" at the regional conference of home economists in Memphis, Tenn (Feed Bags, Once Sad Sacks, 13).

Feed Sack Memories

A relative of mine who worked in a grocery store in Arkansas during the 1940s reported his experience serving female customers shopping for flour sacks. "While in high school I worked at a local grocery store. Flour came in 25 lb. sacks. There was usually 30 or 40 sacks on hand. It became my job to 'dig through' the pile because a lady wanted matching bags, and of course they were scattered thru out the pile... this was 1949."[3]

Laney remarked, "I certainly remember my mom and grandmother making our dresses from feed sacks or flour sacks. Most of our clothing was made at home and we were allowed to go to the stores and pick out the sacks we liked the most. I will look for photos" (Figure 5.1).[4]

A cousin in the Midwestern USA added:

> Yes, Nan, I wore feed sack dresses all the time. Mother was a sewer and made all of my dresses. I had some really pretty ones. One in particular was a white background with tiny green leaves. I really liked that dress and wore it until it literally fell apart. Mom did both the bias tape and rick rack... not on the same dresses though.... Sometimes she would use lace as well. I believe she made some of my brother's short sleeved shirts as well. She would get the plain white ones, hem them and used them as dish towels. Our feed sack came with chicken feed as we had chickens.[5]

Post-War Feed Sacks

Cotton bag manufactures continued to market the bags as dress cloth, producing more and more pamphlets on the uses of the bags, and by the early 1950s offered a greater variety of fabrics including "percale, chambray, cambric,

FIGURE 5.1: *Laney dressed in a sun suit made from feed sack fabric dyed turquoise and trimmed with rick-rack*, 1946. Courtesy Laney.

denim, and toweling fabrics" (Connolly 1992, 28). I remember shopping in the small local grocery store in Monterey, California with my mother in the late 1950s and early 1960s. I was fascinated by the piles of pretty floral printed cotton sacks full of rice. My mother sewed my clothing but never suggested buying any bags of rice to use the fabric for dresses. Her memories of growing up in Kansas during the Great Depression probably predisposed her to reject the idea.

During the 1960s, increasing prices for cotton, combined with competition with less expensive paper bags, forced the demise of cloth bags. Today reproductions of the original feed sack prints are popular for quilting, a form of sewing that has remained very popular in spite of the decline of the home sewing industry. Vintage printed feed sack fabric can be found for sale on the auction web site Ebay, usually individual empty bags selling for approximately $20.00 or more a yard. Multiples of a print are rarely offered, limiting sewing projects to children's clothing or quilting. I often study the prints in the quilt cover that Lois Brieda gave me and imagine what dresses I could make if I only had a few empty bags (Color Plate 14).

Even for weddings, sewing, repurposing, and creativity were required skills while hurriedly planning the special day. The next chapter continues to explore creative skills used when planning a wartime wedding.

NOTES

1. Leila (born 1926, Emporia, KS) in discussion with the author, May 22, 2015.
2. "Celebrating 100 Years of Rit," Rit Dye, 2018, https://www.ritdye.com/100-years-of-rit/.
3. Aaron (born 1932, Garfield, AR) email communication with the author.
4. Laney (born 1933, Missouri) in discussion with author, Monterey, CA, April 22, 2016.
5. Lily (born 1935, Garfield, AR) email communication with the author.

6

Wartime Weddings: Falling in Love During Wartime

Austerity and rationing made wartime wedding planning in Napoli, Italy extremely difficult for Francesca Sorvillo Stewart. Stores in postwar Italy were empty, hard-hit by shortages. Even if Francesca had the coupons or money, wedding party necessities were impossible to buy. She turned to friends and family to find creative solutions to make her wedding to her American soldier fiancé memorable (Color Plate 15).

Francesca explained the situation:

> *Now we concentrated on our wedding:*
> *How about a wedding dress? Forget buying one, none available.*
> *How about material to make one? No luck.*
> *So, my mother decided to use a brand-new linen bed sheet.*
> *A bed sheet? I didn't like the idea period.*
> *A lady friend of the family came to the rescue, "We can dye it any color you want!"*
> *Her family owned the plant where they dyed material in bulk. She suggested for me to pick a color, which I did—Sky Blue.*
> *The plant was closed for the war, but her husband opened it and called a worker to come in and dye the material. This was her wedding present to me.*
> *How about announcements and invitations? Again, another present from a family friend who was a director of a newspaper.*
> *How about the veil? We had a piece of tulle left over from a curtain, and we made a veil.*[1]

The hardship of living through World War II caused many traditional customs of social life to be put on hold for the duration. Sometimes, however, feelings of anxiety, fear, excitement, and urgency intensified the desire to live life in the moment (Probert 1984, 40). Falling in love was a wonderful escape from the stress and worries of the unknown future. Romance often developed quickly as young men stationed all over the world met young women who they never would have had the opportunity to encounter during peacetime (Shukert and Scibetta 1988, 8, 10, 125). Authors Tobin, Pepper, and Willes (2003) noted the differences between wartime and peacetime weddings:

> In peacetime, weddings could be planned for months ahead, and the dress, trousseau and flowers carefully chosen. Wartime weddings were often arranged on the spur of the moment, when the long-awaited telegram announcing the bridegroom's arrival on forty-eight-hour leave spurred a rush to obtain a license.
>
> (106)

The American edition of *Vogue* (October 15, 1942) featured a fashion spread on wartime weddings with the following advice:

> Furlough wedding—if he's in the ranks. Leave wedding—if he's an officer. War wedding, anyway—and that means *quick* wedding, nine times out of ten. It means setting the date at the drop of a telegram; making arrangements practically overnight; shopping for a wedding-dress while the champagne cools for the reception.
>
> ("Furlough Wedding," 40)

Symbolism and Creativity

In Western culture, wedding attire often reflected social codes, status, privilege, or scarcity (Davis 1992, 12–13). During wartime, wedding dresses also symbolized faith in a peaceful future. The emotional poignancy of a wartime wedding imbued the clothing with special value, so that often the dress was kept and treasured for the rest of the bride's life. Many women who were interviewed still have their dresses, now part of the lore of a very distant and romanticized past (Wagner 2015, 109). Fashion historian and author Lou Taylor made the following comment about treasured clothing kept forever:

> From time to time clothes are kept long after their owners stop wearing them because they become repositories of deeply valued personal memories [...] A deep, joyful, emotional attachment rests within certain types of personal clothing such as wedding, party and christening robes, which survive in large numbers, whereas mourning dress and indeed maternity clothes do not.
>
> (2002, 5)

Dressing a wedding party was especially problematic due to apparel and fabric shortages, especially silk. Creativity in outfitting the event was a common theme that transcended culture, social class, and nationality. Repurposing, borrowing, and sewing all came into play. Drapery, mosquito netting, tablecloths, and old clothes were dyed, ruffled, embroidered, and embellished to create dresses. Friends or future in-laws volunteered to lend the bride previously worn dresses, hoping their packages would arrive in time. Silk or nylon parachutes were saved by soldiers or found by friends, then given to the bride-to-be to fashion into a wedding dress.

Shortages and austerity affected people across all socioeconomic classes. However, wedding couples belonging to minority groups, who experienced discrimination ranging from suspicion of collaboration with the enemy to imprisonment in concentration camps, had even greater hardship planning a wedding.

This chapter discusses the symbolism and creativity embedded in wedding attire during World War II. These stories of wartime weddings are drawn from interviews of women from a cross section of both Allied and Axis countries who all turned to creativity to outfit their special day. Women who were interviewed for this research showed great pride in reporting how they resolved the issues of scarcity by improvising fabrics and dresses. Many of the women who shared their stories are members of the Northern California Bay Area War Brides Association. The group organized an exhibit at the Dr. Martin Luther King Library in San Jose, CA called the *Bay Area WWII War Brides Past & Present Exhibit*, which ran from January 2013 to June 2013. The exhibit featured a display of the wedding dresses that the women had carefully saved as treasured memories.

Choosing a Dress

Wedding dresses have historically followed fashion and cultural trends. During the decades preceding World War II, wedding dresses also reflected fluctuating global economics. The 1920s experienced global prosperity, while the 1930s experienced economic depression. During the 1920s, the fashionable, lean, dropped-waist silhouette, with elaborate beading and detail, was reflected in wedding dresses (Fogg 2013, 238–41). After the economic crash of 1929, excessive embellishment gave way to more simple lines and austere details. The silhouette of the 1930s transitioned to a feminine shape with a wasp waist and padded shoulders, also reflected in wedding dress design (Laver 1969, 240).

Before Germany invaded in 1940, France had been the global fashion leader. German occupation cut it off from the free world and created a void in the fashion world (Steele 1998, 266; see also Gustafson 1982, 12). Hollywood movie style, already popular, filled the void as the global fashion leader, influencing wedding style as well. Luxurious white silk satin wedding dresses, often seen in black and white Hollywood movies in the 1930s and 1940s, became a major fashion trend that continued throughout the war years (Probert 1984, 28; see also Summers 2016, 143).

Helen, born in Greece in the 1950s, moved to the USA for a career in engineering and education. She remembered that her mother and mother-in-law, both married in Greece in the 1940s, each selected a Hollywood style white satin dress, markedly different from the traditional wedding style of prewar Greece based on classical heritage.[2] Helen felt that American movies were the major influence on her relatives' wedding dress selection.

The Meaning of Color

During World War II, the color of a wedding dress could represent different values. A sensible suit or day dress worn for the wedding could reflect the need for practicality during a time of scarcity (Nicol 2010, 137). A traditional white gown, a cultural icon of hope and faith, could symbolize trust in a better future when peace returned. A white dress, often in satin, was a dream that many war era brides did not want to give up (Figure 6.1) (Probert 1984, 41).

Queen Victoria, who married Prince Albert on January 25, 1858, at the age of 21, is sometimes believed to be the originator of the custom of wearing white to symbolize "innocence, purity and implied virginity" (Tobin, Pepper, and Willes 2003, 48; see also Shari Sims 2015). "The white wedding dress became the standard symbol for innocence and romance" after Victoria wore white for her wedding with Albert (Dunne 2017). White wedding dresses constituted just one of a range of colors or prints worn during Queen Victoria's era. Author Edwina Ehrman (2011) reported:

> At the highest levels of society silver, [or] white and silver, vied with white as the most prestigious and fashionable bridal colours until white became the colour of choice in the early nineteenth century.
>
> (9)

After the hard years of the global economic depression during the 1930s, resources and wardrobes were limited. Therefore, if finances allowed for a new dress for the wedding, often it would also have to serve as a "best dress" for years to come. Practicality, durability, and functionality were sometimes more important factors than style. For that reason, a smart daytime suit or dress that could be worn for

FIGURE 6.1: *"Oh Promise Me" Bridal Beauty*, 1940. Celanese Slipper Satin advertisement. *Mademoiselle*, March 1940, 187. Courtesy Celanese.

future occasions would often be selected instead of a traditional white dress (Nicol 2010, 137). Women of lesser means often opted for a more practical colored or printed dress that could be worn multiple times.

Lynn, who married her American fiancé in Southampton, UK in 1945, chose a simple blue dress for her wedding (Figure 6.2). The reason for her decision was documented in *GI Brides*,

FIGURE 6.2: *Lynn chose to wear a simple day dress for her wedding*. 1942. Southampton, UK.

> Then there was the dress—or rather, the lack of it. Wedding dresses were almost impossible to get hold of, and many a wartime bride got married in a borrowed or rented dress—an option that Lynn flatly refused. A friend of the family offered her a dress made from reclaimed parachute silk, but knowing that the material was often salvaged from German pilots who had been shot down, she couldn't bring herself to take it.
>
> (Barrett and Calvi 2013, 135)

Lynn told me that the idea of wearing a dress made from a parachute that first had to be cleaned of the blood of a dead German soldier made her sick.[3] Not her idea of a happy wedding dress. She forwent a white wedding and settled on a pretty light blue dress that she bought with borrowed coupons. Ben's mother sent her silk stockings with seams so she did not have to draw the line up the back of her legs. A coworker loaned her a hat decorated with flowers that matched her bouquet for the November 5, 1945 wedding (137). "My sister agreed to be the maid-of-honor wearing her WAAF (Women's Auxiliary Air Force) uniform." Women serving in the military in the UK were at a considerable disadvantage because they received no clothing coupons. Their uniform had to do for every occasion (Walford 2008, 106). Lynn's wedding story is a wonderful example of the many meanings and symbolism of weddings during wartime.

FIGURE 6.3: *Joan wearing the only dress she owned for her wedding.* Brisbane, Australia. Courtesy Joan.

Joan, who was the youngest of three girls, told me that all her clothing while growing up was homemade and often a hand-me-down. Her father had served in World War I and, therefore, she felt she should sign up. She served in the signal corps and wore her uniform throughout the war. She had met an American service man two years earlier and they married while he was on a one-week leave. She wore a wool dress for the wedding (Figure 6.3). The weather was getting warm, but that was the only dress she owned other than her uniform. She invited three girl friends to stand up with her and her fiancé asked the first American soldier off the street to be his witness.[4]

Symbolism of Loss

Some wedding dresses are kept because they hold a poignant memory. One such dress, held in the Killerton House collection in Devon, UK, was worn by a bride whose husband was killed in action soon after the wedding. The dress is described as a "Romney CC41 model," indicating that it was made as part of the UK's Utility Clothing Scheme developed by the government to conserve precious textiles (Figure 6.4). The notes at the museum indicate that the bride pooled her coupons with friends to buy the dress. Shelly Tobin, the curator at the Killerton Museum, collected the dress from the donor, who remains anonymous (Color Plate 16). Tobin described the dress in an e-mail communication as "a little off-the-peg crêpe utility afternoon dress."[5] In her book written with Sarah Pepper and Margaret Willes (2003), the dress is called:

> One of the most poignant dresses in the Killerton collection is an inexpensive, off-the-peg day dress bought hurriedly for a civil wedding in 1943, before the groom rejoined his squadron, never to return. Although she remarried, the bride never parted with her little blue frock.
>
> (10)

FIGURE 6.4: *The bride wore cotton eyelet,* 1942. Courtesy Betty Reid Soskin.

Although the dress is not a traditional white wedding dress, it embodies the cruel sorrows of war.

The Consequence of Race

Betty Reid Soskin, the oldest park ranger with the United States National Park Service, is stationed at the Rosie the Riveter/World War II Home Front National Historical Park in Richmond, California.[6] The historical park is named for the female ship builders who took over the formerly male-only jobs building airplanes when the men left their jobs to fight the war (Gluck 1987, 11). (For discussion of the origin of the name Rosie the Riveter, see Chapter 3.)

Betty lived in Oakland, California, not far from the Ford Motor Company Assembly Plant in Richmond. Banned from making civilian automobiles, Ford focused on producing military combat vehicles. The nearby Kaiser Shipyards manufactured merchant ships and tramp steamships, "known at the time as Liberty Ships" (Michelson 2005–21). Betty was not hired to be a Rosie the Riveter because African American women suffered racial discrimination and were not employed in the shipyards until nearly the end of the war, when additional workers were desperately needed (Wynn 1995, 354). If they were fortunate to be hired before that, janitorial responsibilities were usually the only positions offered (Anderson 1982, 84). Betty worked as a file clerk for the Auxiliary Lodge Number 36 (A-36) of the International Brotherhood of Boilermakers, Iron Ship Builders, and Helpers of America, a separate union for the black workers hired when "there was a shortage of white men to fill the new jobs opening up in the war effort" (Soskin 2018, 43). Since the 1970s, Betty has worked in local politics, "any field that had relevance to the African-American story" (Hua 2015). She later became involved in the planning process for the Rosie the Riveter park site. As a ranger at the park, she gives guided bus tours and is a very popular speaker, providing "context about economic conditions, social migrations, and other historical events" (Hua 2015). I am very appreciative of the time she gave me sharing her story about her wedding experience during World War II when I visited the center.

Betty married her first husband, Mel Reid, in May 1942. Betty's fiancé was a star player on the San Francisco State University football team. When he volunteered to serve in the military, hoping to fight on the front, the only position offered was as a cook. Mel suggested to the officers that, with his proven athletic and intellectual abilities, he could better serve his country in the infantry. Betty explained that Mel, who had grown up in California, had not experienced the harsh restrictions and segregation of Jim Crow laws prevalent in Southern states. He had not been inculcated by the insidious prejudice that would have informed his decision to question his treatment by the military. His suggestion to the officers that he could best serve his country fighting on the front line than working in the mess corps resulted in four days of questioning, after which he was sent home with an honorary discharge. Betty said the military officers feared that an intelligent young African American, already recognized for his leadership potential, would be a hindrance rather than an asset to the war effort. He might even instigate rebellion. Mel was so shamed by this treatment that he kept it to himself for the rest of his life, only telling his wife.

Mel's experience was not unique. Isabel Wilkerson (2010), in her book *The Warmth of Other Suns: The Epic Story of America's Great Migration,* described the experience of African Americans during World War II:

> They were forced into segregated units and often given the most menial tasks or the most dangerous infantry tours. But they also experienced relief from Jim Crow in those European villages, were recognized as liberating Americans rather than lower-caste colored men, and felt pride in what their uniform represented.
>
> (145)

When planning their wedding, an opulent silk satin wedding dress, the fashionable style at the time was beyond Betty's means. Her sister sewed the bride's and the bridesmaid's dresses, using simple cotton fabrics, cotton eyelet for the bride and cotton pique for the maid of honor. The faded photo of her wedding day shows a very beautiful, formal wedding party in spite of the simple cotton fabrics (Figure 6.4). Mel did not wear a military uniform for the wedding as most men did at that time because due to his rejection by the military, he did not own one. Therefore, he wore a formal tuxedo.

George and Michiko Uchida, young Japanese Americans born in the USA, had been planning to marry after Michiko graduated from the University of California, Berkeley (Ukai 2021). However, after Pearl Harbor and President Roosevelt's signing of Executive Order 9066, which prohibited all "American citizens of Japanese descent [...] from living, working or traveling on the West Coast of the United States," their wedding date had to be pushed much sooner so that they would not be separated when sent to the internment camp (Nakanishi 1993, 7).

Unlike in Germany where war prisoners were separated by gender, Japanese American families were allowed to stay together. Therefore, they quickly planned their wedding, including only the bare necessities and inviting only three guests, just two days before the scheduled evacuation date. Photographer Dorothea Lange, already famous for capturing the effects of the Great Depression, documented the couple's very simple reception (Curtis 1986, 1). The bride wore a daytime dress and the groom wore a dark suit (Figure 6.5). The sole sartorial indications of the specialness of the day were the bride's corsage and the groom's boutonnière. The

FIGURE 6.5: Dorothea Lange, *Wedding of George and Michiko Uchida two days before evacuation to Tanforan Assembly Center*, April 27, 1942. Berkeley, California (2903 Harper Street). Courtesy National Archives.

couple's honeymoon was spent in a horse stall at the Tanforan Racetrack in San Bruno, California, waiting for transport to Topaz Relocation Center (Ukai 2021).

Creativity and Wedding Planning: Repurposing

Dorothy E. Pence Berry met an American soldier in Brisbane, Australia in 1942, and married him in 1943 (Color Plate 17).[7] She reported that wedding dresses were still plentiful in the early days of the war, before prewar stocks were depleted:

> I started planning for our wedding and went to my favorite dress shop that sold Elizabethan style wedding dresses. One had caught my eye, so I bought it along with a matching pink bridesmaid dress for my friend, Frances. I was very frugal with my

> money and was able to pay for both. I loved my dress. It was old-fashion and made with organdy material with love knot pattern all over it. At the waist two love knots were tied and hung down the side of the dress. The sleeves were ruffled, large and puffy and I wore above the elbow, high, silky, crocheted fingerless gloves.
> (*Bay Area WWII War* 2013)

Finding a veil in 1943, however, required some creative repurposing: "I couldn't find a veil and netting or tulle could not be found in all of Brisbane, but mosquito netting was plentiful. So, I made my veil out of mosquito netting" (*Bay Area WWII War* 2013).

Due to the climate in Australia, mosquito netting was commonly hung over bed frames, and an abundant resource. Author Paula Dunlop (2015) wrote about the symbolism of mosquito netting for a wedding veil in "Beauty, Duty, and Hope:"

> The domestic "everydayness" of the mosquito net wedding veil, made during a time of unprecedented difficulty and uncertainty, represents the resilience and hopefulness of those on the home front. The double-layer of mosquito netting—possibly salvaged from atop a bed frame [...] It is a symbol of courage and resistance in the face of goods shortages, rationing, the absence and loss of loved ones and fear of invasion.
> (60)

A very different situation existed in Germany when scarcity became so extreme in 1942 that the government requested that civilians donate their wedding veils to be used as mosquito nets by soldiers serving in Africa. Irene Guenther (2004), in her book *Nazi Chic*, described the shortages in Germany:

> Faced with deficient clothing supplies and a war that would not end, women were asked to sacrifice very personal belongings to the war effort. Radio announcements in the spring of 1942 requested that women's used bridal veils be donated to the German nation so they could be utilized as mosquito nets for the Africa Korps.
> (221)

Nina met her American soldier husband in the Philippines (Figure 6.6). They married on December 2, 1945. She shared the difficulty of finding wedding attire:

> Mom's friends found a piece of off-white rayon crepe material that was large enough to make me a short, above the knee, wedding dress, with short sleeves. I helped make fourteen or fifteen buttons for closing in the back, as there were no zippers in the Philippines at that time. Then another friend found an old first communion veil that was cut and gathered at the top to make my veil. I didn't have any white shoes, so I wore a wooden shoe like a clog with a fabric top (no leather available) and carved heels. In the Philippines, these shoes are known as "bakya."[8]

FIGURE 6.6: *Nina's wedding,* December 2, 1945. San Antonio de Padua Parish, Singalong Manila Philippines. Courtesy Nina Edillo.

Regina, a young woman in California, recounted the story of her grandmother, Sabrina, who grew up on the Azores Islands, off the coast of Portugal.[9] Sabrina wore a beautiful silk satin dress, handmade by a local seamstress, for her wedding during the war. At the end of the war, the couple wanted to immigrate to the USA. To do so, they moved to Lisbon, but had to wait a year before they could book a flight over the Atlantic on a small plane. They had a much more active social life during the year in Lisbon than they had on the tiny island. Sabrina did not have many clothes, so she repurposed her wedding dress to wear as a cocktail dress. Dyed bright red and cut short, it lived another life, which now only exists in the family's remembrances and stories.

Repurposing Parachutes

Silk or nylon parachutes, either owned by a serviceman, found in the fields, or purchased as surplus at the end of the war, were often used to make clothing. Stories of wedding dresses made from parachutes are some of the most romanticized accounts of World War II. Costume history books refer to the dresses as made from "parachute silk" (Walford 2008, 106). The fiber is more often nylon than silk, especially dresses made from American parachutes. Du Pont's entire production of nylon fiber was requisitioned by the military on February 10,

1942, "for vital military uses—parachutes, and later military tires, flak vests" (E. I. du Pont de Nemours & Co. 1976). (For discussion of the role of textiles in the war, see Chapter 2.)

Band of Brothers (1992), by Stephan Ambrose, the true story of Easy Company, the 506th Parachute Infantry Regiment of the 101st Airborne Division, featured an account of a parachute wedding dress. First Lieutenant Harry F. Welsh carefully saved his reserve parachute for his fiancée, carrying it in his backpack throughout the Normandy campaign, and presenting it to her when he returned home. Welsh was quoted as saying: "I wanted to send it back to Kitty to make a wedding gown for our marriage after the war" (86).

Many parachute silk wedding gowns are displayed in museum collections around the world today, including:

- The Imperial War Museum, London, UK (Figure 6.7).
- The National WWII Museum, New Orleans, USA.
- The Smithsonian National Museum of American History, Washington DC, USA.
- The Victoria and Albert Museum, London, UK.

FIGURE 6.7: *A wedding dress made from a silk parachute.* Ministry of Information Second World War Official Collection. Courtesy Imperial War Museum © IWM (UNI 1052).

- The USA Holocaust Memorial Museum, Washington DC, USA.
- The 489th Bomb Group Museum, Halesworth, UK.
- The Airborne and Special Operations Museum in Fayetteville, North Carolina, USA.

Borrowing

Brides forced to plan their weddings on short notice often borrowed clothing, a common solution to issues of scarcity. Sylvia Smith Harris met her American soldier husband in Liverpool, UK.[10] She wrote about their romance in the *Bay Area WWII War Brides Past & Present Exhibit*. "I met Jack November 8, 1944, which was his birthday. We got engaged February 18, 1945 and married May 1, 1945 in Liverpool at Princes Road Synagogue. My son Louis was born in Liverpool." She wrote about her borrowed dress, "I was absolutely thrilled. It was white satin with a beaded neckline and six-foot train" (2013). Her veil was borrowed. "I also had a gorgeous hand-made Belgian lace veil, loaned to me by my aunt's next-door neighbor, along with several yards of tulle and coronet" (Figure 6.8)[11]

FIGURE 6.8: *Jack and Sylvia Harris—wearing her borrowed wedding dress.* Courtesy Harris family.

Vincent Schoenstein (2019) told the story of meeting his future bride, Moira, while attending a ten-week technical school in England before joining the US army of occupation in Germany.[12] Vince described his experience:

> I arrived at the school in mid-November. I had a cousin in England at the time and we planned to meet and spend Christmas together. On Christmas Eve, 1945, we were to meet at the Red Cross Club in Liverpool. The events of that night changed the direction of my life forever. While waiting for my cousin, I met a girl on the dance floor. Not just any girl, but a super beautiful girl with intelligence, poise and charm that swept me off my feet. One week later, after being with her only three times, I told her I was going to marry her. Four months later we were formally engaged when I gave her a ring. We planned to be married during July or August of 1946.

Soon after becoming engaged, Vincent received orders to ship out to Europe.

> Moira wrote me a letter with the worrying thoughts that she would be unable to get a wedding dress and accessories together for the July 27 date we had planned on. Understanding her dilemma, and without consulting her, I immediately sent a letter to my sister and family in San Francisco. Did Victoria still have her wedding dress from 1940? Could it, and the rest of a wedding trousseau, be sent to Moira in England by the end of July? I felt sure my sister and Moira were physically the same size. The folks at home set to the task immediately. My sister wrote to Moira and explained to her what they were doing and hoped she would receive and accept the gifts in the same spirit as they were being offered. My mother wrote me a letter and said that the packages had been mailed and were on the way and that she had included a pair of PJs for me. How very thoughtful of her.

Vincent wrote about their wedding day:

> I was stationed in Marseilles when I was given twenty days furlough to be married. I arrived back in England on the 25th of July and the packages had not arrived yet. The afternoon of the 26th, just about when we had given up hope, the mailman arrived with two packages. Were we glad to see him! The scene in the household was more like Christmas than the eve of our wedding: They even found nylon stockings and a full-length slip. There was also a bag of cake mix flour, cheese and two bags of dried pea-sized tapioca that could be used for the reception dessert. [...] Moira was the happiest woman in the world to get that dress.

Moira borrowed a veil covered with embroidery from a neighbor, which she wore with the headpiece sent from San Francisco (Color Plate 18). Vincent described it as "a delicate crown made of wax flowers that were sweetheart shaped like the dress" (Schoenstein 2019).

Luise A. Van Dyne met her future American serviceman husband, Harold, in Tokyo, September 27, 1947 when she worked as a typist for the American military.[13] When planning her wedding, she was fortunate to be able to shop at the military Post Exchange for wedding attire (Figure 6.9).

> I had no wedding gown, like so many war brides in the same dilemma. Harold took me to the PX (Post Exchange) in Tokyo and I found an evening gown that looked like a bridal gown. How lucky I was! My mother-in-law sent me a veil and my white shoes.
>
> (*Bay Area WWII War* 2013)

Edna Hannell Lindley married her American sailor fiancé in Lutwyche, Queensland near Brisbane, Australia on October 28, 1944. When she looked for a wedding dress, she discovered that "because of strict rationing, I couldn't use ration stamps for a wedding dress, so I checked the *Brisbane Telegraph* every evening looking for a second-hand dress. After several weeks, I found one. I bought the dress from the lady without having tried it on and luckily it fit perfectly without any alterations."[14]

FIGURE 6.9: *Luise Van Dyne wedding*, September 27, 1947. Courtesy Luise Van Dyne.

Her sister, Mavis, was her matron of honor and wore a dress she had purchased before the war. Edna's beautiful silk satin dress was exhibited at the War Brides reunion in San Diego in September 2019 (Figure 6.10 and 6.11).

FIGURE 6.10: *Edna Hannell Lindley's wedding portrait.* Courtesy Edna Lindley.

FIGURE 6.11: *Edna Hannell Lindley standing in front of her wedding dress displayed at the World War II War Brides Association reunion.* October 2019. San Diego, CA. Courtesy Edna Lindley. Photo by Nan Turner.

Home Sewing

Sewing did not resolve all the issues of clothing shortages since fabric, thread, and patterns were scarce. When planning her wedding, Jean could not find any fabric to make the dress for her marriage to an American Service man. Jean's future American mother-in-law sent her satin yardage from the USA for her wedding dress. Jean went to the local dressmaker's shop, which was also busy sewing uniforms for the war effort. She reported, "The dressmaker could make a dress if the customer supplied the material." Her sister had designed the perfect dress for her that she hoped to have made. "I took the material to them thinking I could choose a pattern. Not so, they had one pattern, take it or leave it. I took it and it turned out I was very pleased with the results."[15] The style resembled the Hollywood-influenced satin gowns popular in the 1930s and 1940s (Figure 6.12). Jean still has her dress, which was displayed at the War Brides exhibit in San Jose, CA in 2013 (Figure 6.13).

FIGURE 6.12: *Jean wearing her wedding dress made from the only available pattern*, July 4, 1945. Hertfordshire, UK. Courtesy Jean.

FIGURE 6.13: *Jean holding her wedding dress at the Bay Area WWII War Brides Past & Present Exhibit*, 2014. Courtesy Jean. Photograph by Nan Turner.

Knitting

Andriani Chalkiadakis, a young woman who lived in Greece during the war, collected the white and greenish brown cords of parachutes left on the ground after the massive German airborne invasion during the Battle of Crete on June 20, 1941 (Seyferth 2014, 52-55). Later, she hand-knit her wedding dress out of the suspension cords. Andriani untwined the cords, each about 69 feet long, to obtain yarn that she could use to knit the dress. She engineered the two colors of the cords to create a striped pattern. She had to "weave in" the ends of each relatively short piece of fiber, a time-consuming process. An intact piece of the cord became the belt. Andriani wore the dress, now displayed in the Maritime Museum of Crete, for her wedding on October 18, 1941. The dress is exhibited at the museum as a testament to creative solutions during a time of scarcity (Color Plate 19).

Post-War Wedding Attire

Although the war ended in September 1945, rationing and shortages continued as manufacturers scrambled to shift their focus from war munitions to civilian products, not an easy transition. Shortages, scarcity, and the astronomical price tag of waging war were all factors that continued to affect the supply of consumer goods. Europe fared much worse than the USA. The *New York Times* on August 19, 1945, reported, "It is hard for Americans to picture the devastation, the disruption and dislocation of life and the awful crippling shortages that this war has left as a heritage to those who survived it. These people are short of everything—of food and clothing, of shelter, of transportation, of medicine, and even of time and faith and hope" (Daniell, SM8). American retail buyers however did still experience merchandise shortages well into 1946 for "all lines dependent upon fabrics of any type, either cotton or rayon" ("Scarcity to Continue Well into Next Year," 67).

Women from several countries reported that finding anything after the war was difficult; wedding apparel especially continued to be problematic. Adelaide lived in The Hague during the war. She reported that when her sister got married in the Netherlands in 1946, textiles and clothing were still scarce. Adelaide said, "Of course all that shortage did not evaporate right after liberation. We still had rationing for about one year afterwards."[16] Adelaide's sister's dress reflected the extreme shortage of fabric. "She had a gown made out of paper. I don't know where she got it. Kind of a lace type of fabric. Like a doily. It was a full length dress."

Paper fabric, the type used for Adelaide's sister's dress, had been developed in Germany after World War I, when fabric shortages had intensified the need to develop substitutes for wool and other raw materials. Paper-based thread as well was developed to make men's suits, work garments, aprons, dresses, and clothing. Paper fabric, fortunately resistant to water and very inexpensive, was woven from narrow strips of paper twisted into yarn and woven on a loom (Daugherty 2018).

Doris, an art student from Cleveland, Ohio reported,

> Everything was hard to come by. It had to be a left-over thing. People who formerly made wedding dresses wanted to get going but were not set up yet. You couldn't find cars or dresses or fancy stuff. No complaining though. Everyone was proud they had won the war (Figure 6.14).[17]

Elena, who grew up in Monterey, California, spoke about the difficulty of finding wedding attire for her nearly late war wedding date, January 25, 1945. She described the nearly impossible effort to find a wedding dress in her small Northern California hometown. In San Francisco, 120 miles to the north, she had better luck when she spotted a jewelry store display mannequin still clad in a white lace wedding dress. She begged the store owner to sell it to her, and fortunately, it fit perfectly. Elena found her bridesmaid's dresses in a store in

FIGURE 6.14: *Doris's wedding*, June 29, 1946. Cleveland, Ohio. Courtesy Doris' family.

San Jose, California, but white satin shoes were impossible. She had to settle for white satin bedroom slippers (Figure 6.15). "They worked just fine. No one suspected I was wearing bedroom slippers!"[18]

Ellen Miller Coile got married in London after the war but rationing was still going on in the UK. Ellen's friends chipped in and offered her fabric coupons so that she was able to buy dotted swiss cotton fabric to make her wedding dress (Figure 6.16).[19]

Conclusion

Food, fuel, and clothing rationing was a hardship for all during World War II. For those who were planning weddings, it was especially difficult. After apparel manufacturers shifted to war work, civilian clothing of any kind was scarce.

Brides who were lucky enough to shop early could find old stock, but as the war progressed, resources were depleted. Shortages and rationing motivated brides to use ingenuity and creativity to outfit their wedding. These efforts symbolized, as did the marriage itself, hope for a happy and peaceful future, when life would return to normal. After the war, innumerable stories, as well as carefully preserved

FIGURE 6.15: *Elena wearing a store display dress and bedroom slippers for her wedding*, January 25, 1945. Monterey, CA. Courtesy Elena.

dresses, remain as a testament of their difficult, but hopeful wedding days, 70–75 years ago.

The hardship and effort required to maintain simple basic needs of life, such as finding clothing, are very difficult for people living in today's developed societies to imagine. Although war has not become a thing of the past, as hoped for after World War II, most civilians have little contact with current conflicts beyond scant coverage on television. Although the hardships of the war seem to many people to be forgotten facts in history books, the memories of World War II are still within the lifetime of some people, although the group is rapidly dwindling. This book is an attempt to save and share these memories.

Current consumer trends in wedding planning are lavish and costly, totally opposite from the austere preparations during World War II when a practical bride might wear a sensible wool suit because it was something she could wear in the future. The idea of sharing or borrowing wedding dresses during World War II

FIGURE 6.16: *Ellen Miller and Russell Coile's wedding*, December 1951. London, UK. Courtesy Jennifer Coile.

is very different from current day practices of searching for the perfect dress to be worn for only one day. Television shows like *Say Yes to the Dress* feature extravagant new dresses at extremely high prices. *Something Borrowed, Something New*, another popular wedding show, proposes the choice of either buying a new dress or having a professional designer remake the bride's mother's dress. The bride-to-be usually chooses the new dress, giving various reasons for not selecting their mother's now totally redesigned dress. However, the economic or sustainable value of selecting the redesigned dress is rarely one of their reasons.

During the war, rationing, scarcity, and the prioritizing of factory work for the war effort made new dresses almost totally unavailable. Natasha, the bride married in Paris mentioned in the introduction to this book, and the other women interviewed did not have much choice in selecting a dress. They simply had to wear what was offered. Wartime brides often had to borrow a wedding gown that had been worn in the past, economize by wearing a day dress that could be worn again, or wear their service uniform.

Today, consumer spending has been promoted as a method of building prosperity and to drive the economy (Pusca 2009, 370). However, in view of the limited resources of our finite planet, unbridled spending and consumption cannot continue indefinitely. Awareness of the increasing need to resolve issues of over consumption so that the needs of future generations will not be compromised, is evident in society today. The motivation to curtail consumption is difficult when abundant, affordable clothing is so accessible. Learning about the conservative practices of brides outfitting their wedding parties during World War II can be an inspiration for consumers concerned about sustainability and reducing consumption and waste.

NOTES

1. Francesca Stewart (born 1917, Naples, Italy) in e-mail communication to the author, June 28, 2014.
2. Helen (born 1954, Greece) in discussion with the author, Davis, CA, 2014.
3. Lynn (born 1926, Southampton, UK) in discussion with the author at the Northern California War Brides Association lunch, Campbell, CA, March 24, 2017.
4. Joan (born 1923, Brisbane, Australia) in discussion with the author during the War Brides Association Reunion, San Diego, CA, October 9, 2019.
5. Shelly Tobin, in e-mail communication with the author, March 28, 2017.
6. Betty Reid Soskin (born 1921, Detroit, MI) in discussion with the author at the Rosie the Riveter Center, 2015. See also: Betty Reid Soskin, *Sign My Name to Freedom: A Memoir of a Pioneering Life*, ed. J. Douglas Allen-Taylor (Carlsbad, CA: Hay House, 2018).
7. Dorothy E. Pence Berry (born 1923, Australia) *Bay Area WWII War Brides Past & Present Exhibit*, Dr. Martin Luther King Jr. Library, 150 E. San Fernando St. San Jose, CA, Jan–June 2014.
8. Antonia B. Edillo (born 1928, Philippines) in discussion with the author at the Northern California War Brides Association lunch, Campbell, CA, March 12, 2014.
9. Regina (born 1960, CA) in discussion with the author, Davis, CA, 2011.

10. Sylvia Smith Harris (born 1918, Liverpool, UK) *Bay Area WWII War Brides Past & Present Exhibit*, 2014.
11. A coronet is a simple crown-like headdress.
12. Vincent Schoenstein (born 1925, San Francisco, CA) in discussion with the author and in unpublished memoir: *Moira's Recycled Wedding Gown*, 2019b.
13. Luise (born 1929, Tokyo, Japan) in discussion with the author, Sacramento, CA, August 17, 2017.
14. Edna Lindley's life story is an extract from an unpublished article written for the World War II War Brides Association.
15. Jean (born 1927, Welwyn Garden City, UK) in discussion with the author at the Northern California World War II War Brides Association lunch, March 24, 2017, Campbell, CA.
16. Adelaide (born 1927, The Hague, Netherlands) in discussion with the author, November 20, 2014.
17. Doris (born 1925, Cleveland, OH) in telephone discussion with the author, July 2014.
18. Elena (born 1924, Monterey, CA) in telephone discussion with the author, July 2014.
19. Information supplied by Jennifer Coile, daughter of Ellen Miller Coile, June 21, 2020. Ellen reported her friends shared coupons for her to be able to buy the fabric for her wedding dress in 1951 although clothing rationing ended in the UK in 1949.

7

Costumes Go to War: Clothing in Hollywood and British Film

Clothing can tell a story about the past, the present, and the future. Its silhouette, color, line, and construction hold clues about the person who wore the clothing, as well as the history of the time in which it was worn. Clothing can be an "observation point from which to view the political, economic and cultural environment of an historical period" (Veillon 2002, vii).

The film industry has always understood the value of clothing to tell a story. Dorothy's dress from the film *The Wizard of Oz* is one of the most iconic costumes in the history of film, especially since it was the only garment that Judy Garland wore throughout the entire movie.

Reflections on Seeing Dorothy's Dress

I had the good fortune of seeing the actual dress worn by Judy Garland in *The Wizard of Oz* at the *Hollywood Costume* exhibit in Los Angeles (2015). The dress had a hard-pressed horizontal crease a few inches above the bottom hem of the skirt that I interpreted as evidence the hem had been let down (Color Plate 20). This visible crease mark reminded me of Vera, growing up in London during the war, who reported in Chapter 4 that, "My skirts always had hemline creases where they had been lowered."[1] I can envision Dorothy's Auntie Em sewing clothing for the family. Dorothy, growing up during the Great Depression on a poor farm, would have had to wear her dresses for years, even if she outgrew them. I imagined Auntie Em making the dress with a deep hem to be let out as Dorothy grew, just as Vera's mother had done in London. This would have been an authentic detail for the costume Dorothy wore in Dust Bowl ravaged Kansas during the Great Depression.

Auntie Em would also have carefully bundled up all the yardage leftover from sewing her families clothing to use for patching and mending. My mother, born in

1927, also grew up in Kansas during the Great Depression. She carefully bundled up the remnants of the dresses she made for me and for herself. In the prosperous 1960s, when I was growing up, my outgrown dresses were donated to the church rummage sale and my mother made me a new one. I did not have to wear clothing with hems let out and panels added to the hem as I grew.

Dr. Deborah Nadoolman Landis, the curator of the *Hollywood Costume* exhibit, told me that at least 16 versions of Dorothy's gingham dress were made.[2] Multiples of costumes are always required, she explained, in case the dress ripped or needed washing or to fit the stand-in. The dress I saw in the exhibit might not have been representative of the others. The pressed crease above the hem might only have reflected that there was limited yardage for that particular dress. Furthermore, there is no documentation supporting my theory that the dress purposely reflected the Gale family's poverty level. Dr. Landis did concur that she too could imagine Auntie Em carefully washing, pressing, and letting out the hem of Dorothy's dress as she outgrew the dress.

Movies in the 1930s and 1940s

Clothing scarcity impacted civilians all over the world during the 1930s decade of global depression and the 1940s war years. Movies made during those years provide witness of the hardships of that time. This chapter explores the representation of shortages, rationing, and scarcity represented in *The Wizard of Oz*, released in the USA in 1939 and *Millions Like Us* and *The Gentle Sex*, both released in the UK in 1943.

Hollywood and the Great Depression

The Great Depression, caused by a complicated combination of global events, is sometimes blamed on the USA stock market crash of 1929. The real cause was possibly more complicated. Acute stock market gyrations had ravaged the economies of a global collection of countries even before the USA stock market crash.

One example of global instability before 1929 was Germany's economy, devastated by runaway hyperinflation and reparations demanded by Allied countries for the destruction caused by World War I. The German stock market crashed in 1927 (Temin 1989, 24–25). Unemployment rose from 8.6% in 1928 to 43.8% in 1932 (Galenson and Zellner 1957, 455). Germans, furious with the government's handling of the Armistice and the economy, "brought Hitler to the Reich Chancellery, on January 30, 1933," with the campaign promise that he could make Germany great again (Taylor 2013, 343).

Ultimately, the USA stock market crash in October 1929 struck a final blow that "undermined the world credit system and thus was the proximate cause of the depression" (Rothermund 1996, 48). Unemployment in the USA increased from 5.5% in 1929 before the crash, to over 20% by the mid-1930s (Coen 1973, 52). Complicating matters, the Dust Bowl, a severe seven-year drought in the center states of the USA, added to suffering across the country.

During the Great Depression, even though Hollywood was believed to be "recession proof" because "consumers will always be willing to spend on entertainment to escape," film profits dwindled when the hugely popular pastime of going to the cinema became a luxury for the majority of the population (Chmielewski and James 2008). Movie studios, forced to lay off workers, let go of up to 20% of the workforce (Balio 1995, 15). As the Great Depression years rolled on with little relief, several studios, including RKO, Fox, and Paramount, declared bankruptcy (Balio 1995, 15). In the end, Hollywood proved not to be recession-proof as movie studios experienced firsthand the deprivation and scarcity suffered by millions of people throughout the world during the 1930s.

Hollywood Successes

The fortunes of the USA movie industry turned a corner in 1939 and 1940, creating banner years. The film industry seized the opportunity to regain profits and produced critically acclaimed and very successful films, including *The Wizard of Oz* made at Metro-Goldwyn-Mayer studios (Jurca 2008, 6). The film was shown around the world to tremendous acclaim. The theme of survival and tenacity in the struggle to return to a beloved home struck a heartfelt chord for civilians and military serving around the world during World War II.

The Wizard of Oz: *The Book*

The Wonderful Wizard of Oz, published by Frank L. Baum in 1900, became the bestselling children's book of the Christmas season that year (Baum, Denslow, and Hearn 2000, xli). Baum set the story in rural Kansas, a region similar to South Dakota where he and his wife, Maud, had experienced a disastrous drought during the 1890s. The couple moved to South Dakota after a few unusually wet years, which made farming prosperous. Unfortunately, a decade of drought and hard winters followed, during which farms failed and foreclosure brought economic depression and hardship, similar to the cruel effects of the Dust Bowl on Kansas in the 1930s (Selcer 2010, 56). Many homesteaders, forced to file bankruptcy, fled the region like Midwesterners would do in the 1930s (Rahn 1998, 5). Disheartened by the relentless drought that extended for several years, coupled with the danger of Native American uprisings, Baum relocated to Chicago in 1891 to write for the *Chicago Evening Post* (Baum, Denslow, and Hearn 2000, xxiii–xxiv; see also Harmetz 1977, 313). His experience living through the drought and a treacherous tornado in South Dakota later inspired *The Wizard of Oz*.

Kansas experienced a period of unusually favorable wet weather during the 1920s, similar to the temporary climate change that enticed the Baums to move to South Dakota. Farmers, motivated by the high prices they could obtain for wheat, plowed the natural grasslands under to plant cash crops. When normal dry conditions returned, without the protection of the deep-rooted grasses to hold the dirt in place, high winds created dust storms that carried off the barren topsoil. Farmers in Colorado, Kansas, New Mexico, Oklahoma, and Texas suffered from years of drought during the 1930s, similar to what Baum experienced during the 1890s in South Dakota.

Like the Baums, who left South Dakota due to the impossibility of earning a living on the drought-savaged plains, during the 1930s "thousands abandoned the land and migrated west to California to look for work; these were not Hollywood hopefuls but starving 'Okies'" (Loncraine 2009, 283). A government-sponsored documentary: *The Plow that Broke the Plains,* made in 1936, brought attention to the plight of these farmers (Lorentz). Shown commercially in major theaters along with feature films, the documentary alerted the public to the tragedy in the Midwestern states. The *Los Angeles Times* (July 20, 1937) reported on the plight of Dust Bowl refugees,

> Many are said to be near starvation; the problem of schooling the children is acute, and sanitary conditions are such that there have already been three outbreaks of typhoid. Conference on problem was set for next week in Los Angeles to be presided over by Gov. Frank F. Merriam.
>
> ("California Puzzles Over Problem," 10)

Gilbert Adrian, known professionally as Adrian, the costume designer for *The Wizard of Oz*, as well as the director, Victor Fleming, probably were aware of the environmental refugees looking for work or a handout in Southern California during the late 1930s. The clothing of these Dust Bowl refugees announced their poverty; faded after long-term wear and washings, handed down to younger children as it was outgrown, hems turned down, patches or leftover scraps added in places where more length or room was needed (Figure 7.1).

The Wizard of Oz: *The 1939 Film*

Shot in black and white, the opening scenes of *The Wizard of Oz* captured the grayness of Kansas and the grim character of life on the prairie. The harsh, dry,

FIGURE 7.1: Dorothea Lange, *A sharecropper and his family stalled in the desert as they enter California*, 1937. Library of Congress, Prints & Photographs Division, FSA/OWI Collection, (reproduction number, e.g., LC-USF34-9058-C).

and barren landscape resonated with Americans who had been "left with little means by the Great Depression, the drought, and the dust storms" (Hagen 2018). Rebecca Loncraine (2009) noted that the film "would reflect the realities of the thirties in the opening Kansas scenes, and then whisk audiences away with Dorothy to a lush, colorful wonderland" (283). Once Dorothy arrived in Oz, the scenes changed to vivid Technicolor.

Dorothy's faded gingham dress silently told the story of Kansas and the hard life on the farm. The costume was faithfully based on Baum's description:

> Dorothy had only one other dress, but that happened to be clean and was hanging on a peg beside her bed. It was gingham, with checks of white and blue; and although the blue was somewhat faded with many washings, it was still a pretty frock.
>
> (Baum, Denslow, and Hearn 2000, 56)

Her shoe wardrobe was equally spare:

> Then she looked down at her feet and noticed how old and worn her shoes were.

> "They surely will never do for a long journey, Toto," she said. And Toto looked up into her face with his little black eyes and wagged his tail to show he knew what she meant.
>
> At that moment Dorothy saw lying on the table the silver shoes that had belonged to the Witch of the East.
>
> "I wonder if they will fit me," she said to Toto. "They would be just the thing to take a long walk in, for they could not wear out."
>
> She took off her old leather shoes and tried on the silver ones. Which fitted her as well as if they had been made for her.
>
> (56)

Moviegoers in the 1940s, who had suffered through the Great Depression, recognized Dorothy's worn-out and refashioned dress as representative of their own wardrobes. Dorothy's dress, carefully laundered, mended, and repaired during a decade of deprivation, provided witness to difficult lives of common people all over the world during the 1930s and 1940s. Several women interviewed for my research who lived through the era expressed similar habits of thrift and often stated: "We saved everything, string, rubber bands, nothing was thrown out."[3]

British Film Industry

In the 1930s, approximately 40% of the British population went to the cinema at least once a week (Aldgate and Richards 1986, 3). In fact, the British spent more on going to movies than any other country, especially as the economy improved after the Great Depression (Kuhn 2002, 1). During the war, movies provided a way to escape from the stress of nightly bombings and the fear of eminent invasion.

When war broke out, all theaters, cinemas, music halls, and other places of entertainment were closed for fear that they would become "deathtraps" in case of an air attack (Chapman 1999, 36; see also Aldgate and Richards 1986, 1). Film studio executives, eager to save their industry and their incomes, successfully fought to have the theaters reopened, arguing that British films were essential for wartime morale. Theaters were allowed to reopen two weeks after they were ordered closed, perhaps because the Germans had not attacked, or the strong efforts of the film studio executives had convinced the government of the importance of movie theaters (Morgan 1948, 14; see also Aldgate and Richards 1986, 1).

Jean, who lived near London during the war, reported: "The movies were such an important part of everyone's life. We didn't have TV then. We went at the very least two times a week."[4]

Rae, serving in the Auxiliary Territorial Service (hereafter abbreviated ATS), said that she went to the cinema at least once or twice a week: "Well, that is where we spent most of our time."[5]

Thereafter, theaters stayed open, even during the Blitz and provided moviegoers a temporary reprieve from the fear and anxiety of daily attacks (Aldgate and Richards 1986, 1). Jean said that going to the cinema helped provide an escape, even for a short time, "They were great for morale and cheered us up. We just came out of the movies and had to say: Oh, well, back to real life. They taught us something."[6]

Joy Beebe, in her memoir *Snapshots of a War Bride's Life* (2015), wrote,

> By 1942, people were getting used to the way things were going. Shortages were serious and there was no end in sight. I think people started to think that if this was the way life would be, we had better start relaxing and enjoy things while we still could. People queued up for hours to go to the pictures; cinemas were booming, theatres ran matinees and evening performances, and famous stars could be seen for small prices. (118–19)

Joy told me that going to the movies was so popular that people queued up to a film and, if they could not get in, waited in line for the next showing. "There was nothing else to do," she said.[6] Films were good for the morale of both soldiers and civilians, allowing a little time to escape from the harsh realities of wartime, therefore considered essential.

Lucy worked as a movie theater film projectionist in Nottingham, UK, during the war. She reported that her job was considered essential to society since going to see films was so important for morale.[7]

Keeping movie houses open turned out to be a nearly insurmountable task. In addition to staff shortages due to universal conscription; bombings, and evacuations often disrupted screenings (Lant 1991, 26). In spite of these hardships, the British film industry survived and filled a need of the national audience, "A sense of recognition, a feeling of being a person spoken to by a film" (5).

British cinema served not only as a diversion from the stress of wartime but also as a vehicle of propaganda (Chapman 1999, 35) Films that reflected the spirit of the populace banning together to defend their country, in what was presented as "a People's War," fueled patriotism (15). The Minister of Information (MoI) advised studios of the type of films to produce:

> Realistic films about everyday life dealing with matters not directly about the war, but featuring events in various phases of life in factory, mines, on the land etc., are advocated by the Films Division of the M.o.I. Special support will be given to the

> production of such films. A balance between war and non-war propaganda is desirable, emphasis should be given to the positive virtues of British national characteristics and the democratic way of life.
>
> (Richards 1987, 130)

These propaganda films encouraged civilians to accept rationing and austerity of all kinds, including clothing, as a challenging point of honor. Films featuring women dealing with clothing austerity, rationing, military service, and war work, while looking attractive in uniforms or factory garb, encouraged female moviegoers to picture themselves accepting these challenges as their patriotic duty (Chapman 1999, 33–35; see also Robb 2017, 158). Widespread poverty, experienced during the Great Depression years, had already promoted the need to "make-do." During the war, civilians were encouraged to continue "making-do" as an act of patriotism (Kuhn 2002, 122).

Gainsborough Pictures, founded in 1924 by Sir Michael Elias Balcon (grandfather of current day actor, Daniel Day Lewis), became well known for its popular "costume melodramas" (Street 1997, 31). The logo shown at the beginning of each film featured a tableau vivant-type image of a woman elaborately costumed in the typical fashion of a Thomas Gainsborough portrait from the second half of the 18th century (Figure 7.2). His painting, *The Morning Walk*, is emblematic of his portrait style.[8]

Gainsborough Picture's contemporary dramas, portraying the challenges of life during wartime, received critical acclaim, especially after 1942, when victory was a little more certain. Sarah Street (1997), a film professor at the University of Bristol, UK, surmised, "The films stressed pulling together in the face of national emergency, requiring individual sacrifice and a suspension of demands which conflicted with those of the state" (48). In the UK, Gainsborough's films even rivaled the popularity of Hollywood movies in "both critical and popular acclaim" (Morgan 1948, 26; Kuhn 2002, 2). James Chapman (1999), professor of Film Studies at the University of Leicester, UK, believed, "Social historians have seen in films such as *Millions Like Us* evidence that British audiences had developed a taste for realism and had rejected the fictional fancies of Hollywood" (60). Hollywood could not compete in this realm (34).

Millions Like Us, produced by Gainsborough Pictures, and *The Gentle Sex*, produced by Two Cities Films, both in 1943, displayed aspects of clothing austerity and rationing as challenges that strong women fighting on the home front faced with dignity and often humor. For example, Maggie, in the movie *The Gentle Sex*, pulled out her knitting on the train ride to camp, illustrating that she was using every spare moment to contribute to the war effort. Other women knit in bed before lights out, on trains, and in other travel scenes, mirroring the viewing audience's home front commitment to doing their part.

FIGURE 7.2: *Gainsborough Studios film opening logo*. Gainsborough Film.

Millions Like Us

Millions Like Us, a semi-documentary propaganda film, sought to increase patriotism and civilian support of the war effort (Color Plate 21). The film followed the Crowsons, a fictitious working-class British family representing "millions like us," as they lived through the war. The family struggled with rationing and clothing shortages throughout the film, encouraging viewers to accept their own duty to support the war effort.

The film began with the family, Mr. Crowson (Dad), sisters Phyllis and Celia, and brother Tom, preparing to travel to their annual seashore vacation near Brighton, UK. They had lodged at the same bed and breakfast for the past 22 years, a subtle reference to the disruption caused by World War I, which had ended just 21 years before. In 1939, war again hovered on the horizon. Soon after their arrival, air raid sirens signaled the start of World War II. Coastal towns were evacuated and the Crowson's vacation was cut short.

When we next see the Crowson family, each member had signed up to do their part: Tom off fighting on the Egyptian front, Dad in the Home Guard, working three nights a week, and Phyllis and Celia accepting inscription in the Women's Corps. Phyllis signed up to work as an auto mechanic in the ATS and Celia to work in an aircraft factory. Mr. Crowson, left at home to fend for himself, comically demonstrated his dependence on womenfolk by displaying a large hole in his sock. The pile of dishes in the sink, along with his worn sock, illustrated the disruption of traditional gender roles caused by female conscription.

Phyllis broke the news to Dad of the sisters impending conscription by saying that her friend had joined the service, "[She's] in the ATS and she quite likes it. I don't care for the stockings, of course, or the skirt. The coats cute." Her motivation to enlist seemed to be the attractiveness of the uniform jacket.

Traditional society valued women's appearance over their ability; therefore, the military purposely designed flattering women's uniforms to increase their motivation to join up (McEuen 2011, 140–42). The ATS's uniform, however, was not considered very attractive. (Summers 2016, 46).

Celia reported, with some trepidation, to the Ministry of Labor and National Service for her intake interview. The waiting room walls were covered with recruitment posters that set Celia dreaming of her future role in the war (Color Plate 22). In her daydreams she was dressed in a flattering military uniform or a nurse's dress, helping handsome soldiers, and finally being offered an engagement ring by a wounded soldier who she cared for. Antonia Lant, a film professor at New York University's Tisch School of the Arts, suggested, "Her fantasies traverse all four branches of the women's Forces, providing a veritable military fashion parade" (1991, 101). However, when the actual interview started, the positions offered were not as Celia imagined. The female officer told her: "You can help your country just as much in an overall as you can in a uniform these days." Celia's fantasy of dressing in an attractive uniform turned out to be only a dream. Placed in a factory job, she worked on aircraft components wearing an apron over her simple dress and her hair in a kerchief.

Millions Like Us addressed the issue of traditionally defined social class in pre-World War II Great Britain, which was often indicated by clothing, language, or profession. "Seemingly minor items such as gloves, ties, braces or hats, if incorrectly chosen or worn, had clear social significance and could betray a person's lack of breeding" (Horwood 2005, 121). The difference between the social classes became apparent when Celia arrived at the factory and was assigned a roommate in a local hostel. Gwen Price, Celia's roommate, described her life before the service, indicating her lower-class background. Gwen said: "Dad's a miner, a wonderful time we had on the dole." She described her home in a "depressed area, you know with lovely damp patches of fungus blossoming on the wallpaper."

By contrast, Jennifer Knowles' arrival by taxi at the hostel, dressed in a well-tailored windowpane plaid suit with a matching hat, along with many trunks of clothing, indicated her position in the wealthy class (Figure 7.3). Annie Earnshaw, her assigned roommate, spoke with an accent, pegging her as not an equal to Jennifer. Seeing the amount of clothing that Jennifer brought, Annie accused her of illegal stocking up, or hoarding, in anticipation of the war.

A subsequent exchange between the two about clothing again highlighted the difference between classes. Jennifer, shocked when she saw Annie get into bed

FIGURE 7.3: *Jennifer arrives at the hostel in a suit that sets her apart from the other women*, 1943. Film. Gainsborough Pictures, UK. Frame enlargement from *Millions Like Us*. ITV/Shutterstock.

with her underwear on, asked: "Aren't you going to undress?" Annie answered: "Why, I'll just put my clothes on over the underwear in the morning." Wealthy people with abundant wardrobes, like Jennifer, wore pajamas to bed. The lower class, like Annie, slept in their underwear and put the same clothes on the next morning.

The women attended a local dance where Celia met a young man in the Royal Air Force (RAF) and quickly fell in love. The couple planned to marry before he shipped out. Celia's friends discussed the difficulty of putting together wedding clothes with rationing coupons during lunch in the canteen:

> Gwen, "Still struggling with the coupons?"
> Celia, "And I had my [...] of the underwear, all the pink gloves I saw in Springfield. Or a night dress."
> Jennifer, "Take my advice and put the night dress first, after all that is what counts."
> Gwen agreed, "Cross off the walking shoes and put down the night dress."
> Celia, "What about the spare set of underwear?"
> Jennifer, "I've got a pair of blue lace here that don't fit me. You can have those if you like."

The theme of doing without and the effect of scarcity continued in a scene with Dad, serving in the Home Guard. He entered a dark bomb shelter during a raid and a woman's voice was heard: "I can't find a pair of stockings anywhere so its slacks or nothing." Women were not only doing without stockings they were also engaging in activities that made wearing skirts impractical. The coveralls, overalls, and slacks they wore to work in factories disrupted the norms of gender separation that traditional clothing had historically provided. (For discussion of gender issues related to clothing, see Chapter 3.)

The Gentle Sex

The Gentle Sex follows a group of seven women as they enlist in the ATS and travel to Queen's Camp, Guildford, Surrey, to start their training (Color Plate 23). Rae Brewer Zurovcik, whom I met at the 2017 War Brides Association convention in Las Vegas, Nevada, served in the ATS. Her experience in the war is chronicled in the book: *GI Brides* (Barrett and Calvi 2013, 53-62).

Rae was very proud of the fact that 17-year-old Princess Elizabeth (now Queen Elizabeth) also served in the ATS in 1943 (Color Plate 24) (Murphy 2000, 154). In July 2005, Rae was invited to London for the unveiling of the Monument to the Women of World War II ("Memorial to War Women Unveiled" 2005) (Figure 7.4). Queen Elizabeth was also in attendance and Rae told me that she was very happy to meet her.

Actor and director Leslie Howard, the film narrator, first appears in the film with his back to the camera, observing women at Victoria Railway Station, London.[9] He was in the process of selecting seven women, representing a cross-section of British social classes indicated by clothing, language, or profession. Howard described the women he selects: Betty, an immature only child afraid to leave her mother; Ann, a beautiful blond with her colonel father; Maggie, a working class Scottish woman accompanied by her mother; Dot, a hairdresser with her boyfriend; Erna, a Czech refugee; Joan, a teacher with a difficult temperament; and Gwen, a Cockney waitress. They were dressed in an assortment of suits and coats, ranging from functional and ordinary to stylishly fitted. Dot, the hairdresser, stood out in her fashionable turban and well-placed brooch.

When the women finally arrived at camp, they were issued "kits," or uniforms. Ann remarked, "No coupons, no cash, it'll seem like heaven," referring to the UK's clothing rationing system that had been in place since 1941. Uniforms solved the problem of clothing shortages and ration books. Upon arrival at the camp, their social class differences diminished as uniforms replaced their civilian clothing.

Several scenes focused on the women carefully polishing their shoes and using a button stick to protect the leather while polishing, illustrating the care needed

FIGURE 7.4: *Monument to the Women of World War II*, June 26, 2011. Whitehall, London, UK. Photo by Nan Turner.

to make their uniforms last. Rae told me that she prided herself on the look and upkeep of her uniform. She had her collars, which were separate from the shirt, professionally cleaned and pressed even though the military provided laundry service. Rae wanted her dress uniform to be perfect. The process of learning to wear and take care of their uniforms represented the women's transformation from a disparate group into a functional military unit (Lant 1991, 103–04).

The first evening at camp, as the women prepared to sleep in the bunkhouse, further indications of class differences became apparent. Dot, wearing a fashionable robe, spent time combing her hair as she prepared for bed. In a playful conversation, Dot declared that she would rather be dead than not have fun in the ATS. When Dot removed her robe to get into bed, revealing her sleeveless bias-cut gown, Maggie cried out, "So, you will be, Dot Hopkins! If you don't cover yourself up! Makes me shiver to look at you!" Maggie, a working-class woman from a colder climate, obviously only familiar with functional sleepwear, considered Dot's gown inappropriate.

The same evening, Maggie quizzes Ann, who arrived late:

> "Where have you been? You missed roll call!"
> "I've been fighting my way into a bath."

> "On a Friday! We take ours on a Saturday, after the flue's been swept. My mother adds a hot kettle after each one, but the last, that gets a bit cold."
> Joan snipes: "You don't say that you use the same bath water?"
> Maggie: "Aye, we do. Where's the harm? It's all in the family!"

Maggie's comments are very revealing about her working-class family background as well as illustrating the differences between the women drawn together in the ATS.

Reporting for inspection the next morning dressed in their new uniforms, it is obvious that some of the women will need some time to get it right. Most managed to correctly wear the uniform and hat, but others were missing their jacket and one even wore her civilian floral skirt. Attempts at marching as a unit were equally haphazard; a few did not seem to understand the word "halt," and finally a solitary figure marched off mistakenly in the wrong direction. Soon after, they were sent off on a long march through the countryside in their "clumpy lace-up shoes" (Barrett and Calvi 2013, 17). That evening the girls are all shown soaking their painful feet after having had to hike for miles in their brand-new leather shoes (Figure 7.5).

Rae described experiencing the same treatment in *GI Brides*:

> Once the girls were kitted out, they were led into the parade ground for their first drill practice. [...] After a good half-hour, the girls felt ready for a break, but instead they had to set off into the Scottish countryside to wear in their new shoes with a five-mile march.
> (Barret and Calvi 2013, 17)

Rae reported that the purpose of the hike was to break in the shoes by walking in them. Walking five miles or more in brand-new leather shoes would be extremely uncomfortable. Rae said they had no choice, but that evening, as in the film, most of the girls had very sore feet (Figure 7.6).

The women in *The Gentle Sex* sang a song while they marched that Rae also sang in the ATS: "She'll Be Wearing Khaki Bloomers." The lyrics referred to the "passion killer underwear" they were issued (17). The song originated in the army to poke fun at the ATS, but was later appropriated by the women who made it their own, however eschewing several "racy" sexist stanzas in the original version:

> She'll be wearing khaki bloomers when she comes, when she comes
> And we're goin' to take them off when she comes, when she comes
> She'll be wearing striped pajamas when she comes, when she comes [...]
> (Dinan 2015, 335)

When training finished, the women were given their postings, half to drive lorries (trucks) and the other half to a heavy anti-aircraft (ack-ack) regiment.

FIGURE 7.5: *Day Long Comfort for the Feet— Marketed to women in service*, 1945. Ever-Rest Shoe advertisement, UK. *Picture Post*, January 6, 1945, 4.

At their new assignment, Ann and Maggie attended a dance dressed in their uniforms (Figure 7.7). Ann remarked that she would prefer to be dressed in an evening gown:

> "I wish we were wearing evening dresses; it would be fun to feel fluffy again!"
> "Oh, would it? I've never had an evening dress," answers Maggie.

Maggie again showed her working-class disadvantage, admitting that she never owned an evening dress. Yet their uniforms eliminated any outward appearance of class distinction and they appeared as equals, at least on the outside.

The female lorry drivers were assigned to an important secret mission to deliver "a vast quantity of mechanical transport and war material" to an undisclosed location for shipment abroad. The drivers assembled dressed in their uniforms;

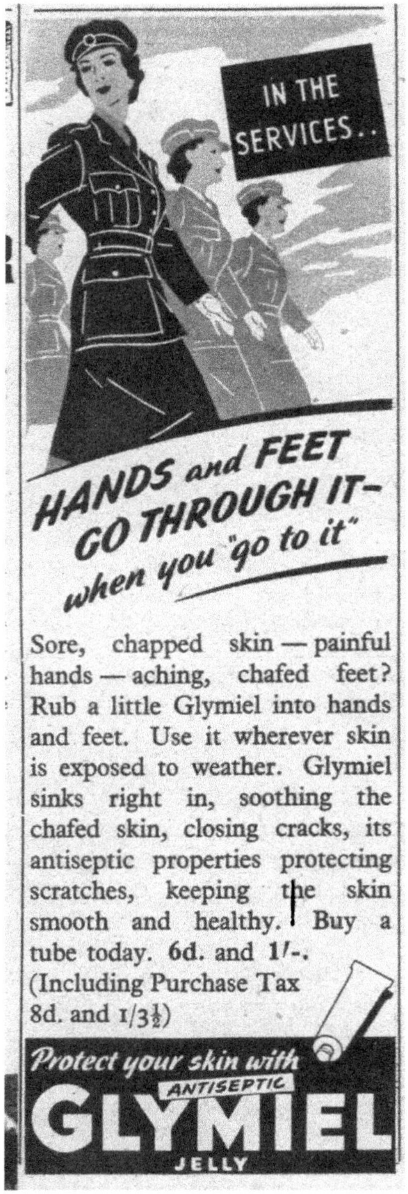

FIGURE 7.6: *In the Services—Hands and Feet Go Through It—when you "go to it,"* Glymiel advertisement, UK. *Picture Post*, March 8, 1941, 34.

however, this time, the majority wore slacks instead of skirts. A female officer accompanied them on a motorcycle. Leslie Howard's voice-over stated, "That dispatch driver, I keep forgetting it's a girl," referring to her masculine appearance

FIGURE 7.7: *In uniform, the women appear to be equals in spite of social class differences*, 1943. Film. *Two Cities Films*, UK. Frame Enlargement from *The Gentle Sex*. Courtesy ITV/Shutterstock.

driving a motorcycle dressed in slacks. Howard's statement underscored the limited acceptance of women wearing slacks, even when a skirt would be particularly uncomfortable or dangerous. On the return train ride after the mission was accomplished, the women all changed back to their skirts, even though they had to sleep lying on the floor of a boxcar.

The lorry drivers' mission became arduous when the deadline to deliver the trucks was pushed back six hours. The women had to forgo their scheduled rest stop and drive all night in the rain. At the shipment destination, the men in charge condescendingly questioned the women's ability to accomplish their mission, insinuating that women did not have the steel to accomplish an important military assignment:

> First man, "How about these […] lorries? They should have arrived by now."
> Second man, "I expect they have stopped to have their hair waved."
> First man, "I shouldn't wonder."

To the men's surprise, the lorry drivers arrived at the station right on schedule, proving their ability to do a man's job.

The Gentle Sex ended with the women reunited at a mess call after succeeding at their assignments, happy and exhausted. Dressed in their uniforms, they looked like a confident, unified group working together for the war effort, all signs of class differences eliminated.

Conclusion

Movies were an important morale builder during World War II because they provided a short escape from the realities of wartime. Some films, however, were not only entertaining but also influenced audiences to accept their duty toward the war effort. These films present images of women using creative means to extend their limited wardrobes during periods of scarcity caused by economic depression and wartime.

The *Wizard of Oz* was internationally popular during the war. Dorothy's love of her family and home resonated with people serving in the military, who also dreamed of returning to an idealized home (Carpenter 1985, 37, 44). Pilots flying for the RAF and Australians fighting in the Libyan desert chose "We're Off to See the Wizard" as their theme song (44).

Many viewers of *The Wizard of Oz* today might not have noticed the extension on the hem of Dorothy's dress, or would have mistaken it for a design detail. Dorothy's family, living on a drought-stricken farm, barely scraped-by. With no extra money for clothing, steps had to be taken to make their clothes last. The bias band of gingham on Dorothy's skirt could have been inserted to increase the length or to disguise the hem extension added after she started to outgrow her dress.

Propaganda films, *Millions Like Us* and *The Gentle Sex*, encouraged the rigid social classes of Great Britain to join together to defeat Hitler. The films presented the combined effort necessary to win the war as the female stars made-do, shared their limited clothing resources, dressed in slacks, and supported each other in spite of class differences (Turner 2019, 171).

Today, movie viewers in prosperous countries have lived most or all of their lives during an era of abundance and waste. The idea of doing without, conserving what one has, and sharing clothing may be unfamiliar. However, a renewed interest in Do-It-Yourself, or DIY, in an effort to reduce consumption for the good of the environment has emerged in recent years. The current DIY revival possibly foretells a renewal of interest in the creative handiwork of women during World War II, who used creativity and resourcefulness to create clothing in spite of the austerity and shortages caused by war. (For discussion of the renewed interest in DIY, see Chapter 9).

NOTES

1. Vera (born 1929, London) in e-mail communication with the author, March 8, 2012.
2. Dr. Deborah Nadoolman Landis, in telephone discussion with the author, June 6, 2015.
3. Betsey (born 1940, Metuchen, NJ) in discussion with the author in Davis, CA, November 2017.

4. Jean (born 1927, Welwyn Garden City, UK) in discussion with the author at the Northern California Chapter of the World War II War Brides Association lunch, Campbell, CA, April 22, 2018.
5. Rae Brewer Zurovcik (born 1923, Holloway, UK) in telephone interview, June 2, 2018.
6. Joy A. Beebe (born 1925, Sidcup, London, UK) in telephone conversation with the author, June 13, 2018.
7. Lucy (born 1930, Nottingham, UK) in discussion with the author at the Northern California World War II War Brides Association lunch, Campbell, CA, November 11, 2017.
8. Thomas Gainsborough, *The Morning Walk*, 1785, oil, London, The National Gallery.
9. Leslie Howard was a very successful and popular British film star and director. *The Gentle Sex* was his last movie. The plane he was traveling on was shot down over the Bay of Biscay on June 1, 1943. For more information on his life, see Ronald Howard's 1981 book: *In Search of My Father* (London: William Kimber).

8

Clothing as Commerce: Hoarding, Bartering, and the Black Market

> Food was scarce, but we did not go hungry. Lilo rode on an old bicycle round the villages to barter for food: my old flying boots for a small sack of flour, fur gloves for a few kilos of beef, tea for a pot of lard. Everything that we could manage to do without in the household Lilo exchanged for food. She bartered and haggles as though she had learned the art in an Oriental bazaar.
>
> Heinz Knoke, *I Flew for the Führer: The Story of a German Fighter Pilot*

Coupons and ration tickets did not resolve all issues caused by consumer shortages during World War II. When government efforts to provide fair shares for all fell short, alternative methods of commerce, including hoarding, bartering, and the black market, flourished. Government attempts to provide fair shares by rationing limited resources and controlling inflation actually fueled these semi-legal, side markets. Ultimately, shortages intensified as merchants hoarded goods knowing they could make a profit on the black market (Taylor 1997, 160).

When money lost all value, textiles and clothing and other scarce commodities could be bartered in exchange for necessities. This chapter explores the value of textiles and clothing in the semi-legal and illegal alternative markets that developed in many countries during World War II.

Hoarding

Hoarding, motivated by the fear of shortages or price increases, was the act of stocking up products in anticipation of future shortages. Ration "scares" or anticipated scarcity could motivate bulk shopping as wealthy people stocked up, creating shortages for others and ultimately diminishing the success of the rationing scheme (Rostow 1942, 496). For example, in the USA in 1943, rumors of clothing rationing caused a run on apparel sales and hoarding soon after the restrictions were enacted on shoe sales. During the first week of shoe rationing, stores in New York City experienced a 53% increase in clothing purchases (Lingeman 1970, 243). Shoppers who bought in bulk justified their acquisitions by claiming that they were just "saving them for a rainy day" (Enssle 1993, 13). Some governments even shut stores for a period of time while rationing was initiated to avoid a run on buying during the transition period.

Hoarding was considered evil (Figure 8.1). It prevented others from having their fair share. In spite of the general public's resentment, many people indulged in the act whenever possible. A common saying was, "I'm just stocking up before the hoarders get there" (Lingeman 1970, 247). Unfortunately, people who did not hoard "suffered particular deprivations" since amounts allotted by government-controlled programs were not sufficient to fill the basic needs (Enssle 1987, 498–99).

Propaganda films like *A Letter from Bataan*, a 1942 "Victory Short" documentary by Paramount Pictures, attempted to shame hoarders by revealing the serious consequences for soldiers on the front. The Bataan Peninsula in the Phillipines was the location of an intense battle between invading Japanese forces and American and Filipino troops (Brinkley and Haskew 2004, 9). 12,000 American and 63,000 Filipino soldiers surrendered to the Japanese army, mainly due to a lack of supplies. The USA military were forced to surrender when due to "starvation and sickness, less than a quarter were able to fight" (276). The infamous Bataan Death March followed the defeat in which the captives were forced on a "horrendous march to prison camps that killed thousands of Americans and Filipinos" (261–62). The film tells the story of two US soldiers, Johnny and Pete, trying to escape Japanese bombers in the Bataan jungle (Beevor 2012, 274–76). Pete suffers cramps and becomes incapacitated, while Johnny suffers night blindness and fails in his attempt to shoot a Japanese plane down. Later, Johnny awakens in a hospital during surgery. The doctor, lacking anesthetic, amputates his leg. Johnny bemoans the fact that he could not see well enough to shoot down the enemy attack, resulting in Pete's death. The doctor comments that due to the lack of fresh vegetables in the solder's diets, Johnny suffered from "night blindness." Pete's cramps were also caused by the lack of vegetables.

The scene changes to two older American women, one shelling peas and the other knitting. The knitter, Mrs. Jackson, brags about how smart she was to stock up ahead of time, boasting, "They didn't catch me napping. I stocked up! You just 'otta' see that cellar of mine! I've got 28 cases of canned goods and 200 pound sacks of sugar and all." The women are interrupted by a whistle, signaling a delivery for Mrs. Lewis, a letter from her son Johnny. Mrs. Lewis calls Johnny's wife, Mary, played by Susan Hayward. The entire family listens to Mrs. Lewis reading the letter. The ghost of Johnny appears on the porch and reads the letter aloud:

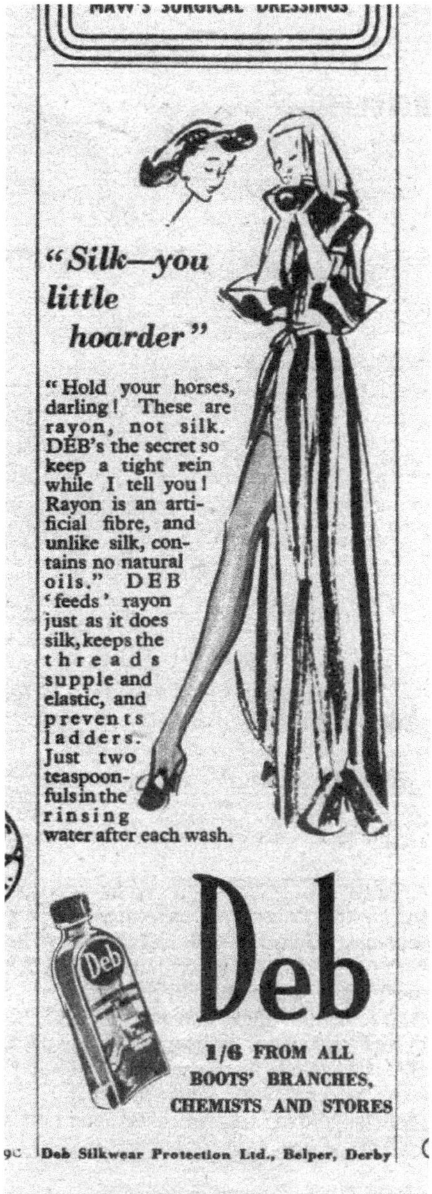

FIGURE 8.1: *The Shame of Being Accused of Hoarding*, 1941. Deb advertisement, UK. *Picture Post*, April 26, 1941, 8.

> It will be lack of food and equipment and medicine [...] We did not have enough of anything [...] Mom, Pete died because we didn't have the things we needed [...] You folks will have to go without the little things so they can have the bombers and guns and tanks that we didn't have. We know we can count on you. No other American boy is going to die in a strange land because somebody at home didn't go without.
>
> (Pine 1942, 7:19 to 11:12)

A telegraph is delivered immediately after the letter is read, alerting the family of Johnny's death. The hoarder, Mrs. Jackson, realizing the error of her ways, breaks down in tears and runs off. The 14-minute film ends with the revelation that the date Johnny's letter was written was the day after he was declared dead. Noting that the letter was written in the past tense, the film suggests that the letter came from heaven.

Using hoarding for profiteering was rampant in countries that suffered monetary devaluation and economic hyperinflation, like Germany and Japan. For example, people who believed that a product's value might increase due to hyperinflation might stockpile large quantities. A tidy profit could be made by selling their stockpile after the value increased. Clothing was easy to hoard, because unlike food, it did not spoil. Hoarders might be tempted to stockpile clothing in anticipation of scarcity. Once the item became scarce, it could be sold for a profit (Zweiniger-Bargielowska 2000, 177).

Bartering

Bartering was a method of commerce based on trading. It was convenient when money and coupons were in short supply, often conducted among a group of trusted friends. A. A. Milne, the author of *Winnie the Pooh*, described bartering in the UK in an article in the *New York Times* in 1946: "Today England is a land of barter. Buying and selling—retail trade—is too difficult. Coupons, queues, permits, priorities, 'export only' are hurdles which few of us have time or ability to negotiate. Barter is the short-cut which brings satisfaction to both sides" (44). His statement did not just apply to the UK but was also true for civilians in many countries during the war. Clothing was a good item to use for bartering because it was scarce and could be traded for food. At the end of the war, when starvation was a reality in many war-torn countries, this was especially true (Maines 1985, 40, 43).

Alice, an Estonian woman now living in the USA, described her experience bartering clothing when neither coupons nor money was left. She said, "We had no coupons to buy clothes. We formed a group and one day a month pulled all our clothes together and selected the dresses we wanted to wear. We shared our clothes to get around the shortages of wartime."[1]

Sisters Kath and Sophie in Weston-super-Mare had a second source for coupons. Sophie related, "My mother knew a very poor family with lots of children and she would exchange clothes that we had worn and did not wear again for coupons." Kath added, "About once in three or four months it happened. Because she was so poor, I think we gave her money as well."[2]

Karin Yount fled East Prussia on foot with her mother. They had nothing of value except her grandfather's heavy gold watch chain that:

> Fed us many months through refugee camps. We slept in ruins on railroad stations, empty farms and cement foundation ruins and hitched on horse and wagons [...] [The chain] was getting shorter by the time we reached Bavaria; we traded one heavy gold link for bread or a piece of pork fat.[3]

Ingrid told me a sad story about bartering in her family toward the end of the war in Germany when money no longer had value. The family home needed painting so a workman was hired to make the repairs. Money had no value so the workman negotiated a barter to pay for his efforts. He requested a baby buggy and Ingrid's plastic baby doll, Hildie, wearing a dress that her mother had made from fabric scraps. He wanted to give his grandchild a gift. Ingrid's mother agreed to the deal and the man left with the baby buggy and doll. "Ta, ta Hildie," cried Ingrid softly as the workman left with her doll. Ingrid's mother always regretted the sacrifice she made by bartering the baby doll.[4]

Families often did not have enough coupons to clothe growing children. In the UK, 30 coupons a year bought only one suit, one pair of shoes, one shirt, and one pair of socks, hardly enough for a growing child. Sally Reston, an American correspondent for the *New York Times* who lived in London during the war, reported that the barter system solved the problem: "The busiest stores in Britain in the past few days have been the children's clothing exchanges, which through an ingenious barter system are helping to solve the problem of outfitting youngsters for the current school year" (1943, 27). The exchange stores, set up by the Board of Trade, assigned a point value to clothing based on quality and amount of wear. All donated clothing had to be freshly washed and mended. The donor could then use the points to select other clothing. Reston reported that the clothing barter system coupled with rationing was so successful that Britain was getting by with only 45% of the prewar supply of clothing (27).

Gray Market

The "gray market," sometimes referred to as the "under-the-counter" market (Calder 1969, 406–07; see also Hancock and Gowing 1949, 511), usually involved trade among friends to help others get by (Roodhouse 2013, 51). It was composed of "all those offences considered illegal but socially acceptable" (16). Gray market dealings avoided regulations and rationing on a smaller scale and was more morally acceptable than black-market dealings (50). They in fact existed to a greater extent than black markets. People rationalized that something they had made, like clothing or other handicraft, belonged to them, and therefore was not subject to government controls and could be freely bartered for necessities (52).

Gray Market—Rural Versus Urban

Bartering was essential for city dwellers who were dependent on stores to buy necessities. With store shelves nearly empty, city dwellers needed to find an alternative resource for survival. Jill Norman (2007) noted that "People living in the country fared better when it came to food, urban dwellers had more choice when buying clothes" (9). As a result, illegal commerce developed between the city and the countryside (Smith 2010, 16). City folk used their abundance of clothing to barter for food with country dwellers, benefiting from access to gardens and livestock. This "marche amical" or friendship market, used barter economics as a method of payment (16). To ensure confidentiality and avoid arrest, prices were often based on relationships. Strangers had to pay more. By happenstance or deception, urban dwellers sometimes rediscovered quasi-country cousins who could provide them with food. Farmers were able to supplement the meager diet of urban dwellers with fresh vegetables, eggs, milk, and sometimes meat in exchange for clothing.

Adelaide, in the Netherlands, mentioned, "If you had things like linen, that was a good barter item. There were farms in Holland and they were supposed to give everything to the Germans. People from the city went to the country to see if they could get some food in exchange for sheets or towels. They returned with a sack of potatoes."[5]

Black Market

The most illegal of all alternative forms of commerce was the black market, a mode of business that existed outside of government regulations and rationing. It developed in nearly every nation during World War II as a shadowy side market that almost everyone interviewed for this book had experienced.

Adina, who grew up in Austria, remembered the black market: "If you wanted to have certain things you had to go on the black markets. My parents bought things. Whatever you could get."[6]

Vera, in London, UK, remembered, "There were men, from India or Pakistan, who came door to door with bulging suitcases of blouses, etc., silk-like, rayon, or cotton. This was black market and my mother didn't approve but did buy a few things."[7]

Lydia, in Germany, reported: "Hoarding and black market were no no's, but people will do it. If you had to, if you sold your jewelry [...] You really do not want to do it, but you do."[8]

Like hoarding and bartering, the black market was fueled by scarcity, as well as government price controls and price ceilings set to regulate the fair distribution of limited resources (Taylor 1997, 156; see also Casdorph 1989, 71). Scarcity provided the opportunity and black marketeers could demand extortionist prices for goods that were no longer available. Black-market businessmen with connections to products in short supply could set their own prices, as high as the market would bear. Lynne Taylor (1997), in *The Black Market in Occupied Northern France, 1940-4*, called it: "The free market at its most brutal" (153).

The black market developed out of necessity. As a result, people found ways to get around rationing to "secure cigarettes, gasoline, scarce food items, or rationed clothing" (Casdorph 1989, 126). Profit, at the deceit of others, was also an objective. On April 11, 1943, the *New York Times* explained the difference between the two sides of black-market operations:

> On the one hand, there are outright crooks who sell stolen coupons or secret stores of merchandise with every intention of making a big profit by breaking the law. On the other hand, there are black markets, more prevalent at present, where an ordinarily honest man is driven by extraordinary circumstances to a violation of the law in order to stay in business. Black markets are as old as wars and famines. Whenever there have been extraordinary shortages of essential commodities and whenever an attempt has been made to fix prices or regulate distribution, there have been deserters who put their own profit before the public good.
>
> (Solmssen, SM14)

Dealings in the black market were considered unpatriotic. Fern Hobson, of Tacoma, Washington, shared her opinion about the black market in an oral history. She described how growing up during the Depression made scarcity part of her life:

> Rationing was odd: sugar, meat, and coffee were rationed. We had ration cards for shoes and clothing, but for someone who had grown up during the Depression, being able to buy two pairs of shoes per person per year was luxury. The same was true of clothing. With our boys dying overseas, living in wet, cold, muddy foxholes,

> or roasting in the desert during the day and freezing at night, swatting bugs in the jungle, and eating cold food out of tins, it seemed that we lived in immoral riches. The black market where you could buy "anything for a price" was positively sinful.
> (Davis 2008, 85)

Many people shared Fern's opinion that the black market was immoral. However, at times during the war, it provided the only means of survival.

Black marketeers used many methods of subterfuge, including passing off lower quality products as higher quality, and at a higher price. This practice was called "upgrading" (Clinard 1952, 16–17). In his 1952 book *The Black Market*, Marshall Clinard stated that "quality deterioration in the form of upgrading was particularly prevalent in the apparel field" (20). The following are some examples:

- A pair of men's shorts made of cheesecloth, with 50% added sizing to give it form until washed;
- A women's slip made of practically unwearable coarse, heavily sized muslin;
- A pair of baby's pants, allegedly water-resistant, which permitted a third of a glass of water to leak through after being laundered once;
- And a cotton sweater that was too loosely knit to hold its shape (20).

These examples were extreme forms of passing-off shoddy merchandise as higher quality because they seem to be purposely constructed to fool the customer, while making a higher profit for the seller. The trustworthiness of black-market vendors was questionable and the secretiveness of the black market made it nearly impossible for customers to get any product information (Hammock and Carden 2007, 6).

Black Market—Paris

When Germany invaded France, intense rationing was immediately established. Extreme scarcity, already an issue in France, became more severe when the occupiers ordered huge shipments of materials to be shipped to Germany. French men as well were sent to Germany to work, including thousands of apparel workers. Dominique Veillon (2002) reported that, "one-and-a-half million [French] prisoners of war were held in Germany and they included tens of thousands [formerly] employed in the textile and clothing industry" (39). The shortage of apparel industry workers compounded issues of clothing scarcity in France.

Nearly everyone in France participated in the black market, city or country dwellers, buyers or suppliers, on a large or small scale (Taylor 1997, 156). It was described as "an overt challenge to the authority and control of the Occupation forces" (156). It was also a crime and "the consequences could be considerable" (160) (Figure 8.2).

Kathleen Cannell (1944), a dance and fashion correspondent for *The Christian Science Monitor,* who remained in Paris for nearly four years after the German occupation, wrote about the hardships of life. She focused on scarcity and the consequential black market, reporting at the time that "at least 60 percent of the population is declining into anemia because of undernourishment, although the black markets provide almost anything that money—lots of money—can buy" ("Paris Ghost City, Repatriate Says" 4). Cannell reported that clothing had become a valuable commodity: "'Clothes bandits' have arisen because of the textile shortage and they operate with absolute impunity, specializing in female apparel. People are stripped of their furs and other clothing in the streets" (4).

Cannell described the black-market businessmen, who specialized in profiting from the spoils of wartime and made no effort to hide their ill-gotten riches. The expensive dress of their wives and girlfriends displayed the racketeer's wealth. Cannell related,

> While representative serious French women are working and worrying, the black market molls dance over this volcano. They defy restrictions with monumental hats that take two outsized felts or six meters of fabric to erect. They complete pure silk or wool costumes in extravagant silhouettes with wooden shoes, bare legs and an odd pint of assorted jewelry-real or false. They buy their dresses by the dozen at an average price of 20,000 francs a piece. They fight to order 5,000-franc hats at the leading Parisian modistes and roll round the town in horse cabs at 500 francs a course, lest they be mobbed by indignant crowds in the subway.
>
> (4)

Chicago Defender reporter Edward Toles (1944) who traveled with an artillery battalion, continued to report on life in France after Cannell left Paris in May 1944 (14). Unfortunately, peace did not put an end to scarcity, hardship, or black markets. A little more than a month after the end of World War II, he wrote: "The high cost of living in Paris, once a city where a person could live like a king on an income of $500 a year, is the only topic of discussion among housewives today" (Toles 1945, 13). Food was scarce, but available for a high price: "If you were known, you could have food, but it was obtained at le prix de la marche noir, the black market" (13). Toles described the shopping experience of Monsieur and Madame Saintonge, owners of a beauty salon: "When Madame Saintonge goes shopping, her earnings vanish into thin air for food alone. One doesn't attempt to buy clothes and shoes" (13). This revealed that clothing and shoe purchases were beyond the economics of the average person like the Saintonge's.

After the war, the critical lack of new clothing combined with the extortionist prices of the black market turned into a crisis. Surviving prisoners of war, dressed in rags, found that the coupons they were given to buy clothing and food were worthless. Food and clothing was only available "on the black market, where prices run as high as $300" (Sage 1945a, 6). Riots ensued as unrest "based on the continued rise of living costs and official red tape, incompetence, and inaction" escalated (6). To resolve the shortages, the French government "dispatched 100 trucks, protected by armed guards, to requisition all remaining stocks of wearing apparel in Paris stores" (Sage 1945b, 1). The attempt to pacify the rioting returning former prisoners resulted in eliminating any hope of buying new clothes or shoes anywhere except on the black market, in spite of having ration tickets (1). The government paid for the clothing that they had taken from the stores but at the rationed price, defeating the dreams of vendors hoping to hoard their stocks and sell them for huge profits on "le Marché Noir."

Black Market—UK

Lord Woolton, head of the Ministry of Food, claimed that the UK had "little or no [black] 'market'" (Smithies 1982, 58; Woolton 1959, 230–31). Woolton (1959) believed that the British public supported rationing and considered it a "necessary and sensible provision" (230). Any evasive activity, he suggested, resulted as a matter of random, unconnected coincidences. In spite of Woolton's belief that the "British public disapproved of black markets," it did exist (230). Penalties for black-market activity in food regulations included a "fine of five hundred pounds with or without two years of imprisonment" (231). At the minimum, the contraband products were confiscated. Black-market traffickers also risked prison sentences if caught (Grenard 2008, 107).

Illegal market activity in the UK was centered on goods "in short supply (clothing, cloth, razor blades, soap and electrical products)" (Smithies 1982, 59). Black marketers took advantage of shortages to price-gouge consumers who could not get products in any other way. For example, the limited availability of blackout cloth, mandated to cover windows at night after Germany started flying nightly raids over the UK, provided an opportunity to trade on the black market, offered at sky high prices.[9] Motivated by the illegal manipulation of blackout cloth prices, the government instituted price controls in an attempt to restrict profiteering (Hancock and Gowing 1949, 158).

One trick used by the black-market traders was to claim that an item was coupon-less. The seller could make more money claiming that no coupons were required. Therefore, the seller did not have to report the sale to the control board and could charge a higher price and make a higher profit. For example, a vendor who sold artificial silk (rayon) stockings, an item in high demand, claimed that the stockings were defective and, therefore, did not require a coupon to be sold (Smithies 1982, 80). These transactions were risky because shop owners needed to return any coupons received to the control board, along with money, to justify all purchases. If they did not do so, they could not get more stock to sell in the future. Therefore, coupon-free sales could indicate ill-gotten goods.

Jean, living in Welwyn Garden City, UK, recalled her experience with what she believed might have been the black market.[10]

FIGURE 8.2: *Marché Noir—Crime Contre la Communauté*, 1943. Affiche de propaganda. Courtesy AKG-Images.

> I was window shopping in London and admired a lime green blouse in a shop window. The owner came out like they did and asked me if I was interested in the blouse. I said I was but did not have any coupons. He told me that was okay and invited me in. He sold me the blouse without coupons. Was that black market? I always remember it because that was the blouse I was wearing when I met my husband-to-be. I was wearing it with the leopard print skirt that my mother had made for me.

Scarcity affected shopkeepers as well as consumers. Sales were limited because merchandise was limited, therefore, profit was limited as well. The blouse was most likely procured illegally, possibly through barter, and the salesman made extra profit by selling it to Jean and not having to report that sale.

When Joy Beebe was planning her wedding in the UK, her brother showed up one day with a dress. He was 17 at the time. Joy asked him where he got it and he replied, "Don't ask." Joy always wondered if it was the black market.[11]

Clothing ration coupons developed value on the black market (Hargreaves and Gowing 1952, 326; see also Roodhouse 2013, 8, 23). Each year, as scarcity increased, fewer coupons were allocated to each consumer. Coupons' value traded on the black market increased along with their scarcity. Clothing coupons had an advantage over food coupons, which were only valid for two weeks. Clothing coupons were valid for one year. Their longer life commanded a higher price. The illegal exchange or sales of coupons could be tricky since each person was only allotted a fixed number and they could only legally be exchanged with a family member (Roodhouse 2013, 53). Furthermore, only a store clerk at the point of sale was allowed to cut the coupons out of the book. This regulation restricted the exchange of loose coupons that could then be sold for a profit, especially if the legal owner did not want or need that specific coupon (Color Plate 25).

People caught dealing in illegal coupons faced prosecution and usually had to pay a fine or even serve jail time (Smithies 1982, 82–83). Their penalty depended on the severity of their dealings. The public abhorred the black market, and in March 1942, members of the press and the House of Commons suggested "such dire penalties as floggings, life imprisonment, and even death for the 'black marketeers'" (Backman 1943, 61).

The Times, February 17, 1942, reported an example of profiteering using clothing coupons ("305,500 Coupons for Clothing," 2). Two men in Glasgow, apprehended at the Regent Palace Hotel, were charged with "being concerned in stealing 305,500 Board of Trade clothing coupons from some person or persons unknown, and, alternatively, with receiving the coupons knowing they had been stolen or unlawfully obtained" (2). A detective overheard their discussion about the profit they could make by selling the coupons, "We can get half a million of them if you can take them," said one of the men (2). The detective then saw one

FIGURE 8.3: *Kill the Black Market with Ration Stamps. Remember: It Takes Two to Make a Black Market* (1941–45). Office for Emergency Management. Courtesy US National Archives (514829).

man hand a packet of 159,000 coupons to the other. When the detective questioned them, one of the men denied any illegal dealings, claiming, "You have made a mistake. We have no coupons" (2). His plea did not work and the two were charged with stealing coupons and ordered to appear in court for sentencing.

Another example of an illegal coupon scheme involved a barmaid, found by the police in a drunken state at the railroad station at Camberwell Green in South London. She had used a double identity scheme to make a profit selling coupons by living under two different names for five years, and drawing twice the legal number of coupons (Figure 8.3). She realized a considerable profit selling the excess coupons that she did not use. The woman received a three month sentence in jail for her transgression (Smithies 1982, 85).

Black Market—Clothing Regulation and Subterfuge in the USA

As the USA prepared for war, the government needed to reduce civilian consumption of resources needed by the military. A request was made for women to "self-ration" and stop buying clothing so the military would have enough raw materials. The request backfired, producing a rash of "scare buying" instead of the hoped-for reduction of clothing consumption. The *New York Times* called this "a type of insanity" ("Rush for Clothing Alarms Retailers" 1943, 18). The article suggested that "if the women would only stop to think, they would realize that the quickest way to bring on such rationing is by hoarding and buying unnecessary goods" (18). An announcement that 75,000,000 pounds of wool fiber that had been held for military uniforms was going to be released to manufacturers did not assuage the fear of impending clothing rationing. The article attempted to appeal to women's vanity by suggesting that stockpiling clothing would only result in "'Milady the Hoarder' [...] find[ing] herself wearing outmoded attire by the next season" (18).

The black market was especially tempting in the USA (Color Plate 26). Many people who had lost their jobs during the Great Depression found employment working for the war industry. The *New York Times* reported on April 17, 1943, "The cost of living in the USA, [...] had gone up 22.6 per cent and food prices had increased 42.9 per cent, while average weekly earnings had risen 70.7 per cent" since the beginning of the war in Europe (Lawrence, E3). American workers' earnings and employment levels were higher than they had been in a decade. However, rationing and the prioritization of all manufacturing for the military left limited products available for civilians. If a consumer was fortunate to find something they wished to buy in a store, they had to have a coupon in addition to money in order to make the purchase (Figure 8.4). The black market, where anything could

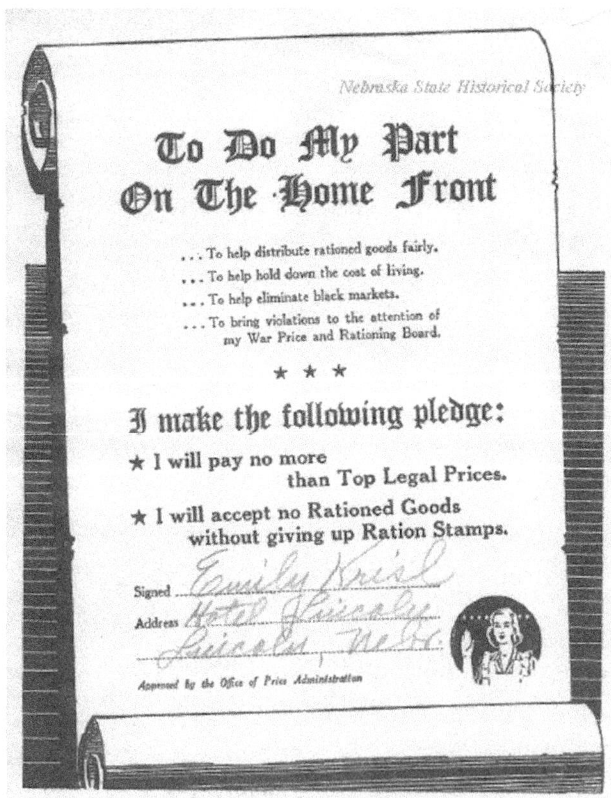

To Do My Part
On The Home Front

. . . To help distribute rationed goods fairly.
. . . To help hold down the cost of living.
. . . To help eliminate black markets.
. . . To bring violations to the attention of my War Price and Rationing Board.

★ ★ ★

I make the following pledge:

★ I will pay no more than Top Legal Prices.

★ I will accept no Rationed Goods without giving up Ration Stamps.

Signed ...

Address ...

Approved by the Office of Price Administration

FIGURE 8.4: *To Do My Part On The Home Front [...] To help eliminate black markets*. 1940s. Courtesy Nebraska State Historical Society, 10019-9-(1).

be purchased at a price, allowed people to enjoy their new prosperity. The *New York Times* (1943) explained American's rationale for buying on the black market:

> Millions who now have incomes which look large to them—the woman who used to buy a pound of hamburger meat and now demands two pounds of steak; the man who, after buying his rationed pair of shoes, can still afford another two pairs because his wartime earnings are high; the war worker who, knowing that the plant cannot afford to spare him, takes the risk of being caught wasting gasoline—these are the ultimate supporters of black markets.
>
> (Solmssen, 36)

The black market quickly grew to "immense proportions" (Clinard 1952, 27) and became "responsible for nearly one-quarter of all retail business during the war" (Brinkley and Haskew 2004, 388). Approximately 25% of Americans dealt in the black market (Lingeman 1970, 270) (Figure 8.5).

Not all Americans were wealthy. Margo, a teenager during the war, remembered that "our family was so poor that we rarely had enough money to buy shoes and did not use the shoe coupons. We used them to trade with neighbors for other necessities, like food."[12]

Black Market Portrayed in Movies—The Third Man

Passing off inferior or faulty products was one of the most dangerous forms of illegal commerce. Graham Greene's late 1940s book and movie, *The Third Man,* illustrated an extreme example and a caution to people tempted to deal in the black market. The story, which took place in post-war-torn Vienna, focused on a black-market racketeer, played by Orson Wells, who sold watered-down stolen penicillin to hospitals desperate to save children's lives. As a result, many sick children, given the incorrect medication, died from meningitis. Well's character goes into hiding to avoid arrest but dies in the end, a suitable sentence for dealing in the most villainous of crimes.

Japan—Black Market and Defeat

"For more than a decade, from the late 1930s to the late 1940s, the black market increasingly dominated the lives of the Japanese people, expanding in inverse proportion to Japan's deteriorating war condition" (Griffiths 2002, 825). Financial instability developed toward the end of the war in Japan as prices soared, doubling between 1936 and 1944 (Harrison 2000, 261). Economic problems created by Japan's failing war efforts were intensified by black markets and hoarding (Griffiths 2002, 829). Hoarding grew to epic proportions as both individuals and store owners anticipated future shortages. Dealings in "Yami torihiki" or "bargaining in the dark," a euphemism for the black market, were rampant (Byas 1940, 57).

Bartering was one of the only methods of commerce when money had lost all its value. Keiko, who grew up on Kyushu, Japan's southernmost main island, told me how her family bartered to keep from starving.[13] The war did not really affect them until the later years after their home was destroyed in a bombing. Nearly starving, they traveled to the country to buy food from farmers. The only currency they had was their silk kimonos, which the farmer accepted in trade for food.

Nobue's situation was very different from Keiko's. Her father was a farmer and they lived in the country.[14] Nobue's daughter told me stories that her mother had told her about life during the war. People from the cities came to the country to try to buy food by trading their silk kimonos. Nobue said that her grandfather had so many silk kimonos at that point, given to him in trade from city dwellers, that he did not need or want anymore, however, he took them anyway to help them out. Nobue was very smart and skipped many grades, going to high school after graduating from elementary school. She was hired as a substitute teacher at an elementary school even though she was very young because many teachers in Japan had been sent to fight the war.

Black Market—Philippines

Mary McKay Maynard (2002), the author of *My Far Away Home: An American Family's World War II Tale of Adventure and Survival in the Jungles of the Philippines*, dealt with hoarding and bartering during the two years that her family hid in the jungle from the Japanese. Her father had managed the Mindanao Mother Lode Gold Mine. Japan invaded the Philippines on December 8, 1941, one day after Pearl Harbor. The Maynard family, along with other Americans working at the mine, went into hiding in the jungle for the next two years until they could escape to Australia. They fortunately had stocked up on canned food, clothing, textiles, and sewing supplies, and used these to barter for food. Money had no value. Therefore, scraps of fabric became precious. Clothing was so valuable that "a pair of men's pants was worth a horse in some parts of the island" (190). Mary said, "The demand for cloth was so great and our supply so small that my mother ripped the ticking off a mattress left in the empty rooms. She put the kapok stuffing in a *cambo* [a woven storage basket] and washed the cotton ticking fabric cover in the river" (189). Cloth was so valuable that some vendors who walked by excitedly wanted to buy it.

Mary described an incident when her family traded a scrap of fabric for potatoes as they left the jungle in a small *baroto*, or boat. Bags were scarce, so the potatoes were simply unloaded into the boat. Mary wrote that "Ah Hing emptied a sack of camotes into the *baroto* for a *despedida* [farewell] gift. He couldn't spare the potato sack; there were so few" (199).

Mary's mother saved a package of sewing needles to last for the duration. She traded her last sewing machine needle for eggs. The tradesman was so desperate that he accepted the trade even though the needle did not fit his sewing machine. Mary's mother said,

> I had tried to tell him so at the time, but since he thought I was trying to keep him from getting it, I gave it to him for thirty eggs. Today he wanted reparation for a bad bargain. I gave him a pair of Mary's socks to unravel and let him keep the needle. He was delighted even though the eye is in the wrong end. It will sew better than no needle at all.
>
> (199)

Black Market and the Military

American soldiers based in Europe were in a slippery position after the war. The Post Exchange stores carried products, such as cigarettes and nylon stockings, that were in high demand in war-torn countries. These stores were only accessible to US government employees, their wives, and their children. The goods were sold at very low prices. It was a perfect setup for servicemen who wanted to make some additional money by selling on the black market. Soldiers could make a huge profit by purchasing "ten packs of cigarettes for 50 cents at the Post Exchange and sell them for $100" (Ruffner 2002, 3).

American servicemen's easy access to products that reaped high rewards and opportunities to get rich quick in the black market resulted in undermining discipline and creating a morale issue (3–4). *Life* (1945) magazine reported on American soldiers dealing in the black market in Germany ("Black Markets Boom in Berlin" 51). The article stated:

> The biggest, most open and most international black market in Europe is located in the famous wooded Tiergarten in the center of Berlin. Here crowds of soldiers and civilians gather daily for trade, both legal and illegal. Germans, who traipse

> hopefully to the Tiergarten with their household goods in prams and rucksacks, want food, cigarettes and foreign currency. Red Army men, who lug along suitcases of bills representing their back pay for several years, want cameras, clothing, and especially watches. The Americans, British and French, who drive up with pockets bulging with salable gadgets, want money.
>
> (51)

American soldiers had been selling watches to Russians for $1,000. However, the article concluded that "when a trade flourished to the point where some enterprising GIs sent home for boxes of watches, the Army had to clamp down" (51).

An American soldier stationed in Vienna after the war, named here with the pseudonym "Bruce," told me about his dealings on the black market.[15] His daughter knew about my research and suggested that I talk to her father. However, when I called, I could tell that he was still fearful of the consequences of black market dealing and hesitated to tell me anything. At first, he downplayed his dealings, saying: "No, there was nothing big, I just sold a couple of cigarettes. I bought the cigarettes at the Post Exchange and sold them to people."

As Bruce became more comfortable talking with me, the stories started to come out.

> We sold to the Russians at the end of the war who got paid in military script. They could not take the script home, so they bought things from the black market. The script had no value in Russia, so soldiers were interested in exchanging their pay for valuable products that they could resell at home.

Russian soldiers were interested in buying high-value objects, particularly watches, that could be resold back home in Russia. Bruce, who had access to watches at very low prices at the Post Exchange, told me he sold, "Gold watches. For good money—$800.00" (Ruffner 2002, 3).

Silk, rayon, or nylon stockings, also purchased at the Post Exchange became "the object of a considerable black market" (Veillon 2002, 52). Prices averaged four times the price determined by the legally rationed rate (52). A gift of stockings from an American soldier was very attractive. Bruce told me that he bought a pair at the Post Exchange. "I sold a pair of stockings to a lady in Vienna [...] I bought them at the Post Exchange. They only had one pair."

Bruce's hesitancy to reveal his black market dealings, even after so many decades, was not without reason. The following report of prison sentences received by soldiers dealing in illegal markets is quite severe.

The *Chicago Daily Tribune* (1944) reported that American soldiers in postwar Paris supported themselves through black-market earnings selling cigarettes, smoking tobacco, gasoline, American food, and other supplies ("Black Market Deals of U.S. Soldiers Told," 3). Three AWOL (Absent Without Official Leave) soldiers were caught with 11,000 packages of American cigarettes that they claimed were bought from a truck driver. The three received sentences for illegal possession and sale of government property ranging from 10 to 15 years of imprisonment. Another soldier caught and convicted of desertion and selling a government pistol and clothing to a French civilian was sentenced to 25 years (3). These severe sentences were proof that dealing in the black market was considered a very serious crime.

Conclusion

Winning the war was the primary goal. Often, to achieve this goal, governments were forced to limit resources provided to civilians so that the military would have what they needed to fight. Civilians varied in their acceptance of the inevitable suffering that went along with scarcity. The morality of involvement in side-commerce varied depending on the scope of illegal dealing. Helping one's self and others by bartering or trading was a common way to reduce the hardship of wartime scarcity. Conversely, profiting from scarcity by setting prices as high as possible, as in illegal black-market dealings, increased suffering for others. These illegal dealings ultimately hindered the efforts of wartime governments to provide fair shares.

These marginal forms of exchange ranged from simple deals with friends to get by, to criminal activity for private profit. Reporter Sally Reston (1943) wrote that clothing exchanges, a system of bartering used clothes, resulted in great relief to the population of the UK who were getting by with only "45 percent of their pre-war supply of clothing" (27). In contrast, hoarding and black-market dealings, common in all countries, had negative effects on populations, especially when operated to earn a profit. Civilian morale was damaged when black marketeers gouged customers with sky-high prices, eradicating the ideal of a unified effort to win the war.

Most countries frowned on hoarding and black-market activities since they were not only illegal, but increased scarcity for all. Fines and imprisonment could be severe for participants. The black market was especially cruel if it resulted in the loss of goods needed by the military, thus hurting the war effort.

NOTES

1. Alice (born 1928, Estonia) in discussion with the author at the Northern California War Brides Association lunch, Campbell, CA, October 11, 2014.

2. Kath and Sophie (born 1924 and 1925, Weston-super-Mare, UK) in discussion with the author, Weston-super-Mare, UK, June 11, 2010.
3. Karin Yount (born 1923, Yalta, Crimea), answer to the questionnaire passed out at War Brides Reunion on the Queen Mary, Long Beach, CA, November 4, 2015.
4. Ingrid (born 1926, Fürstenfeldbruck, Bavaria, Germany) interviewed at the War Brides Reunion, 2017 in Las Vegas, NV and 2019 in San Diego, CA.
5. Adelaide (born 1927, The Hague, Netherlands) in discussion with the author, Davis, CA, November 20, 2014.
6. Adina (born 1928, Austria) in phone conversation with the author, March 21, 2019.
7. Vera (born 1930, UK) in e-mail communication with the author, March 8, 1929.
8. Lydia (born 1929 in Sudan, German/Chinese, lived in Germany during the war) in discussion with the author during the War Brides Association Reunion, San Diego, CA, October 9, 2019.
9. Blackout fabric was used to cover windows to block any light that might be used by an enemy pilot to locate a target on the ground. It was used in the UK and the USA. See Levine and Levine (2011, 435).
10. Jean (born 1927, Welwyn Garden City, UK) in discussion with the author, San Jose, CA, April 13, 2019.
11. Joy A. Beebe (born 1925, Sidcup, UK) in discussion with the author during the War Brides Association Reunion on the Queen Mary, Long Beach, CA, November 2015.
12. Margo (born 1935, Missouri) in discussion with the author, Davis, CA, March 2017.
13. Keiko (born 1928, Japan) in conversation with the author, Seaside, CA, January 12, 2013.
14. Nobue (born 1928, Japan) her daughter told her story to the author in Pacific Grove, CA, January 12, 2013.
15. Bruce (not his real name), telephone interview with the author, Danville, CA, 2012.

9

Make-Do and Mend: Once Forgotten, Now Reborn

> Well into the twentieth century, clothes were pricey and precious enough that they were mended and cared for and reimagined countless times, and most people had a few outfits that they wore until they wore them out.
>
> How things have changed. We've gone from making good use of the clothes we own to buying things we'll never or barely wear. We are caught in a cycle of consumption and waste that is unsettling at best and unsatisfying at its core.
>
> Elizabeth L. Cline, *Overdressed: The Shocking High Cost of Cheap Fashion*

Until just a few decades ago, clothing was considered a long-term investment. Good quality was appreciated and particularly important during World War II when clothing really had to last (König 2013, 573). Most women were skilled at "domestic arts," including mending, sewing, careful hand washing, and other skills needed to prolong their clothing's life. Every bit of leftover fabric was saved to mend, remake, or refit garments if necessary, all part of every homemaker's job. Additionally, many kinds of professional services were available to repair shoes, invisibly reweave holes, and custom-fit apparel.

Many of the women interviewed for this book spoke with pride about their efforts to do their part for the war by sewing, knitting, mending, repairing, repurposing, and finding a use for everything they owned. Nothing was thrown away. When several of these women were asked if they still practiced the skills they used during the war to make their clothing and possessions last, some replied no, but several answered that they still knit, mend, and wash their clothing carefully by hand, even some clothing recommended to be dry cleaned. Lisbeth replied to a survey question, "My husband still darns his socks today!"[1] Ruby replied, "I think I still do all of those things. I started a knitting group at church to knit blankets for babies."[2] Elizabeth answered, "I still mend and alter clothes and bedding."[3]

This chapter focuses on cultural changes after World War II in relationship to apparel ownership and the rise of inexpensive ready-to-wear clothing known as "fast fashion." These changes resulted in the "domestic arts" disappearing from practice in the mainstream culture of industrialized countries (Gwilt 2014; Clark 2008, 434-5). Since the end of World War II, businesses have become focused on a "relentless expansion of material consumption" (Fletcher and Grose 2010, 100). The unending attitude of a throwaway society, continuous disposal, and buying new, has exponentially crammed landfills with unneeded waste, resulting in detrimental consequences to the environment.

Jill Norman (2007), in her book: *Make Do and Mend: Keeping Family and Home Afloat on War Rations* comments: "Now, with more awareness of carbon emissions, green issues and the changed geo-political environment, we are belatedly realizing that some far-reaching measures are needed"(8). She concludes that "there are lessons to learn" from the practices of World War II and "the global urgency to act is just as necessary as was the wartime effort" (8). Fortunately, a movement based on traditional or "slow" making has started in reaction to overconsumption and waste. Interest in the revival of traditional handcrafts, similar to those practiced during World War II, bids well for a future that will remedy problems that arose from the excess and waste of the past few decades.

Transition to a Peacetime Consumer Economy

When World War II ended in 1945, the general belief promoted by the press was that "once the war is over, women should return home; that is where they belong" (Margerum 1999, 203–04; see also Lowe 2017, 126–27). Women's wartime employment was considered temporary, and the returning soldiers deserved to get back their prewar jobs (Figure 9.1). Women had faced the same consequence after the end of World War I, when "the rights women gained during the war were revoked as soon as the Armistice was signed. Repopulating the country was more important than female suffrage in the interwar period—French women had to wait until 1945 to have the right to vote for the first time" (Bass-Krueger 2019a, 65).

Although some women were happy to return to "normal" life, many wanted to keep their employment (Leder 2006, 146–48; see also Buckland 2000, 149). Nella Last had volunteered in a canteen run by the Women's Voluntary Service in the UK. Although the organization continued to exist until 1966, Nella's canteen closed. She wrote in her diary about the good times the women had working together and her feeling of loss after the war, "Yet now we are all like an untied bundle of sticks, all tired and busy with household tasks and worries we took in our stride or made them fall into the pattern that was our life for so long" (Malcolmson and Malcolmson 2008, 117).

FIGURE 9.1: *Stronger Women—Or Lighter Work?* 1945. Northern Aluminium Co. Ltd. advertisement, June 14, 1945, 3. *The Times* Digital Archive.

Post-War Fashion

The feminine silhouette of Christian Dior's debut couture collection for spring/summer 1947 was perfectly timed to capture the spirit of the postwar years and fulfill cultural desires for change; or a return to prewar traditional norms (Charleston and Koda 2004; Pochna 1996, 138). Women were ready to re-embrace a feminine silhouette, replacing the skimpy skirts, uniforms, or work coveralls they had worn during the war (Charleston and Koda 2004; see also Buckland 2000, 149). Called "such a new look" by fashion editor Carmel Snow, the silhouette was not really new but actually took up right where the French couture styles had left off in 1940 (Howell 2012, 26; see also Walford 2008, 191). The silhouette featured "an overtly feminine silhouette with nipped-in corseted waists and long, full flowing skirts reaching to the ankles" (Biddle-Perry 2017, 110–11).

The indulgence of wearing yards of fabric required for the long full skirts, hems reaching to just 14 inches above the ground, caused some outcry after the shortages of the war. The UK, where clothing rationing continued until the spring of 1949, was still suffering from austerity (Wood 1989, 69). *The Times* reported in September 1947, after Dior's second collection which continued to show full skirts,

> Mr. J. B. Rogers, chairman of the [United Committee of Light Clothing] association, said that shortage of materials was still one of the industry's biggest difficulties. He hoped we were not going to follow the so-called creators of fashion in Paris and New York who were trying to bring in really long skirts. To go to such extremes now was not in the national interests.
>
> ("Wasteful Long Skirts," 2)

In Paris, women dressed in the New Look were sometimes attacked in the streets, their new clothes torn to shreds by people dressed in rags still suffering from wartime austerity and outraged by the waste of scarce textiles in a country "still paralyzed by strikes, rocked by government crises, and seemingly doomed to perpetual gloom" (Pochna 1996, 138).

The American version of *Vogue*'s coverage of the Spring 1947 Paris Haute Couture collections, including Christian Dior, was very positive. The article declared, "evolving in spite of the shutting down of electricity; in spite of a cold that stiffened fingers and froze everything but ideas. In line this look has been unforced femininity—a polished continuation of the rounded line that has been seen in Paris ever since the first post-Liberation collections" ("Fashion: Paris Collections" 137).

Many women were happy for a change after the bleak years of the war. Maggie Wood (1989), author of *We Wore What We'd Got,* quoted a young British woman, "We very much wanted to get back to before. I was in my twenties and was very conscious that we'd had to patch and darn, patch and darn; you wanted to get back into nice clothes" (69). Sarah, in Weston-super-Mare, UK, said: "We were all so ready to dress up again and loved the New Look."[4] In Germany, Lydia, when asked about her awareness of Dior's New Look, replied, "Oh sure! That the style has changed. There is no style when you just try to keep yourself warm."[5]

Post-War Handicrafts

During the 1950s and 1960s, many women still relied on their needle skills to make clothing at home and maintain the family wardrobe. These decades were considered the "Golden Age" of home sewing (Stevens 2016). Women with limited financial resources relied on their traditional needle skills as a way to acquire fashionable looks beyond their means, often inspired by Dior's collection (Black and Idle 2013, 25). Women's magazines promoted home sewing, relying on the skills women had learned during the war (Reynolds 1999, 337). The American version of *Vogue* stated in their February 15, 1947 issue: "Probably a quarter of women in America right now are scheduling an important part of their wardrobes on a design for dressmaking basis" ("*Vogue* Designs for Dressmaking: Spring" 1947b, 160). This issue of *Vogue* would have gone to press before editors had attended Dior and the other French designers' Spring 1947 shows. Therefore, the dresses offered in the issue do not feature the new long, full skirts. The anticipated new length is addressed as something still yet unknown, recommending, "Sewing takes time; this spring it means a straight line of thoughtful choice—from the time you first consider the new and now-returning wealth of materials to the fitting, when the final, new length of hem is decided" (160).

By September, the influence of Dior's New Look was seen in the sewing patterns offered in *Vogue*. Describing two dresses with billowing skirts nearly touching the ground and tightly held waistlines, *Vogue* advised: "Trace with your finger the outline of each of these dresses, and you'll have touched upon their news. It is shape, pure shape, of the most beguiling sort" ("*Vogue* Designs for Dressmaking: Dressmaker" 1947a, 188).

The End of Make-Do and Mend

The USA economy experienced a growth boom in the 1950s and 1960s, but by the 1970s it was slowing (Reich 2011, SR6). Middle-class wages flattened as automation, technology, and outsourcing started to replace manpower (SR6). One salary was no longer sufficient to keep a family out of debt (SR6). The "two-income family" became the solution as women realized they had to get a job so the family could at least break even (Warren and Tyagi 2004, 30). Women entering the workforce struggled for the right to equal wages (Friedan 1963, 520).

These new working women no longer had time to sew for the family or teach their daughters the skills many had learned from their mothers (Hackney 1999, 89). Their precious and now limited free time was better spent doing other things than home sewing (Margerum 1999, 193). Further putting an end to the "domestic arts," women who were part of the feminist movement in the late 1960s and early 1970s viewed sewing, mending, knitting, and other needle skills "as domestic drudgery" and symbols of oppressive and unpaid domestic labor (Bain 2016, 6). Author Anna König (2013) noted that women sometimes are proud to claim

"'I can't sew a button on' in the same way that claiming not to be able to boil an egg is the indicative of a rejection of a traditional domestic role" (576).

In the later 1950s and early 1960s, high school and college home economics departments that had offered sewing lessons started to be considered old fashioned (Thompson 2018, 77). *The San Diego Union-Tribune* reported that:

> Sewing clothes was once considered a basic, practical skill, but it began to fall out of fashion with the baby boomer generation. Mothers were working and had less time for such tasks, and the price of clothing was plummeting. By the time boomers had their own children, their memories of such skills were faint and increasingly unnecessary.
>
> (Meiling 2020)

Today, most schools do not teach home economics and "millennial-aged Americans (and younger) never learned the skill at all" (Meiling 2020). Author Elizabeth Cline, herself born in 1990, noted, "My mother learned how to sew from her mother and made an outfit from scratch in home economics class in high school [...] I never learned how to sew. In a single generation the skill was lost" (Cline 2012, 193).

Ready-Made Clothing Replaces Homemade

Clothing sold in the majority of stores today is much less expensive than it was during World War II or the two decades after (Summers 2016, 26; see also Waldinger 1986, 69). Clothing prices started to plummet in the late 1960s when manufacturers in the USA and Western Europe came up with a clever way to increase their profits by making ready-to-wear less expensive. Moving production to Japan, where workers made a small fraction of the salary paid in advanced countries, afforded manufacturers the ability to produce less-expensive clothing with higher markups and increased profits (Waldinger 1986, 74). Over a period of several decades, almost all clothing manufacturing has been moved to lower wage countries. One of the last holdouts in the USA, traditional clothing manufacturer Brooks Brothers, recently closed their last domestic factory in the USA (Palmieri 2020; see also Friedman and Maheshwari 2020). Subsequently, the United States Bureau of Statistics reported that, "Food and apparel made up about 46 percent of the weight of the index in 1950, compared with about 18 percent in 2013" (Reed 2014).

Japanese manufacturers also realized the profit potential of exporting inexpensive clothing to economically developed countries (Elson and Pearson 1981, 89).

As Japan's economy grew as a result of profits made by exporting, production prices and wages increased, making Japanese factories too expensive for Western manufacturers seeking to increase profits. Manufacturers moved their production to Hong Kong, Taiwan, and South Korea where prices were lower (Waldinger 1986, 74). As the standard of living in these countries increased as they had in Japan, western manufacturers moved on to China, Vietnam, Bangladesh, and India. In these locations, wages were "often ten times lower than in comparable factories in developed countries, while working hours per year are up to 50% higher" (Elson and Pearson 1981, 90). Corporations continued to compete in the contest of continually moving production to countries with lower minimum wages and poorer standards of living, setting off what has been named: "the race to the bottom" (Rivoli 2009, 89; see also Tokatli 2008).

Fashion historian Rachel Worth, in an article about the history of one of the earliest haberdasheries in the UK, John Lewis, remarked, "Not only has ready-made changed the way we produce clothing, but it has affected how we feel about our clothes, along with the attachments we have—or don't have—to them" (2017, 27).

What Happened to Make-Do and Mend?

Author Judith Woods wrote about coming across her grandmother's sock darner, a wooden tool that looks like an egg on a stick, in an article called: "Make Do and Mend? Children Don't Know What That Even Means" (2020). When Judith offered it to her teenage daughter as a lovely gift from a previous generation, the girl revealed that not only did she not know what the object was, she had never even heard of darning. Woods concludes "mending and making-do is yet another life skill that has atrophied away."

Author Franklin Habit wrote in the Fall 2020 issue of *PieceWork* magazine about his grandmother's darning egg that he found in her sewing kit after she died (Figure 9.2). He said his grandmother "was a person for whom 'make do and mend' was a lifelong necessity, but even she ceased to mend holes in socks. Flimsy, modern socks seldom stand up to darning, so she used them as dust cloths. With a worn-out sock over each hand, a person could get through dusting twice as fast" ("The Egg and I: Tools for Darning," 13). Vince Schoenstein remembered that his wife Moira "kept a wooden stand full of socks to darn in the evening."[6]

For people born after the war, who never experienced the decades of austerity and shortages, their parent's, grandparent's, or great grandparent's ideals of saving, mending, remaking clothing, and abhorring waste may seem foreign. Lydia told me in an interview: "We still have the round egg, the glass egg for mending socks. Even today, I remember, I made a rug out of nylon stockings, you know,

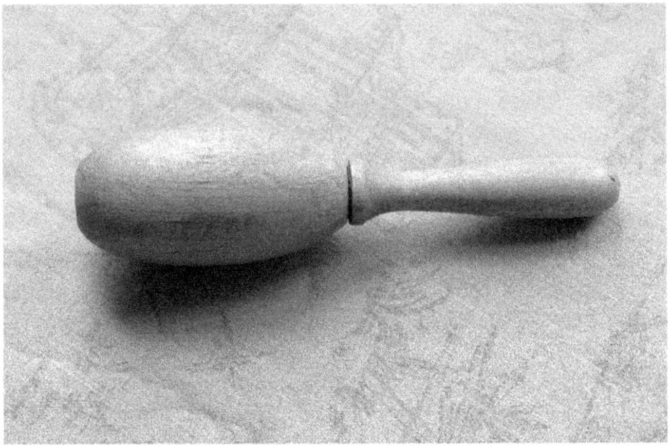

FIGURE 9.2: *Wooden mending egg*. Courtesy Franklin Habit.

just braid it and sew it together. And I always think about that time. When we threw nothing away, nothing. It is really hard to see the waste here. I still think, I don't need to, but I still do."[7]

Fast Fashion

Today, most developed countries have outsourced apparel production to third world manufacturers to take advantage of low labor costs. As a result, stores all over the Western world are filled with an abundance of inexpensive clothing (König 2013, 570). This modern clothing phenomena is called "throwaway fashion" or "fast fashion," named for its promotion of mass-produced, quick production, and low prices (Bhardwaj and Fairhurst 2010, 165). Holly McQuillan (2011), described fast fashion as "a system that taps into our desire for change and fulfils it at a price point we can easily justify spending our hard earned or borrowed money on" (96). In today's world, "fast production must be matched by fast consumption. This is the basic quandary of post World War II capitalism, in which a puritan ethic of savings is replaced by an ethic of spending, aided by credit" (Agger 2015, 17). Many affluent countries promote shopping and the need to continually update products and possessions as a means of fuelling their economy (Claudio 2007). Jo Cramer (2011), a designer who studies garment use and longevity, reports, "Today the fashion market is driven by rapidly changing trends and saturated with cheap ready-made clothing of relatively poor quality. These garments are deliberately designed only to last for the few seasons they are in fashion, forcing the continual purchase of new garments" (1). Rachel Worth, writing in *Selvedge* magazine, remarked, "'slow' home dress-making, along with the given expectation that people's clothes are made to be worn for more than just a few weeks, became lost in the pursuit of instant gratification, encouraged by the juggernaut that is 'fast fashion'" (2017, 27).

During World War II, domestic skills were used to economize or save money (Gwilt 2014). Today, the low cost of store-bought clothing has made the high cost of fabrics and notions needed to create a homemade garment more expensive than buying ready-made. Fast fashion has become so prevalent globally that it no longer pays to sew, knit, or make anything at home. Consumers realized the low price of outsourced ready-to-wear made home sewing obsolete. Furthermore, since clothing is so inexpensive, people can afford to buy much more than in the 1940s. As a result, very little gets used enough to become worn out (Gwilt 2014).

Clothing has become a cheap commodity, instead of a valued possession treated with care (Fletcher 2010, 260). Consumers thrilled by the availability of low-price clothing, regardless of where it came from, have shifted their interest from quality to bargain-hunting (Cramer 2011, 1). Consumers' wardrobes have grown in size and the need to repair or alter clothing has become unnecessary (Gwilt 2014). The idea of mending a cheap knit garment, like a T-shirt, the current wardrobe staple, rarely comes to mind. There is no need. When a garment has a hole, it is now normal to discard it (Gwilt 2014). The price to replace a T-shirt is so minimal that mending is not worth the effort.

Turning old clothing into rags to use for cleaning, as older generations did, has also become obsolete. Paper towels are so convenient and widely used that very few people would think of cutting up their unwanted clothing to use as rags. Instead, unwanted clothing usually gets tossed out or donated (König 2013, 569). Unfortunately, the reality is that the majority of donated clothing ends up in landfills (Cline 2019). As clothing has become less expensive, quality has inevitably been reduced. As a result, contemporary cheap clothing is worth very little second-hand (Cline 2019).

Changing Attitudes Promoted by Environmental Awareness

Toxic pollution is part of the hidden cost of fast fashion's outsourced clothing production and single-use disposable products. In the USA, textile waste, of which only about 15% is donated as used clothing, adds about 10.5 million tons a year to landfills (Cline 2014). The cost of the growing mountain of thrown away textiles can be measured in "pollution, resource depletion and climate change" (Fletcher and Grose 2010, 126). Jason Kibbey of the Sustainable Apparel Coalition was quoted in *Newsweek* (2016), speaking about the toxic effect of clothing disposed of in landfills:

> Natural fibers go through a lot of unnatural processes on their way to becoming clothing [...] They've been bleached, dyed, printed on, scoured in chemical baths [...]
> (Wicker 2016)

Furthermore, the article reports, those chemicals can leach from the textiles and—in improperly sealed landfills—into groundwater. Burning the items in incinerators can release those toxins into the air.

Handicrafts Today—Revival of "Domestic Crafts"

Debbie Stoller, a feminist and the author of *Stitch'n Bitch: The Knitter's Handbook* (2003), has worked to revive traditional domestic arts. She took up knitting in public and wondered how people would react to seeing her with needles in hand knitting on the subway:

> Soon it occurred to me that if I had told folks I'd been playing soccer, or learning karate, or taken up carpentry, they most likely would have said, "Cool." Because a girl doing a traditionally male activity—now, that's feminist, right? But a girl doing a traditionally female activity—let alone one as frivolous and time-wasting as knitting—well, what were they to make of that?
> (7)

Crafting has been "reclaimed by women as liberating feminist action rather than as subjugating work" (Fletcher and Grose 2010, 149). Handicrafts have taken on a sense of political activism, both similar and different to the World War II housewife who knit to do her part on the home front to win the war (149). The movement has been fueled as a backlash against fast fashion and the exploitation of underpaid factory workers and unsustainable, environmentally damaging practices (259; see also Chansky 2010, 681). Fashion professor and sustainable fashion writer Sass Brown (2010) argues that "a quiet revolution has been slowly growing in fashion since the outcry against sweatshop and under-age labour in the 1990s" (9). She contended in a more recent publication, "The onslaught of garment factory disasters has drawn attention to the true cost of fast fashion, and nothing but distaste for over-consumption" (2019, 1).

Author and editor Betsy Greer (2014) coined the term "craftivism" in 2003 to describe the use of craft as a method of protest (8). The most widely recognized aspect of "craftivism" was the global movement of the Pussyhat Project, initiated in the USA to protest the American president during demonstrations after the 2016 presidential election. The largest march was held on January 21, 2016, when nearly one million men and women marched on Washington, DC.

Domestic arts today are no longer seen as the job of the homemaker but a creative platform of self-expression, "social justice and community-building" (Bain 2016, 1; see also Chansky 2010, 681). No longer considered purely a feminine domain, both men and women have rediscovered the joy of creating something by hand, especially in a world that has become so automated (Bain 2016, 2–3). Computers have taken over most jobs and filled lives with hours of screen time. The revival of a desire to use our hands to create homemade objects can be seen as a reaction to "an exploitative corporate culture" that so many people experience (Stoller 2003, 10).

Similar to the practice of women during World War II, traditional crafts, local materials, season-less styling, caring for clothing, prices that reflect the time and effort necessary to construct a quality garment, are once again starting to be valued (Fletcher 2010, 262). Consequently, the craft skills of women living during World War II, have become "deeply hip among their twenty- and thirtysomething granddaughters" (Matchar 2013, 3).

Jill Norman (2007) comments, "Recycling, more popular in today's 'green' society than at any time since the years of wartime austerity, was the order of the day in the forties, with paper, old pots and pans and all manner of scrap salvaged to help the war effort" (5). New terminology has replaced old, now called upcycling instead of repurposing, repair instead of mend, and sometimes sewist instead of sewer (Bain 2016, 9-10). These terms are considered less gendered since both men and women are crafters.

American *Vogue*'s September 2019 issue discussed the current importance of sustainable practices to American designers in an article titled "Calling Planet Earth" by Emily Farra (2019). The mantra of this movement, according to *Vogue*: "Reduce, reuse, recycle [...] repeat" (386). Clearly a reference to the efforts during World War II to "make-do." Upcycling was defined as "turning something old into something new. Repurposing old fabrics or cutting a vintage dress into a shirt means extending the life cycle of a garment, thus reducing its carbon footprint." This is good news for the planet as Farra concludes: "After decades upon decades when the vast majority of our clothing ultimately sits in landfills, the notion of creating heirlooms is, almost shockingly. Of the moment" (396). Jill Norman (2007) also comments: "Now, with more awareness of carbon emissions, green issues and the changed geo-political environment, we are belatedly realizing that some far-reaching measures are needed [...] The global urgency to act is just as necessary as was the wartime effort" (8).

The Changing Role of Handicrafts on a New Platform

A resurgence of "lost" domestic crafts, fueled by social media: Facebook groups, bloggers, Instagram, and dedicated sites like *Ravelry* for knitters, *Etsy* for crafters, and *Textillia* for sewers, has taken off with women in their 20s and 30s today (König 2013, 569; see also Hackney 2013, 171). A positive sign of the revival, noted by Debbie Stoller (2003), "after years of watching knitting stores go out of business, we suddenly saw new, lively ones begin cropping up" (10).

Inspiration found in the handicraft skills and fashion of World War II abound on social media. Vintage sewing patterns, available to purchase online, are in demand (Color Plates 27 and 28). The WWII USO (United Services Organization) Preservation Association, an online living history or re-enactment society, lists 33 links to sites that sell vintage patterns, listed by decade. The 1940s section offers images of patterns produced by *Vogue*, *McCall's*, *Hollywood*, *American Weekly*, and *Anne Adams* among others.

The Victoria and Albert Museum in London provides 1940s knitting patterns to download. Among the offerings is the "Victory jumper." The knitting instructions state, "This jumper is worked in one of the most simple lace-stitch patterns, consisting of two rows, so it is easily learned and quickly worked" (1940s Knitting Patterns). Many other sources for free vintage knitting patterns can be found on the internet (Figure 9.3). *Betty Sparkle's Vintage Knitwear Emporium*, on Facebook, offers reproductions of 1940s knitting patterns. Each newly knit sweater is photographed alongside the original image, adding authenticity to the new handknits (Figure 9.4 and 9.5).

Creative Repurposing of Old T-shirts

Websites abound with clever ideas using creative mending, repurposing, or sewing techniques to keep worn T-shirts out of landfills. Professor Pincushion's blog offers a "How to Repair a Hole in a T-Shirt" video. His slogan, "toss it, wear it with a hole or repair it," is reminiscent of World War II slogans (2016).

A website called: *Wonder What to Do With Old T-Shirts? Here are 15 Things Beyond Turning Them into Rags* shows how to take a pair of scissors to a T-shirt

FIGURE 9.3: *Vintage knitting pattern archive*: *1940's Ladies Sweater—Patons 114—free vintage knitting pattern*. https://vintageknittingpatternarchive.com/free-vintage-knitting-patterns/1940s-ladies-sweater-patons-114-free-vintage-knitting-pattern/.

FIGURE 9.4: *Betty Sparkle's Vintage Knitwear* Emporium, March 23, 2018. Brighton and Hove, UK. https://www.facebook.com/1836750023230013/photos/pcb.2028319720739708/2028319587406388/?type=3&theater.

FIGURE 9.5: *Betty Sparkle's Vintage Knitwear* Emporium, March 23, 2018. Brighton and Hove, UK. https://www.facebook.com/1836750023230013/photos/pcb.2028319720739708/2028319614073052/?type=3&theater.

to create a new design (Weiner 2020). Projects include weaving strips of old T-shirts into a basket, making a toy for your pet, or sewing them into quilts (Figure 9.6).

Mending Has a New Look

During World War II and before, women were taught to mend a garment so it would look like new. As mentioned in Chapter 1, Jean's sister in the UK earned money mending silk stockings with a latch tool that would make the hosiery look new. Even though people wore patches on their patches, and it was unpatriotic to dress extravagantly, care was taken when mending to make the patch as invisible as possible. Keeping up appearances by taking care of holes and stains on garments was considered good for wartime morale. Today, "visible mending," which does not try to hide holes but actually to glorify them, has become an artform and taken a political stance. "Showing off your patches, visible menders say, draws attention to the way a garment's life span has been extended. It also subverts the notion, long held, that mended clothes are worn by the poor, while the height of luxury is buying a new wardrobe every season" (Enrich, Abrams, and Kurutz 2020).

British author Kate Sekules, originator of the online secondhand site *Refashioner*, described a technique she uses to visibly mend a greasy spot on a T-shirt. She creates a chain stitch border in a contrasting color thread around the spots, emphasizing them instead of hiding them. She states that they look "like tiny maps" (Enrich, Abrams, and Kurutz 2020).

Along with the trend of "visible mending," blue jeans manufactured with very large holes, patches, and worn spots sell for high prices. Daniel Miller writes: "Distressed blue jeans are an extraordinary phenomenon. The point about these jeans is that, in effect, someone somewhere is spending their time simulating the wearing out of your clothing, replicating the effect of you spending months or years wearing them" (Miller 2009, 157).

Garment Longevity

Knitwear designer and academic Amy Twigger Holroyd, born in Huddersfield, UK in 1979, learned to knit from her grandmother. Her goal, she states on her web site, is to build awareness of social and environmental problems caused by "today's consumerist and ultra-wasteful fashion system" (Twigger Holroyd). Her knit line, *Keeping & Sharing*, encourages people to reduce consumption by wearing things longer or in different ways. Garment longevity, Holroyd surmises, is one of the factors of the current fashion system that needs to be reassessed.

> Quite obviously, a garment needs to be well-made and pleasant to wear, so I knitted and finished my items with great care and aimed to use quality yarns that would age well. I also offered a repair service (along with a handwashing service, for those scared of shrinking their precious woollens) to help keep the pieces in use. Another key question is the ability of a garment to transcend passing trends.

Holroyd's statement is very reminiscent of World War II practices when good-quality clothing was appreciated and treated with special care so it would last. Furthermore, fashion styles were frozen during the war to increase their longevity so that people would not feel the need to waste or dispose of serviceable clothing each season just because it was out of fashion (Mower and Pedersen 2013, 37).

Garment longevity, as noted in a report compiled by the British association, WRAP (2012), is important because increasing the active use of clothing by just three years could "save £5 billion a year from the costs of resources used in clothing supply, laundry and disposal" (3).

FIGURE 9.6: *National War Savings Committee Poster* No. 7. Previously folded into four horizontal sections, 1916. Courtesy Imperial War Museum © IWM (10122).

Longevity and Personal Attachment

Holroyd believes in the value of a personal connection with clothing. She states on her website, "Ideally, if people would make things themselves, they'll have a whole extra kind of story to it and level of attachment to it that might contribute to them wanting to keep that thing for a long time. Therefore, in addition to selling finished products, Holroyd started selling knitting patterns and holding workshops to teach people to knit. She hopes that by encouraging her customers to create garments with "emotional durability and sustainability," they will also keep and use their garments longer" (Twigger Holroyd).

Having a Choice

During World War II, governments enforced mandatory apparel restrictions and rationing in many countries. Today, people are free to continue buying into the allure of fast fashion overconsumption or to choose to reduce their consumption. Consumers, inspired by the "slow clothing" movement, can return to practices similar to those used during World War II, mending and carefully washing their clothing so they can wear them for a longer period of time. Unwanted clothing can be turned into rags, substituted for paper towels, or even made into useful handwoven baskets (Color Plate 29). Reducing consumption would lessen the need to dump outdated or excess apparel in landfills, thereby helping to diminish humankind's negative effects on the planet.

In the long run, the issues of overconsumption faced today, compounded by the exponential increase in global population, may perhaps be more serious than the issues of deprivation and scarcity faced during the Great Depression and World War II. Is it too late for self-imposed rationing to have an effect? Will the load of the increased population strain the natural resources of our planet to such an extent that someday governments will have to reinstate rationing like in World War II? Or will the efforts of consumer groups and movements to reduce consumerism be sufficient to curtail depletion of natural resources and destructive environmental pollution?

Crafters today can take a stand similar to the "Make Do and Mend" campaign of World War II, changing the slogan to, as Enrich, Abrams and Kurutz (2020) suggest, "Fret about the planet and mend." The practices of women living during World War II, a time when the reduction of consumption and waste was enforced, as well as one's patriotic duty, can serve as a guide and inspiration for consumers today interested in reducing their global footprint.

The resurgence of interest in learning and using the handicraft skills of World War II is encouraging. Although unfortunately this practice is still mainly outside of the majority, it seems to be growing (Gwilt 2014). One sign of the increased interest in reducing consumption is the growing popularity of clothing resale shops for both donating and buying gently used clothing.

Women who lived through World War II were the original eco-fashioners. Lydia spoke about the value of her experience making-do during World War II, "I see it as it prepared me for life. Whatever comes, you know, I can handle it. Because I have been there. And I appreciate that I know how to use left-overs, how to make things from left-overs."

Emma spoke about her efforts to preserve the environment during the war, "Yes, we were very environmental conscious because we did not have tin cans. We never bought any tin because we bottled. We used glass jars. Of course, they were always reused. And there weren't tops to put on them, you put paraffin on them. And then you would save that paraffin, wash it off, use it on another jar. Then having the garden, whatever would be good for the garden, you had your little compost pile. There was nothing thrown away."[7]

Jeanne, whose mother had a coat made from a World War I blanket, described in Chapter 4, recently finished telling me the story about the garment's life.

> You asked what things that were practiced during the war carried on with us? It turned out that my coat became a bit too small, I could not quite fit it anymore. I made a skirt out of it. That was a little bit longer and it was just about the knee because that was the fashion. But, when I came to Canada a year later, I had my first child who was a little boy. And naturally, at the farm, it was very difficult to get one penny out of the land, we had to be very thrifty. That skirt eventually did not seem to be suitable for me, it was too short and it did not fit well. I made a pair of little ski pants for my boy. He was born in 1947 and so it was, winter of 1951, he wore those little ski pants. Four years later came Anna-Lynn. She wore them as pants as well. So that coat, which was actually an American army surplus from just after the war in 1919 was still being worn in 1953. I am not sure if the other sister, who came two years after Anna-Lynn, also wore it. I would say that she probably did, but then I can't remember. So much came from that American army surplus blanket.[8]

Five people in Jeanne's family used that blanket for at least 35 years. The original coat made from the blanket was reincarnated into three or four different garments. Truly an inspiration in terms of reducing one's global footprint and lessening the effect of human consumption on the environment.

NOTES

1. Lisbeth (born 1935, UK), answer to the questionnaire circulated in the UK, 2017.
2. Ruby (born 1923, Australia), answer to the survey question during the War Brides Association Reunion of the Queen Mary, Long Beach, CA, September 2015.
3. Elizabeth (born prewar, UK), answer to the questionnaire circulated in the UK, 2017.
4. Sarah (born 1927, Weston-Super-Mare, UK) in discussion with the author, Weston-super-Mare, UK, June 11, 2011.
5. Lydia (born 1929 in Sudan, German/Chinese, lived in Germany during the war) in discussion with the author during the War Brides Association Reunion, San Diego, CA, October 9, 2019.
6. Vince Schoenstein (born 1925, San Francisco, CA) in discussion with the author at the Northern California War Brides Association lunch, Campbell, CA, October 11, 2014.
7. Emma (born 1925, Auckland, New Zealand) in discussion with the author at the Northern California Bay Area War Brides lunch, Campbell, CA, August 11, 2014.
8. Jeanne (born 1927, Tours, France) in discussion with the author during the War Brides Association Reunion on the Queen Mary, Long Beach, CA, September 2015.

10

Epilogue: Global Pandemic of 2020 Forces Revivals of 1940s Handicrafts

> They are scrounging for fabric, cutting it up, stitching it together. They are repurposing drapes, dresses, bra straps, shower curtains, even coffee filters.
>
> Enrich, Abrams, and Kurutz, *A Sewing Army, Making Masks for America*

The quote above is not another headline about women during World War II, but the reality of a global pandemic in 2020. As I finish this book, the world is locked down in a fight against the novel coronavirus, an invisible enemy. Cable News Network (CNN), the newsbased television channel, has reported that some politicians call it a war (Levenson, 2020). Many similarities between this 21st-century war and World War II come to mind as days turn into months and the lockdown continues. Protective clothing prioritized for front-line workers is in short supply, elastic and fabric to sew facemasks is sold out, store shelves are empty, and many are closed. These are just a few of the issues that hark back to World War II. Toilet paper, hand sanitizer, and bleach disappeared from store shelves quickly, paralleling World War II shortages and hoarding. Adelaide remembered during World War II, "No toilet paper. You used whatever paper was there. Newspaper. There was definitely a shortage. We cut up newspaper."[1]

Modern-day Western cultures most likely never imagined they would have to experience shortages like these. The *Bangor Daily News* advised that "upcycled paper may come in handy if you run out of toilet paper. Try to find white printer paper, catalogs or a phone book, if you still have one, to use. Avoid using glossy magazine pages, as the colored ink might rub off in sensitive places. Newspapers can be used in place of toilet paper, but exercise the same caution with inks" (Schipani 2020). The advice is eerily reminiscent of World War II.

Facemasks, harking back to gas masks required in the UK during World War II, have become mandatory when leaving the house. Joy Beebe

(2015), living outside London during World War II, always had to carry a gas mask. Joy's mother had taught her to knit when she was four years old. She recollected in her memoir: "It was quite fashionable to knit or sew an outer cover for [the gas mask] to match my coat. We would have 15-minute sessions of wearing the masks in class. They smelled awful and steamed up so one could not see" (85). Ellen Miller Coile (2017), also growing up outside London, remembered that her first knitting project at age nine was a cover for her gas mask case (50).

At the beginning of the outbreak, masks were prioritized for frontline workers including doctors, nurses, and other essential staff. Desperate consumers were forced to try their skills at making their own masks. Mae Krier, one of the original Rosie the Riveters, even sewed coronavirus masks (Color Plate 30). Challenges arose. Stores selling fabric and sewing notions were closed. The ubiquitous mending basket, full of scrap fabrics, had disappeared in the 1970s. Elastic was sold out, even on the internet. People were forced to turn to resources from an earlier time. Old clothes, T-shirts, tablecloths, napkins, and scarves were turned into masks covering the nose and mouth. Like women who sewed their underwear during the war from parachutes, self-fabric ties were added to secure the mask around the wearer's face when elastic could not be found. And they still always steam-up, as Joy Beebe remembered.

Hoarding was one of the first reactions to the fear induced by the unknown effects of the global situation. Panic that the shutdown would effect supplies of food and necessities caused a rash of buying. Summers (2016) noted, in the early 1940s in the UK, "The shelves are getting emptier and emptier and many other shops space their goods out to look more than there really is…" (87). I witnessed hoarding and empty shelves in my local neighborhood grocery store. Limits were placed on how many rolls of toilet paper or disinfecting wipes each customer could buy.

As restaurants open slowly now, masks are required except when eating. The *San Francisco Chronicle* calls the facemask, "The accessory/necessity of the year" (Bravo 2020b). A new pandemic fashion is the bag to carry your mask in. *The Baltimore Times* reported, "Perhaps it's just a matter of time before enterprising makers design bags for our masks to keep them at the ready" (Pass 2020).

When the lockdown was first imposed in March 2020, governments closed all movie theaters, concert halls, sporting events, and large gatherings. Summers (2016) recalled practically the same scenario during World War II: "The government immediately ordered all cinemas, theatres and concert halls to close. Race meetings and sporting fixtures were cancelled and people were discouraged from gathering in large numbers" (16). However, unlike during World War II, they remained shuttered into the spring of 2021. One major difference between the 1940s and 2021 is that entertainment at home is far different. The morale boasting

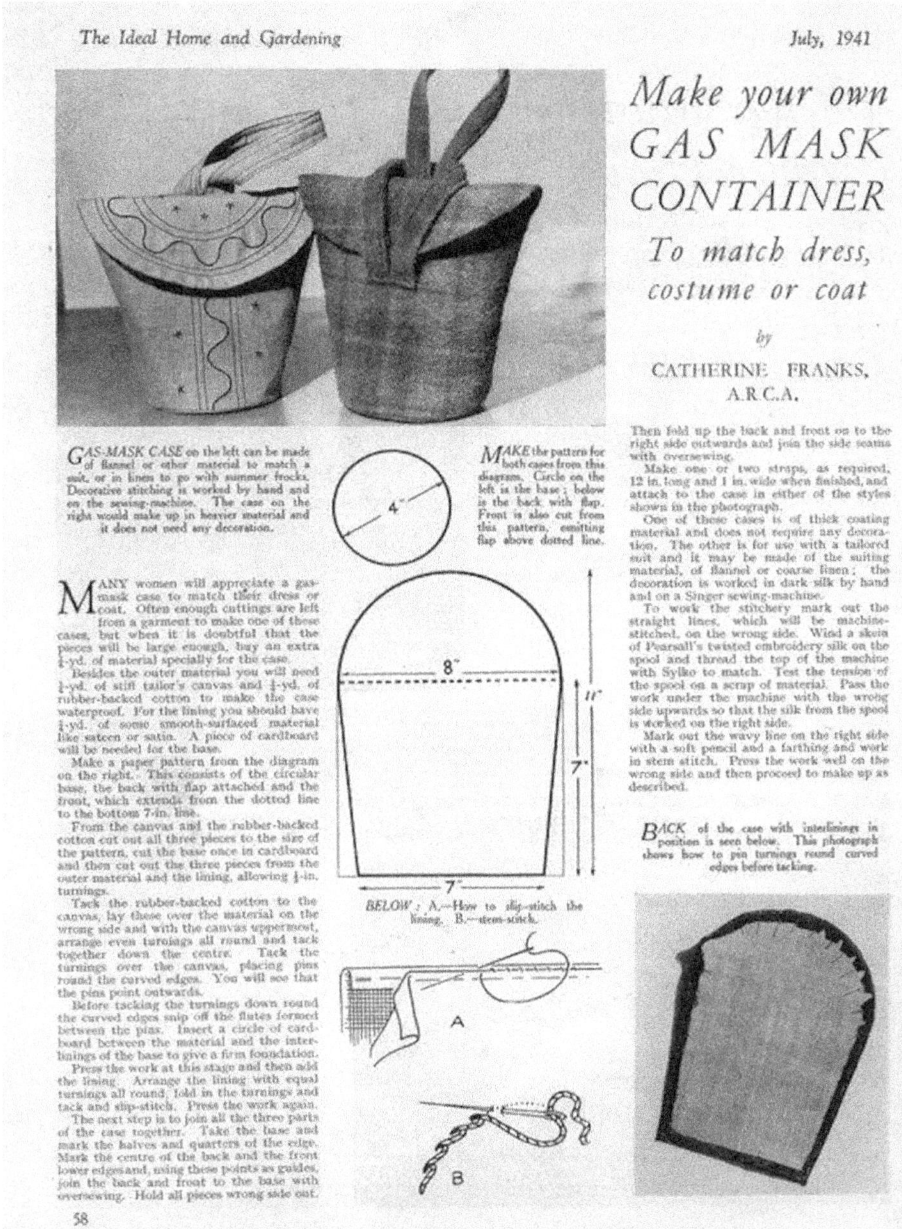

The Ideal Home and Gardening   July, 1941

Make your own GAS MASK CONTAINER

To match dress, costume or coat

by

CATHERINE FRANKS, A.R.C.A.

GAS-MASK CASE on the left can be made of flannel or other material to match a suit, or in linen to go with summer frocks. Decorative stitching is worked by hand and on the sewing-machine. The case on the right would make up in heavier material and it does not need any decoration.

MAKE the pattern for both cases from this diagram. Circle on the left is the base; below is the back with flap. Front is also cut from this pattern, omitting flap above dotted line.

BELOW: A.—How to slip-stitch the lining. B.—stem-stitch.

MANY women will appreciate a gas-mask case to match their dress or coat. Often enough cuttings are left from a garment to make one of these cases, but when it is doubtful that the pieces will be large enough, buy an extra ½-yd. of material specially for the case.

Besides the outer material you will need ½-yd. of stiff tailor's canvas and ½-yd. of rubber-backed cotton to make the case waterproof. For the lining you should have ½-yd. of some smooth-surfaced material like sateen or satin. A piece of cardboard will be needed for the base.

Make a paper pattern from the diagram on the right. This consists of the circular base, the back with flap attached and the front, which extends from the dotted line to the bottom 7-in. line.

From the canvas and the rubber-backed cotton cut out all three pieces to the size of the pattern, cut the base once in cardboard and then cut out the three pieces from the outer material and the lining, allowing ½-in. turnings.

Tack the rubber-backed cotton to the canvas, lay these over the material on the wrong side and with the canvas uppermost, arrange even turnings all round and tack together down the centre. Tack the turnings over the canvas, placing pins round the curved edges. You will see that the pins point outwards.

Before tacking the turnings down round the curved edges snip off the flutes formed between the pins. Insert a circle of cardboard between the material and the interlinings of the base to give a firm foundation.

Press the work at this stage and then add the lining. Arrange the lining with equal turnings all round, fold in the turnings and tack and slip-stitch. Press the work again.

The next step is to join all the three parts of the case together. Take the base and mark the halves and quarters of the edge. Mark the centre of the back and the front lower edges and, using these points as guides, join the back and front to the base with oversewing. Hold all pieces wrong side out.

Then fold up the back and front on to the right side outwards and join the side seams with oversewing.

Make one or two straps, as required, 12 in. long and 1 in. wide when finished, and attach to the case in either of the styles shown in the photograph.

One of these cases is of thick coating material and does not require any decoration. The other is for use with a tailored suit and it may be made of the suiting material, of flannel or coarse linen; the decoration is worked in dark silk by hand and on a Singer sewing-machine.

To work the stitchery mark out the straight lines, which will be machine-stitched, on the wrong side. Wind a skein of Pearsall's twisted embroidery silk on the spool and thread the top of the machine with Sylko to match. Test the tension of the spool on a scrap of material. Pass the work under the machine with the wrong side upwards so that the silk from the spool is worked on the right side.

Mark out the wavy line on the right side with a soft pencil and a farthing and work in stem stitch. Press the work well on the wrong side and then proceed to make up as described.

BACK of the case with interlinings in position is seen below. This photograph shows how to pin turnings round curved edges before tacking.

58

FIGURE 10.1: *Make your own GAS MASK CONTAINER: To match dress, costume or coat*, 1941. *The Ideal Home and Gardening*, July 1941, 58.

value of going out to the movies has been replaced by the vast offerings of Netflix, binge watched in the comfort of home.

New Values

Wearing a facemask has taken on a political aspect, who wears and who does not wear them. The purpose of wearing a facemask is to stop the spread of the coronavirus through respiratory droplets transmitted by an infected person while coughing or sneezing. Fashion editor for the *San Francisco Chronicle*, Tony Bravo (2020a), reported on the fashion evolution of the facemask:

> As the weeks have gone on, people's cloth masks have gotten steadily more aesthetic, a sign not only that creativity has entered the equation but also that we're preparing to wear masks well into the future. While your clothes tell the story of you sheltering from home, your mask is a signal to people that you care about your health and the health of those around you when you go out. Seeing other people wearing masks brings a kind of solidarity to this time of solitude.

Siren Suit

Jumpsuits, both comfortable and "anti-contamination" have become popular (Dyett 2020). These one-piece garments are similar to the coverall garments worn by the Eastlake sisters in Weston-super-Mare, UK, during the 19 to 24 months they slept each night in their basement bomb shelter. The garments provided protection, comfort, and large pockets for caring necessities like a gas mask. Victoria Pass (2020) recently suggested,

> A siren suit could be handy right now for walks around my neighborhood and trips to the store. I can imagine they'd be incredibly practical for grocers, postal workers, and delivery people to protect themselves and easily launder an outer layer at the end of the workday. Well-designed uniforms might be part of a larger set of changes badly needed in the gig economy.

Post-Pandemic Dress

Vanessa Friedman (2020), fashion director and chief fashion critic for the *New York Times*, reassured readers in her article "This Is Not the End of Fashion," stating "it is a truth that may be hard to imagine in a world devastated by illness and economic insecurity, riven by racism and unrest, but we will get dressed again." Visually harking back to post-World War II fashion, the image selected for the article: Christian Dior's *Tailleur Bar*, one of the most iconic styles of his 1947 New Look collection. Friedman asks, "What will our post-crisis identities look like?" Friedman quotes trend forecaster, Li Edelkoort: "We will come out of this, like we come out of a war [...] The buildings are still there, but everything is in ruins. We will want two things: security and to dance. We will be aching for something new, to refresh our personalities, [...] eccentric clothes romantic clothes." Friedman concludes,"It sounds ridiculous: Who cares what we will wear when there has been so much tragedy and economic destruction, when old wounds left to fester have been gashed open once again? But the root of that question is as cyclical as history: What will our post-crisis identities look like?"

Conclusion

World War II can be viewed in hindsight now. By contrast, the current global pandemic is still in our midst, our future unknown. We are stuck in this pandemic for the duration, however long that will be. Keeping diaries has become a popular past time to record this difficult unanticipated time period. Someday, scholars will read those diaries and question the few remaining survivors asking what it was like. Memories will fade. Movies will project a glossy, perhaps romanticized image of what it was. The few remaining nonagenarians who remember living through World War II still carry some psychological effects like saving everything, mending clothing, and hand washing precious clothing. The survivors of the novel coronavirus will carry the stigma of the lived experience throughout our lifetimes as well.

The world will be different once the pandemic has been conquered. Fashion will be different. We wait now, as women waited during World War II, for a return to normalcy. Will we dance in the streets? Will we wear fashions that reflect a remembered time of peace before the pandemic, as Dior's New Look recalled 1930s styles. Will this traumatic time period evolve into a burst of creativity and awaken a new style of dress for those who survive? The aftermath of World War I, which coincided with the pandemic flu outbreak of 1918, as well as the fashion resurgence with Dior's New look after World War II may indicate that a new fashion will be born.

Forecasters predict that pre-pandemic shopping practice of favoring fast fashion and quantity buying will be replaced with a new appreciation of value and quality (Friedman 2020). Timeless fashion that holds its value is already acknowledged by millennials who appreciate products that can be resold on the internet. Will the way people dress post pandemic reflect "the dawning of a new age?" (Friedman 2020). Will our new fashion be called: "Such a new look"?

Mick Lasalle (2020), film credit for the *San Francisco Chronicle* predicts, "Right now, it's difficult—emotionally, spiritually and financially—and that's even if you're lucky enough to not get sick. But just as other generations frequently cited the Great Depression or World War II as pivot points in their lives, people will look back on this precise time as formative" (13).

Hopefully, readers of this book will already know the answers to these questions and will be living in the post-coronavirus era, older and wiser for what they have experienced.

NOTE

1. Adelaide, (born 1927, The Hague, the Netherlands) in discussion with the author, Davis, CA, November 20, 2014.

Bibliography

"$10,000,000 Plant to Make Synthetic Yarn; Major Blow to Japan's Silk Trade Seen." 1938. *New York Times*, October 21, 1938.

"305,500 Coupons for Clothing." 1942. *The Times* (London), February 17, 1942.

"1940s Knitting Patterns." London: Victoria & Albert Museum. Accessed April 13, 2021. https://www.vam.ac.uk/articles/1940s-knitting-patterns.

A Bag of Tricks for Home Sewing. 1945. National Cotton Council, Memphis, TN.

Adams, Frank S. 1942. "Rubber: The Story of a Product That Is All-Vital to the United States in Its Vast War Effort Rubber." *New York Times*, January 11, 1942.

Agger, Ben. 2015. *Speeding Up Fast Capitalism: Cultures, Jobs, Families, Schools, Bodies*. Abingdon, UK: Routledge.

Aldgate, Anthony, and Jeffrey Richards. 1986. *Britain Can Take It: The British Cinema in the Second World War*. Oxford (Oxfordshire): B. Blackwell.

Ambrose, Stephen E. 1992. *Band of Brothers: E Company, 506th Regiment, 101st Airborne from Normandy to Hitler's Eagle's Nest*. New York: Simon & Schuster.

Anderson, David. 1942. "British to Add Cut in Living Standard." *New York Times*, March 4, 1942.

Anderson, Karen Tucker. 1982. "Last Hired, First Fired: Black Women Workers During World War II." *The Journal of American History* 69, no. 1 (June): 82–97. Oxford University Press on behalf of Organization of American Historians. Accessed April 15, 2021. https://www.jstor.org/stable/1887753.

Antelme, Sandy. 2016. *1940–1944: Se Chausser Sous L'occupation*. Lyon, France: Éditions Libel.

Aubrac, Lucie. 2000. *La Résistance Expliquée À Mes Petits-Enfants*. Paris, France: Éditions du Seuil.

Aus Alten Sachen Neues Machen. [1943–45?]. Vobach Album nr. 18. Berlin, Germany: Universalverlag W. Vobach & Co.

Ayling, Keith. 1942. *Calling All Women*. New York and London: Harper & Brothers.

Backman, Jules. 1943. *Rationing and Price Control in Great Britain* 50. Washington, DC: The Brookings Institution.

Bain, Jessica. 2016. "'Darn Right I'm a Feminist... Sew What?' The Politics of Contemporary Home Dressmaking: Sewing, Slow Fashion and Feminism." *Women's Studies International*

Forum 54, (January-February): 57–66. Accessed April 14, 2021. https://www.sciencedirect.com/science/article/abs/pii/S0277539515301424.

Baker, Marjorie M. 2009. *Hand Stitches*. Lexington, KY, University of Kentucky: College of Agriculture, Food and Environment. https://fcs-hes.ca.uky.edu/publications-list/1.

Balio, Tino. 1995. *Grand Design: Hollywood as a Modern Business Enterprise, 1930–1939*. Berkeley, CA: University of California Press.

Barnett, L. Margaret. 1996. "The Conscription of Fashion—Utility Cloth, Clothing, and Footwear, 1941–1952." *Albion* 28, no. 1 (Spring): 171–72. https://aquila.usm.edu/fac_pubs/5622/.

Barrett, Duncan, and Nuala Calvi. 2013. *GI Brides: The Wartime Girls Who Crossed the Atlantic for Love*. London: Harper Collins Publishers.

Bass-Krueger, Maude. 2019a. "Introduction." In *French Fashion, Women, and the First World War*, edited by Maude Bass-Krueger and Sophie Kurkdjian, 38–69. New York: Bard Graduate Center.

Bass-Krueger, Maude. 2019. "The Wartime Fashion Industry." In *French Fashion, Women, and the First World War*, edited by Maude Bass-Krueger and Sophie Kurkdjian, 251–93. New York: Bard Graduate Center.

Baudin, Louis. 1945. "An Outline of Economic Conditions in France under the German Occupation." *The Economic Journal* 55, no. 220 (December): 326–45. https://www.jstor.org/stable/2226017.

Baum, L. Frank, W. W. Denslow, and Michael Patrick Hearn. 2000. *The Annotated Wizard of Oz (The Wonderful Wizard of Oz)*, edited by Michael Patrick Hearn. Centennial Edition. New York: Norton.

Bay Area WWII War Brides Past & Present Exhibit. Dr. Martin Luther King Jr. Library: 150 E. San Fernando St. San Jose, California, Jan - June 2013.

Beebe, Joy A. 2015. *Snapshots of a War Bride's Life*. Salem, Oregon: Salem Printing & Blueprint, Inc.

Beevor, Antony. 2012. *The Second World War*. New York: Little, Brown and Company.

Beevor, Antony. 2002. "They Raped Every German Female from Eight to 80." *The Guardian* (London), May 1, 2002. https://www.theguardian.com/books/2002/may/01/news.features11.

Beveridge, Sir William. 1939. "War Without Waste." *The Times* (London), October 3, 1939, Issue 48426.

Bhardwaj, Vertica, and Ann Fairhurst. 2010. "Fast Fashion: Response to Changes in the Fashion Industry." *The International Review of Retail, Distribution and Consumer Research* 20, no. 1 (June 1): 165–73. Accessed April 15, 2021. https://doi.org/https://doi.org/10.1080/09593960903498300.

Biddle-Perry, Geraldine. 2017. *Dressing for Austerity: Aspiration, Leisure and Fashion in Postwar Britain*. London and New York: I. B. Tauris.

Bixler, Norma. 1945. "Married Women Workers in the War." *The Antioch Review* 5, no. 3: 360–72.

"Black Market Deals of U.S. Soldiers Told: Army Gets Convictions; Offenders Sentenced" 1944. *Chicago Daily Tribune*, December 26, 1944.

"Black Markets Boom in Berlin: Red Army Men Are Biggest Buyers" 1945. *Life*, September 10, 1945.

Black, Prudence, and Jan Idle. 2013. "'It Was Just Something You Did': Mothers, Daughters and Sewing in the 1960s." *Clothing Cultures* 1, no. 1 (October 1): 23–44.

Blanc, Paul D. 2016. *Fake Silk: The Lethal History of Viscose Rayon*. New Haven: Yale University Press.

Bowen, Glenn A. 2006. "Grounded Theory and Sensitizing Concepts." *International Journal of Qualitative Methods* 5, no. 3 (September):12–23.

Brandes, Kendra. 2009. "Feed Sack Fashion in Rural America: A Reflection of Culture." *The Online Journal of Rural Research and Policy* 4, no. 1. Accessed April 14, 2021. https://doi.org/10.4148/ojrrp.v4i1.59.

Bravo, Tony. 2020a. "Fashion During a Pandemic: Sweatpants for Now, Masks for the Future." *San Francisco Chronicle* (California), April 20, 2020. Accessed April 15, 2021. https://datebook.sfchronicle.com/entertainment/fashion-during-a-pandemic-sweatpants-for-now-masksfor-the-future.

Bravo, Tony, 2020b. "Fashion Forward: A Spring of Coronavirus and Social Movements Gives Clothing a Reality Check." *San Francisco Chronicle* (California), July 5, 2020. Accessed April 15, 2021. https://www.sfchronicle.com/culture/article/The-coronavirus-and-social-movements-gives-15383790.php.

Brinkley, Douglas, and Michael E. Haskew. 2004. *The World War II Desk Reference: With the Eisenhower Center for American Studies*. New York: Harper Resource.

"Britain Expanding Control of Goods." 1942. *New York Times*, October 11, 1942.

"Britain Relaxes Rationing of Clothing after 8 Years." 1949. *New York Times*, February 1, 1949.

"Britain Orders Strict Rationing of Clothing: Rigid Rationing Plan Clamped on Clothing in Surprise Order." 1941. *The Washington Post*, June 1, 1941.

Broad, Richard, and Suzie Fleming, eds. *Nella Last's War: A Mother's Diary 1939-45*. Sphere Books Limited, 1981.

Brown, Alfred E., and Kenneth A. Reinhart. 1971. "Polyester Fiber: From Its Invention to Its Present Position." *Science* 173, no. 3994 (July 23): 287–93. Accessed April 14, 2021. https://www.jstor.org/stable/1732359.

Brown, Kathryn. 2010. "Patriotic Support: The Girdle Pin-Up of World War II." PhD. dissertation, University of Akron, History. Accessed April 14, 2021. https://etd.ohiolink.edu/apexprod/rws_olink/r/1501/10?p10_etd_subid=47483&clear=10.

Brown, Sass. 2010. *Eco Fashion*. London: Lawrence King Publishing.

Brown, Sass. 2019. "Global Artisanship Models for the Craft Sector." Accessed April 21, 2021. https://iasdr2019.org/uploads/files/Proceedings/vo-s-1076-Bro-S.pdf.

Brucker, Jérémie. 2019. "Overalls." In *French Fashion, Women, and the First World War*, edited by Maude Bass-Krueger and Sophie Kurkdjian, 238–49. New York: Bard Graduate Center.

Buckland, Sandra Stansbery. 2000. "Fashion as a Tool of World War II: A Case Study Supporting the SI Theory." *Clothing and Textiles Research Journal* 18, no. 3 (June): 140–51. Accessed April 15, 2021. https://doi.org/10.1177/0887302X0001800303.

Burton, Jeffrey F., Mary M. Farrell, Florence B. Lord, Richard W. Lord, and Tetsuden Kashima. 2002. *Confinement and Ethnicity: An Overview of World War II Japanese American Relocation Sites*. Seattle; London: University of Washington Press. Accessed April 14, 2021. www.jstor.org/stable/j.ctvcwnv2x.

Byas, Hugh. 1940. "A Real Peace in China Urgent Need of Japan." *New York Times*, March 24, 1940.

Calder, Angus. 1969. *The People's War: Britain, 1939–1945*. New York: Pantheon Books.

"California Puzzles Over Problem of Oklahoma Dust Bowl Refugees" 1937. *Los Angeles Times*, July 20, 1937.

Campbell, D'Ann. 1984. *Women at War with America: Private Lives in a Patriotic Era*. Cambridge, MA: Harvard University Press.

Carpenter, Lynette, 1985. "'There's No Place Like Home:' The Wizard of Oz and American Isolationism." *Film and History* 15, no. 2 (May 1): 37–45. Accessed April 14, 2021. https://muse.jhu.edu/article/402276/pdf.

Casdorph, Paul D. 1989. *Let the Good Times Roll: Life at Home in America During World War II*. New York: Paragon House.

Cassell, Peter. 1869. *Cassell's Household Guide: Being a Complete Encyclopaedia of Domestic and Social Economy*. vol. 4, London: Cassell, Petter, and Galpin.

Chadeau, Emmanuel. 1993. "The Large Family Firm in Twentieth-Century France." *Business History* 35, no. 4: 184–205. Accessed April 14, 2021. https://doi.org/10.1080/00076799300000133.

Chafe, William H. 1990. "World War II as a Pivotal Experience for American Women." In *Women and War: The Changing Status of American Women from the 1930s to the 1950s*, edited by Maria Diedrich and Dorothea Fischer-Hornung, 21–34. New York and Oxford: Berg.

Chansky, Ricia A. 2010. "A Stitch in Time: Third-Wave Feminist Reclamation of Needled Imagery." *The Journal of Popular Culture* 43, no. 4 (August): 681–700.

Chapman, James. 1999. "British Cinema and 'The People's War.'" In *Millions Like Us? British Culture in the Second World War*, edited by Nick Hayes and Jeff Hill, 33–61. Liverpool, UK: Liverpool University Press.

Chapman, Stephanie, Jessica Keener, Nicole Sobota, and Courtney Whitmore. 2019. *Prisoners at Home: Everyday Life in Japanese Internment Camps*. Digital Public Library of America. Accessed April 14, 2021. https://dp.la/exhibitions/japanese-internment/employment.

Charleston, Beth Duncuff, and Harold Koda. 2004. "Christian Dior (1905–1957)." *Heilbrunn Timeline of Art History*. New York City: The Metropolitan Museum of Art, (October). Accessed April 14, 2021. http://www.metmuseum.org/toah/hd/dior/hddior.htm.

Charlton, Jonathan, 2018. "What's the Story Behind This Dress Made Out of a Nazi Banner?" (video) *Saskatoon StarPhoenix* (Canada), February 28, 2018. Accessed April 8, 2021. https://youtu.be/ZJlma4-83ak.

Charman, Terry. 1989. *The German Home Front 1939–1945*. New York: Philosophical Library.

Chesky, Anne. 2010. "From Sewing to Shopping: Signals of a Shifting Economy." *North Carolina Folklore Journal* 57, no. 1 (Winter-Spring): 20–41. Accessed April 14, 2021. https://digital.ncdcr.gov/digital/collection/p16062coll43/id/8003.

Chmielewski, Dawn, and Meg James. 2008. "Downturn May Not Aid Studios This Time: In a Recession, Online Diversions Could Be a Drain on Hollywood." *Los Angeles Times*, October 29, 2008.

Christofferson, Thomas Rodney, and Michael S. Christofferson. 2006. *France During World War II: From Defeat to Liberation*. New York: Fordham University Press.

Churchill, Winston. 1950. *The Second World War: The Grand Alliance*. Boston, MA: Houghton Mifflin Company.

Clark, Hazel. 2008. "SLOW + FASHION—an Oxymoron—or a Promise for the Future... ?" *Fashion Theory* 12, no. 4 (April): 427–46. Accessed April 14, 2021. https://doi.org/10.2752/175174108X346922.

Claudio, Luz. 2007. "Waste Couture: Environmental Impact of the Clothing Industry." *Environmental Health Perspectives* 115, no. 9 (September): A449–A454. Accessed April 14, 2021. https://doi.org/10.1289/ehp.115-a449.

Clinard, Marshall B. 1952. *The Black Market: A Study of White Collar Crime*. New York: Rinehart & Company Inc.

Cline, Elizabeth L. 2012. *Overdressed: The Shocking High Cost of Cheap Fashion*. New York: Penguin.

Cline, Elizabeth L. 2014. "Where Does Discarded Clothing Go?" *The Atlantic*, July 18, 2014. https://www.theatlantic.com/business/archive/2014/07/where-does-discarded-clothing-go/374613/.

Cline, Elizabeth L. 2019. "Tidying Up Has Created a Flood of Clothing Donations No One Wants." *Slate*, May 13, 2019. Accessed April 14, 2021. https://slate.com/technology/2019/05/marie-kondo-tidying-up-donate-unwanted-clothing.html.

"Clothing Sale Halts in France for Curbs." 1941. *New York Times*, February 14, 1941.

Coen, Robert M. 1973. "Labor Force and Unemployment in the 1920's and 1930's: A Re-Examination Based on Postwar Experience." *The Review of Economics and Statistics* 55, no. 1 (February): 46–55. Accessed April 14, 2021. http://www.jstor.com/stable/1927993.

Cohen, Allen C., and Ingrid Johnson. 2010. *J. J. Pizzuto's Fabric Science*. New York: Fairchild Books.

Coile, Ellen Miller. 2017. *Under Two Flags: A Memoir*. Bloomington, IN: iUniverse.

Colopy, Mary Ann. 2009. "Never Just Sit: Eleanor Roosevelt and a Life of Knitting." *Piecework*, Fort Collins, CO: Long Thread Media, (January–February).

Connolly, Loris. 1992. "Recycling Feed Sacks and Flour Bags: Thrifty Housewives or Marketing Success Story?" *Dress* 41, no. 2: 17–36. Accessed April 14, 2021. https://doi.org/10.1179/036121192805298418

Conrat, Maisie, and Richard Conrat. 1972. *Executive Order 9066: The Internment of 110,000 Japanese Americans*. Special Publication (California Historical Society no. 51. San Francisco, CA.

Cook, J. Gordon. 1959. *Handbook of Textile Fibres—Man-Made Fibres*. Vol. II. Durham, England: Merrow Publishing Com.

Copeland, Morris A. 1945. *The Impact of the War on Civilian Consumption in the United Kingdom, the United States and Canada*. Washington, DC: Government Publishing Office.

"Corset Industry Gets Jitters; Women Start Rush on Stores." 1942. *New York Times*, January 10, 1942.

Cramer, Jo. 2011. "Made to Keep: Product Longevity through Participatory Design in Fashion." *Design Principles & Practice: An International Journal* 5, no. 5: 437–46. Accessed April 14, 2021. doi:10.18848/1833-1874/CGP/v05i05/38170.

Cunningham, Patricia A. 2003. *Reforming Women's Fashion, 1850–1920: Politics, Health, and Art*. Kent, OH: The Kent State University Press.

Curtis, James C. 1986. "Dorothea Lange, Migrant Mother, and the Culture of the Great Depression." *Winterthur Portfolio* 21, no. 1 (Spring): 1–20. Accessed April 14, 2021. https://www.jstor.org/stable/1181013.

"Cut Down Runs in Your New Rayons: Lux Them Nightly." 1942. *Good Housekeeping*, New York, Hearst Magazines, November 1942.

Cutlip, Kimbra. 2015. "How Nylon Stockings Changed the World." *Smithsonian Magazine*, Washington, DC, May 11, 2015. Accessed April 8, 2021. https://www.smithsonianmag.com/smithsonian-institution/how-75-years-ago-nylon-stockings-changed-world-180955219/.

Daniell, Raymond. 1945. "Europe Faces a Black Winter: Unless a Way Is Found Quickly to Repair." *New York Times*, August 19, 1945.

Daugherty, Greg. 2018. "When Paper Clothing Was the Perfect Fit: A War-Weary World Needed a New Wardrobe, and This Cheap, Washable Attire Seemed to Rise to the Occasion." *Smithsonian Magazine*, Washington, DC, May 24, 2018. Accessed April 8, 2021. https://www.smithsonianmag.com/history/when-paper-clothing-was-perfect-fit-180969159/

Davis, Kingsley. 1984. "Wives and Work: The Sex Role Revolution and Its Consequences." *Population and Development Review* 10, no. 3 (September): 397–417. Accessed April 14, 2021. https://doi.org/10.2307/1973512.

Davis, Fred. 1992. *Fashion, Culture, and Identity*. Chicago and London: The University of Chicago Press.

Davis, Judi. 2008. "Oral History of Fern Louise Boswell Hobson's WWII Years." *Tahoma West Literary Arts Magazine* 12, no. 1 (May): 83–87. Accessed April 8, 2021. https://digitalcommons.tacoma.uw.edu/tahoma_west/vol12/iss1/18.

DeLong, Marilyn, Carol Salusso-Deonier, and Kinley Larntz. 1983. "Use of Perceptions of Female Dress as an Indicator of Role Definition." *Home Economics Research Journal* 11, no. 4: 327–36. Accessed April 8, 2021. https://doi.org/10.1177/1077727X8301100402.

"Dependence of U.S. On Silk Continues." 1941. *New York Times*, May 9, 1941.

"Devise Powder Bags with Silk Substitute: Army and Navy Each Studying Problem" 1941. *New York Times*, August 10, 1941.

Dinan, Jacqueline. 2015. *Between the Dances*. Sydney: Jane Curry Publishing.

Dirix, Emmanuelle. 2016. *Dressing the Decades: Twentieth-Century Vintage Style*. Yale University Press.

Domestic Commerce: A Weekly Bulletin of the National Economy. 1942. US Department of Commerce 22, no. 10 (October). Accessed April 8, 2021. https://fraser.stlouisfed.org/title/survey-current-business-46/october-1942-9398.

Doughty, Robert A., and Harold E. Raugh. 1991. "Embargoes in Historical Perspective." *Parameters: Journal of the US Army War College* 21, no. 1 (July): 21–30. Accessed April 14, 2012. https://press.armywarcollege.edu/parameters/vol21/iss1/7.

Dunlop, Paula. 2015. "Beauty, Duty, and Hope." In *Remotely Fashionable: A Story of Subtropical Style*, edited by Nadia Buick, Madeleine King, Ed King: Fashion Archives.

Dunne, Susan. 2017. "CHS Exhibit Reflects Queen Victoria's Influence on Fashion." *Hartford Courant*, August 22, 2017. Accessed April 8, 2021. https://www.courant.com/ctnow/arts-theater/hc-queen-victoria-fashion-hartford-0818-20170817-story.html.

Dyett, Linda. 2020. "They Splurged on Fancy Clothes Before Quarantine. Now What?" *New York Times*, July 8, 2020. Accessed August 18, 2021. https://www.nytimes.com/2020/07/08/style/why-did-i-buy-this.html.

Earley, James S., and William S. B. Lacy. 1942. "British Wartime Control of Prices." *Law and Contemporary Problems* 9 (Winter): 160–72. Accessed April 8, 2021. https://scholarship.law.duke.edu/lcp/vol9/iss1/11.

Easy Ways to Sew and Save: The Latest Sewing Secrets. 1941. The Spool Cotton Company, USA, no. 169.

Edwards, Elaine M. 2010. *Scotland's Land Girls: Breeches, Bombers and Backaches*. Edinburgh: NMS Enterprises-Publishing.

Egan, Charles E. 1942. "Rationing Speeded up as a Wartime Measure: But as Yet Americans Endure Only Few of Restrictions Adopted Elsewhere." *New York Times*, October 4, 1942.

Ehrman, Edwina. 2011. *The Wedding Dress: 300 Years of Bridal Fashions*. London: V&A Publishing.

E. I. du Pont de Nemours & Company. 1976. *Milestones in the Du Pont Company's Textile Fiber History and Some Important Industry Dates*. 12th ed.Wilmington, DE.: Distributed by E. I. du Pont de Nemours & Co., Textile Fibers Dept.

Elson, Diane, and Ruth Pearson. 1981. "'Nimble Fingers Make Cheap Workers': An Analysis of Women's Employment in Third World Export Manufacturing." *Feminist Review* 7, no. 1 (Spring): 87–107. Accessed April 8, 2021. https://doi.org/10.2307/1394761.

Enrich, David, Rachel Abrams, and Steven Kurutz. 2020. "A Sewing Army, Making Masks for America." *New York Times*, March 25, 2020. Accessed April 8, 2021. https://www.nytimes.com/2020/03/25/business/coronavirus-masks-sewers.html.

Enssle, Manfred J. 1987. "The Harsh Discipline of Food Scarcity in Postwar Stuttgart, 1945–1948." *German Studies Review* 10, no. 3 (October): 481–502. Accessed April 8, 2021. https://doi.org/10.2307/1430898

Enssle, Manfred J. 1993. "Five Theses on German Everyday Life after World War II." *Central European History* 26, no. 1: 1–19. Accessed April 8, 2021. https://www.jstor.org/stable/4546314.

Evans, Redd, and John Jacob Loeb. 1942. *"Rosie the Riveter Song with Lyrics,"* edited by Four Vagabonds. YouTube. Accessed April 10, 2021. https://youtu.be/D2E613J9m0I.

Ewing, Elizabeth. 1978. *Dress and Undress: A History of Women's Underwear*. New York: Drama Book Specialists.

Fairchild, Thomas E. 1944. "The Legal Mechanism of Rationing." *Marquette Law Review* 28, no. 1 (Winter): 11–22.

"Farewell to Silk Stockings" 1940. *The Times* (London), October 21, 1940.

Farra, Emily. 2019. "Calling Planet Earth." *Vogue*, New York: Condé Nast Publishing, September, 2019.

Farrell-Beck, Jane. 2011. "Underpinning Depression, Wartime, and Recovery Bras and Girdles, 1935–1950." *Dress* 37, no. 1: 23–38. Accessed April 10, 2021. https://doi.org/10.1179/036121112X13099651318584.

"Fashion: America's Own-Cotton" 1942. *Vogue*, New York: Condé Nast Publishers, February 1, 1942.

"Fashion: A New Heating Plan" 1942. *Vogue*, New York: Condé Nast Publishers, October 15, 1942.

"Fashion: A Primer on Pants" 1942. *Vogue*, New York: Condé Nast Publishers, April 1, 1942.

"Fashion: Foreign Shores" 1938. *Vogue*, New York: Condé Nast Publishers, June 1, 1938.

"Fashion: G. I. Siren for USO Camp Shows" 1944. *Vogue*, New York: Condé Nast Publishers, May 1, 1944.

"Fashion: Paris Collections" 1947. *Vogue*, New York: Condé Nast Publishers, April 1, 1947.

"Fashion: Veils for Legs" 1943. *Vogue*, New York: Condé Nast Publishers, December 1, 1943.

"Feed Bags, Once Sad Sacks, Make Fancy Dresses" 1946, *Chicago Daily Tribune*, May 1, 1946.

Fields, Jill. 1999. "'Fighting the Corsetless Evil': Shaping Corsets and Culture, 1900–1930." *Journal of Social History* 33, no. 2: 355–84. Accessed April 10, 2021. https://doi.org/10.1353/jsh.1999.0053.

Fields, Jill. 2007. *An Intimate Affair Women, Lingerie, and Sexuality*. Berkeley, CA: University of California Press.

"First Offering of Nylon Hosiery Sold Out; Out-of-Town Buyers Swamp Wilmington." 1939. *New York Times*, October 25, 1939.

Fishback, Margaret. 1942. "C'est La Guerre or the Wonderful Alibi—The War." *Woman's Day*. New York: Stores Publishing Co. Inc, December 1942.

Fletcher, Kate. 2010. "Slow Fashion: An Invitation for Systems Change." *Fashion Practice* 2, no. 2: 259–66. Accessed April 14, 2021. https://doi.org/10.2752/1756938 10X12774625387594.

Fletcher, Kate, and Lynda Grose. 2010. *Fashion & Sustainability: Design for Change*. London: Laurence King Publishing Ltd.

Fogg, Marnie. 2013. *Fashion: The Whole Story*. New York: Prestel Publishing, a member of Verlagsgruppe Random House GmbH.

Friedan, Betty. 1963. *The Feminine Mystique*. New York and London: W. W. Norton & Company.

Friedman, Vanessa. 2020. "This Is Not the End of Fashion: History and Human Nature Prove We Will Dress Up Again. What That Looks Like Is the Real Question." *New York Times*, June 4, 2020. Accessed April 10, 2021. https://www.nytimes.com/2020/06/04/style/fashion-industry-dead-or-alive.html.

Friedman, Vanessa, and Sapna Maheshwari. 2020. "Brooks Bros., 'Made in America' Since 1818, May Soon Need a New Calling Card." *New York Times*, June 5, 2020. Accessed April 10, 2021. https://www.nytimes.com/2020/06/05/business/brooks-brothers-factory-closings.html.

"Furlough Wedding" 1942. *Vogue*, New York: Condé Nast Publishers, October 15, 1942.

Fussell, Paul. 1989. *Wartime: Understanding and Behavior in the Second World War*. Oxford (England): Oxford University Press.

Galenson, Walter, and Arnold Zellner, eds. 1957. *International Comparison of Unemployment Rates*, edited by Universities National Bureau. Cambridge, MA: National Bureau of Economic Research (NBER).

"General Limitation Order L-85" National War Production Board. 7 Fed. Reg. vol 7, no. 70, Washington DC. April 10, 1942: 2719.

Glickman, Lawrence B. 2005. "'Make Lisle the Style': The Politics of Fashion in the Japanese Silk Boycott, 1937-1940." *Journal of Social History*, 38, no. 3: 573–608.

Gluck, Sherna Berger. 1987. *Rosie the Riveter Revisited: Women, the War, and Social Change*. Boston, MA: Twayne Publishers.

Gluckstein, Donny. 2012. *A People's History of the Second World War: Resistance Versus Empire*. 20th Century Britain: Economic, Cultural and Social Change. Pluto Press.

Goldin, Claudia Dale. 1988. "Marriage Bars: Discrimination Against Married Women Workers, 1920s to 1950s." *NBER Working Paper #2747*. Cambridge, Mass.: National Bureau of Economic Research.

Goodin, Robert E., and John S. Dryzek. 1995. "Justice Deferred: Wartime Rationing and Postwar Welfare Policy." *Politics & Society* 23, no. 1 (March): 49–73. Accessed April 14, 2021. https://doi.org/10.1177/0032329295023001003.

Goodman, Jill, Greg Knotts, and Jeanne Jackson. 2007. "Doing Dress and the Construction of Women's Gender Identity." *Journal of Occupational Science* 14, no. 2 (September): 100–107. Accessed April 14, 2021. https://doi.org/10.1080/14427591.2007.9686590.

Gordon, Sarah A. 2009. *Make It Yourself: Home Sewing, Gender, and Culture, 1890–1930.* Columbia University Press. Accessed April 10, 2021. http://www.gutenberg-e.org/gordon/.

Grayzel, Susan R. 2019. "'Needles En Avant!': The Militarization of Women's Sewing and Knitting During the First World War in France, Great Britain, and America." In *French Fashion, Women, and the First World War*, edited by Maude Bass-Krueger and Sophie Kurkdjian, 133–67. New York: Bard Graduate Center.

Greene, Graham. 1950. *The Third Man.* New York: Bantam Books.

Greer, Betsy, ed. 2014. *"Craftivism: The Art of Craft and Activism."* Arsenal Pulp Press.

Grenard, Fabrice. 2008. *La France Du Marché Noir (1940–1949).* Paris: Payot.

Griffiths, Owen. 2002. "Need, Greed, and Protest in Japan's Black Market, 1938–1949." *Journal of Social History* 35, no. 4 (Summer): 825–58. Accessed April 11, 2021. http://www.jstor.org/stable/3790613.

Guenther, Irene. 2004. *Nazi Chic? Fashioning Women in the Third Reich.* Oxford, UK and New York: Berg Publishers.

Gustafson, Robert. 1982. "The Power of the Screen: The Influence of Edith Head's Film Designs on the Retail Fashion Market." *The Velvet Light Trap* 19 (January 1, 1982). Accessed April 10, 2021. https://search.proquest.com/scholarly-journals/power-screen-influence-edith-heads-film-designs/docview/1306638683/se-2?accountid=14505.

Gwilt, Alison. 2014. "What Prevents People Repairing Clothes?: An Investigation into Community-Based Approaches to Sustainable Product Service Systems for Clothing Repair." *Making Futures Journal* 3.

Habit, Franklin. 2020. "The Egg and I: Tools for Darning." *PieceWork*, Fort Collins, CO: Long Thread Media, (Fall): 12–14. Accessed April 14, 2021. https://www.scribd.com/article/468929909/The-Egg-And-I-Tools-For-Darning.

Hackett, Lisa J., and Denise N. Rall. 2018. "The Size of the Problem with the Problem of Sizing: How Clothing Measurement Systems Have Misrepresented Women's Bodies, from the 1920s to Today." *Clothing Cultures* 5, no. 2 (June): 263–83.

Hackney, Fiona. 1999. "Making Modern Women, Stitch by Stitch: Dressmaking and Women's Magazines in Britain 1919–39." In *The Culture of Sewing: Gender, Consumption and Home Dressmaking*, edited by Barbara Burman, 73–95. New York: The Berg Fashion Library.

Hackney, Fiona. 2013. "Quiet Activism and the New Amateur: The Power of Home and Hobby Crafts." *Design and Culture* 5, no. 2 (July): 169–93.

Hagen, William M. 2018. "Grapes of Wrath, The." In *The Encyclopedia of Oklahoma History and Culture*. Oklahoma City: Oklahoma Historical Society. Accessed January 9, 2018. https://www.okhistory.org/publications/enc/entry.php?entry=GR010.

Hagner, Anne. 1942. "Clothing Rationing Appears Unlikely, but Market Seeks Substitutes for Cotton and Wools." *The Washington Post*, November 16, 1942.

Hall, Martha L., Belinda T. Orzada, and Dilia Lopez-Gydosh. 2015. "American Women's Wartime Dress: Sociocultural Ambiguity Regarding Women's Roles During World War II." *The Journal of American Culture* 38, no. 3 (September 8): 232–42. Accessed April 14, 2021. https://doi.org/10.1111/jacc.12357.

Hammock, Michael R., and Art Carden. 2014. "The Black Market and the Silver Screen: Economics in the Third Man." In *New Developments in Economic Education*, edited by Frank Mixon and Richard Cebula. Edward Elgar Publishing: 140–147.

Hancock, William Keith, and Margaret Mary Gowing. 1949. *British War Economy: History of the Second World War*. United Kindgom Civil Series. London: His Majesty's Stationery Office.

Handley, Susannah. 2000. *Nylon: The Story of a Fashion Revolution: A Celebration of Design from Art Silk to Nylon and Thinking Fibres*. Baltimore, MD: Johns Hopkins University Press.

Hannon, Laura Bellew. 2012. "The 'Stylish Battle' World War II and Clothing Design Restrictions in Los Angeles." PhD. dissertation, UC Riverside.

Hargreaves, Eric Lyde, and Margaret Mary Gowing. 1952. *Civil Industry and Trade*. London: Her Majesty's Stationery Office.

Hargrove, Charles R. 1940. "New French Decrees Will Lead to Civilian Rationing System: Bank of France's Gold Reserve Revalued in Only Financial Order Sale of Luxury Goods Reduced." *Wall Street Journal*, March 1, 1940.

Harmetz, Aljean. 2013. *The Making of the Wizard of Oz*. Chicago: Chicago Review Press.

Hara, Akira. 1998. "Japan: Guns Before Rice." In *The Economics of World War II: Six Great Powers in International Comparison*, ed. Mark Harrison. Cambridge University Press, 224–67. Accessed April 14, 2021. doi:10.1017/CBO9780511523632.007.

Hartmann, Susan M. 1978. "Prescriptions for Penelope: Literature on Women's Obligations to Returning World War II Veterans." *Women's Studies: An Interdisciplinary Journal* 5, no. 3: 223–39. Accessed April 14, 2021. https://doi.org/10.1080/00497878.1978.9978450.

Heinrichs, Waldo. 1988. *Threshold of War: Franklin D. Roosevelt and American Entry into World War II*. United States: Oxford University Press.

Held, Rhiannon, and Olwen Sanderson. 2020. "Creative Scrimping." *PieceWork*, Fort Collins, CO: Long Thread Media, November 23, 2020, 46–49. Accessed April 14, 2021. https://www.scribd.com/article/468929945/Creative-Scrimping.

Hodgson, Grace. 2016. "Cold." Unpublished.

Hollen, Nancy, Jane Saddler, Anna L. Langford, and Sara J. Kadolph. 1988. *Textiles*. 6th ed. New York: MacMillan Publishing.

Hollywood Costume. 2012. Edited Deborah Nadoolman Landis. Wilshire May Company Building: Academy of Motion Picture Arts and Sciences, October 2–March 2, 2012. Accessed April 14, 2021. https://www.oscars.org/museum.

Horwood, Catherine. 2005. *Keeping Up Appearances: Fashion and Class between the Wars*. UK: Sutton Publishing Limited.

"Hosiery Industry Through with Silk: To Rely Hereafter on Synthetic Yarns." 1942. *New York Times*, January 14, 1942.

Howard, Ronald. 1981. *In Search of My Father: A Portrait of Leslie Howard*. London: William Kimber.

Howell, Geraldine. 2012. *Wartime Fashion: From Haute Couture to Homemade, 1939–1945*. London and New York: Berg.

Hoyt, Elizabeth. 1942. "People and Ideas: How We Live in France." *Vogue*, New York: Condé Nast Publications, December 15, 1942.

Hua, Vanessa. 2015. *Living History*. National Parks Conservation Association. Accessed April 11, 2021. https://www.npca.org/articles/480-living-history.

Iklé, Fred Charles. 1958. *The Social Impact of Bomb Destruction*. Norman, OK: University of Oklahoma Press.

Jones, Lu Ann, and Sunae Park. 1993. "From Feed Bags to Fashion." *Textile History* 24, no. 1: 91–103. Accessed April 11, 2021. https://doi.org/10.1179/004049693793712213.

Jurca, Catherine. 2008. "What the Public Wanted: Hollywood, 1937–1942." *Cinema Journal* 47, no. 2 (Winter): 3–25.

Kimble, James J., and Lester C. Olson. 2006. "Visual Rhetoric Representing Rosie the Riveter: Myth and Misconception in J. Howard Miller's 'We Can Do It!' Poster." *Rhetoric and Public Affairs* 9, no. 4 (Winter): 533–69.

Klein, Maury. 2013. *A Call to Arms: Mobilizing America for World War II*. New York: Bloomsbury Press.

Knit for Defense. 1941. The Spool Cotton Company, United States, no. 172.

Knit for Victory: Warm Wools for the Long Watch. 1943. The Spool Cotton Company, United States, no. 198.

Knoke, Heinz. 1953. *I Flew for the Führer: The Story of a German Fighter Pilot*. UK: Hachette Livre.

Kolkman, Donald. 2010. "US Rationing During WWII Part 8: Shoes." *International Journal of Rationing* 2, no. 1.

König, Anna. 2013. "A Stitch in Time: Changing Cultural Constructions of Craft and Mending." *Culture Unbound: Journal of Current Cultural Research* 5, no. 4: 569–85. Accessed April 11, 2021. https://ualresearchonline.arts.ac.uk/id/eprint/6753/1/cultureunbound.pdf.

Kuhn, Annette. 2002. *An Everyday Magic: Cinema and Cultural Memory*. London, New York: I. B. Tauris.

Kurutz, Steven, 2020. "Now Is When We All Learn to Darn Our Socks Again." *New York Times*, March 12, 2020. Accessed April 14, 2021. https://www.nytimes.com/2020/03/12/style/visible-mending.html.

Lant, Antonia. 1991. *Blackout: Reinventing Women for Wartime British Cinema*. Princeton, NJ: Princeton University Press. Accessed April 14, 2021. https://www.jstor.org/stable/j.ctt7zvkq2.

LaSalle, Mick. 2020. "Virus Can Teach You a Life-Upending Lesson." *San Francisco Chronicle*, July 12, 2020. Accessed April 12, 2021. https://datebook.sfchronicle.com/movies-tv/the-virus-is-teaching-us-what-we-really-want-to-do-with-our-lives.

Lauterbach, Albert. 1944. "From Rationing to Informed Consumption." *The Journal of Business of the University of Chicago* 17, no. 4 (October): 209–19. http://www.jstor.org/stable/2350259.

Laver, James. 1969. *The Concise History of Costume and Fashion*. New York: Harry N. Abrams Inc.

Lawrence, W. H. 1943. "War Powers Are Invoked in War on Inflation." *New York Times*, April 11, 1943.

Lazan, Marion Blumenthal, and Lila Perl. 1996. *Four Perfect Pebbles: A Holocaust Story*. NYC: Avon Books. Accessed April 12, 2021. http://www.fourperfectpebbles.com/.

League of Nations. 1942. *Wartime Rationing and Consumption*. Geneva: Economic Intelligence Service-League of Nations.

Leder, Jane Mersky. 2006. *Thanks for the Memories: Love, Sex, and World War II*. Westport, CT and London: Praeger.

Lejenäs, Harald. 1989. "The Severe Winter in Europe 1941–42: The Large-Scale Circulation, Cut-Off Lows, and Blocking." *Bulletin of the American Meteorological Society* 70, no. 3: 271–81.

Le Maguet, Jean-Paul. 2000. "Ravitaillement Et Système D Sous l'Occupation." In *Le Mémorial de Caen*. Caen, France: Editions Mémorial De Caen.

Levenson, Eric. 2020. "Officials keep calling the coronavirus pandemic a 'war.' Here's why." *Cable News Channel (CNN)*, April 2, 2020. Accessed April 12, 2021. https://www.cnn.com/2020/04/01/us/war-on-coronavirus-attack/index.html.

Levine, Adeline G., and Murray Levine. 2011. "WWII and the Home Front: The Intersection of History and Biography." *American Journal of Orthopsychiatry* 81, no. 4 (October 2011): 433–41. Accessed April 14, 2021. http://dx.doi.org/10.1111/j.1939-0025.2011.01119.x.

"Life Without Silk," 1938. *The Washington Post*. January 28, 1938.

Lingeman, Richard R. 1970. *Don't You Know There's a War On? The American Home Front, 1941–1945*. New York: G. P. Putnam's Sons.

Lloyd, Edward Mayow Hastings. 1942. "Some Notes on Point Rationing." *The Review of Economics and Statistics* 24, no. 2 (May): 49–52. Accessed April 14, 2021. https://www.jstor.org/stable/1924375.

Loncraine, Rebecca. 2009. *The Real Wizard of Oz: The Life and Times of L. Frank Baum*. New York: Gotham Books.

Lorentz, Pare, dir. 1936. *The Plow That Broke the Plains*. Resettlement Administration. Accessed April 12, 2021. https://www.youtube.com/watch?v=hzaV5FdZMUQ.

Lowe, Keith. 2017. *The Free and the Freedom: How the Second World War Changed Us*. New York: St. Martin's Press.

Lurie, Alison. 1981. *The Language of Clothes*. New York: Random House.

Macdonald, Anne L. 1988. *No Idle Hands: The Social History of American Knitting*. New York: Ballantine Books.

MacDonald, James. 1940. "Rations Without Want Introduced in Britain." *New York Times*, January 14, 1940.

MacDowell, Laurel Sefton. 1978. "The Formation of the Canadian Industrial Relations System During World War Two." *Labour/Le Travail* 3: 175–96. Accessed April 14, 2021. https://www.jstor.org/stable/25139912.

Maginnis, Tara. 1992. "'She Saves Who Sews for Victory': Home Sewing on the American Home Front." *Costume* 26, no. 1: 60–70. Accessed April 14, 2021. https://doi.org/10.1179/cos.1992.26.1.60.

Mahlendorf, Ursula. 2009. *The Shame of Survival: Working through a Nazi Childhood*. University Park, PA: The Pennsylvania State University Press.

Maines, Rachel. 1985. "Wartime Allocation of Textile and Apparel Resources: Emergency Policy in the Twentieth Century." *The Public Historian* 7, no. 1 (Winter): 28–51. Accessed April 14, 2021. http://www.jstor.org/stable/3377298.

"Make and Mend for Victory" 1942. *The Spool Cotton Company*, United States, no. S-10.

Malcolmson, Patricia and Robert W. Malcolmson, eds. 2008. *Nella Last's Peace: The Post-War Diaries of Housewife, 49*. London: Profile.

Marcus, Stanley. 1974. *Minding the Store: A Memoir*. Boston, MA: Little, Brown and Company.

Margerum, Eileen. 1999. "The Sewing Needle as Magic Wand: Selling Sewing Lessons to American Girls after the Second World War." In *The Culture of Sewing: Gender, Consumption and Home Dressmaking*, edited by Barbara Burman, 193–205. New York: Berg.

Marion, Jr., George, and Thomas Fat's Waller. 1943. "When the Nylons Bloom Again." Performed in Broadway show: *Early to Bed*, Broadhurst Theatre, Jun 17, 1943 - May 13, 1944.

Matchar, Emily. 2013. *Homeward Bound: Why Women Are Embracing the New Domesticity*. New York: Simon and Schuster.

Mavin, Helen. 2018. *What Is the Cenotaph?* London, UK: Imperial War Museum, May 31, 2018. Accessed April 14, 2021. https://www.iwm.org.uk/history/what-is-the-cenotaph.

Maynard, Mary McKay. 2002. *My Faraway Home: An American Family's WWII Tale of Adventure and Survival in the Jungles of the Philippines*. Guilford, CT: The Lyons Press.

McDowell, Colin. 1997. *Forties Fashion and the New Look*. London: Bloomsbury Publishing.

McEuen, Melissa A. 2011. *Making War, Making Women: Femininity and Duty on the American Home Front, 1941–1945*. Athens: University of Georgia Press.

McNeil, Peter. 1993. "'Put Your Best Face Forward': The Impact of the Second World War on British Dress." *Journal of Design History* 6, no. 4: 283–99.

McQuillan, Holly. 2011. "Zero-Waste Design Practice." In *Shaping Sustainable Fashion: Changing the Way We Make and Use Clothes*, edited by Alison Gwilt and Timo Rissanen. London: Earthscan.

Meiling, Brittany. 2020."Home-Sewn Clothes Are Making a Comeback. But Is It Too Late for Dying Fabric Stores?" *The San Diego Union-Tribune*, January 21, 2020. Accessed April 13, 2021. https://www.dailyitem.com/business/home-sewn-clothes-making-a-quality-inspied-comeback/articled0767cb2-320e-5cf9-bfea-a5e4cf5ed532.html.

"Memorial to War Women Unveiled." *BBC News*, July 9, 2005. Accessed April 13, 2021. http://news.bbc.co.uk/2/hi/uknews/england/london/4667705.stm.

Mendes, Valerie, and Amy De La Haye. 1999. *20th Century Fashion*. London: Thames & Hudson.

Michel, Sonya. 1987. "American Women and the Discourse of the Democratic Family in World War II." In *Behind the Lines: Gender and the Two World Wars*, edited by Margaret Randolph Higonnet, 154–67. New Haven, CT and London: Yale University Press. Accessed April 14, 2021. https://www.jstor.org/stable/j.ctt1cc2m97

Michelson, Alan. 2021. *Kaiser Shipbuilding Company, Richmond Field Hospital, Richmond, CA*. Accessed April 13, 2021. http://pcad.lib.washington.edu/building/18029/.

Milbank, Caroline Rennolds 1985. *Couture: The Great Designers*. New York: Stewart, Tabori & Chang, Inc. Publishers.

Miller, Daniel. 2009. "Buying Time." In *Time, Consumption and Everyday Life: Practice, Materiality and Culture*, edited by Elizabeth Shove, Frank Trentmann and Richard Wilk, 157–69. Oxford, New York: Berg.

Milne, A.A. 1946. "Blue Eyes: Love You Only—Michael." *New York Times*, September 1, 1946.

Milward, Alan S. 1965. *The German Economy at War*. London: University of London, The Athlone Press.

"Miners' Children Face Starvation." 1931. *New York Times*, November 4, 1931.

Ministry of Information. 1943. "Make Do and Mend" (video). Great Britain, Imperial War Museum: NPB 13037. Accessed April 13, 2021. https://www.iwm.org.uk/collections/item/object/1060034062.

Mitchell, Allan. 2008. *Nazi Paris: The History of an Occupation 1940—1944*. New York and Oxford: Berghahn Books.

"More Wool, Less Cotton" 1943. *Washington Post*, June 16, 1943.

Morgan, Guy. 1948. *Red Roses Every Night: An Account of London Cinemas Under Fire*. London: Quality Press.

Mower, Jennifer M., and Elaine L. Pedersen. 2013. "Pretty and Patriotic: Women's Consumption of Apparel During World War II." *Dress: The Annual Journal of the Costume Society of America* 39, no. 1: 37–54.

Murphy, Robert. 2000. *British Cinema and the Second World War*. London and New York: Continuum.

Nakanishi, Don T. 2009. "Surviving Democracy's 'Mistake:' Japanese Americans & the Enduring Legacy of Executive Order 9066." *Amerasia Journal*, 35, no. 3, 52–84.

Nicol, Patricia. 2010. *Sucking Eggs: What Your Wartime Granny Could Teach You About Diet, Thrift and Going Green*. London: Vintage Books.

Norman, Jill. 2007. *Make Do and Mend: Keeping Family and Home Afloat on War Rations*. London: O'Mara Book Ltd.

Overy, Richard J. 1994. *War and Economy in the Third Reich*. Clarendon Press.

Palmieri, Jean E. 2020. "Brooks Brothers: No Longer 'Made in the USA'?" *Women's Wear Daily*, May 19, 2020.

Palmsköld, Anneli. 2015. "Reusing Textiles: On Material and Cultural Wear and Tear." *Culture Unbound: Journal of Current Cultural Research* 7, no. 1: 31-–43. Accessed April 14, 2021. https://cultureunbound.ep.liu.se/article/view/2148.

Panek, Tracey. 2014. *Throwback Thursday: Celebrating 80 Years of Women's Jeans*. https://www.levistrauss.com/2014/09/04/celebrating-80-years-of-womens-jeans/.

Parachute Wedding Dress. 2011. Washington DC: Smithsonian Museum, June 6, 2011. Accessed April 13, 2021. https://www.si.edu/newsdesk/snapshot/parachute-wedding-dress.

"Paris Fashions: First Report from the French Couture since 1940." 1944. *Vogue*, New York: Condé Nast Publications, October 15, 1944.

"Paris Ghost City, Repatriate Says: Kathleen Cannell Describes French Capital after Four Years of Occupation." 1944. *New York Times*, March 17, 1944.

Pass, Victoria. 2020. "Fashion in An Age of Pandemic: History Shows That Significant Shifts Tend to Happen in the Wake of Crisis." *BmoreArt*, (May 4). Accessed April 13, 2021. https://bmoreart.com/2020/05/fashion-in-an-age-of-pandemic.html.

Patnode, Stephan R. 2012. "'Keep It under Your Hat:' Safety Campaigns and Fashion in the World War II Factory." *The Journal of American Culture* 35 no. 3: 231–43.

Pegler, Westbrook. 1942. "Westbrook Pegler." *The Washington Post*, January 11, 1942.

Phillips, Charles F. 1945. "Some Observations on Rationing." *The Journal of Business of the University of Chicago* 18, no. 1 (January): 9–20. The University of Chicago Press. Accessed April 13, 2021. http://www.jstor.org/stable/2349729.

Phillips, Dave. 2019. "To Stand Out, the Army Picks a New Uniform with a World War II Look." *New York Times*, May 5, 2019.

Professor Pincushion. 2016. "How to Repair a Hole in a T-Shirt," YouTube Video, 5:25, March 29, 2016. Accessed April 13, 2021. https://www.youtube.com/watch?v=vvDdzD5pF3M.

Pine, William H. 1944. "A Letter from Bataan," United States: U.S. Office of War Information. YouTube Video, 14:12, September 12, 2009. Accessed April 13, 2021. https://www.youtube.com/watch?v=VbVCuZQ9F9g.

"Plan to Divert All Nylon to Parachutes Reported." 1940. *New York Times*, June 5, 1940.

Pochna, M. 1996. *Christian Dior: The Man Who Made the World Look New*. New York: Arcade Publishing.

Probert, Christine. 1984. *Brides in Vogue Since 1910*. New York: Abbeville Press.

Pusca, Anca. 2009. "'Born to Shop': Malls, Dream-Worlds and Capitalism." *Journal of International Relations and Development* 12, no. 4 (December): 370–77. Accessed August 18, 2021. https://research.gold.ac.uk/id/eprint/3440/1/PuscaJIRDas_published.pdf.

"Putting on the Feed Bag." 1954. *Chicago Daily Tribune,* January 10, 1954.

Rahn, Suzanne. 1998. *The Wizard of Oz: Shaping an Imaginary World*. New York: Twayne Publishers.

Rantisi, Norma M. 2004. "The Ascendance of New York Fashion." *International Journal of Urban and Regional Research* 28, no. 1 (February 4, 2004): 86–106.

"Rationing Made Easy: Why Shoe Rationing?" 1943. *The Washington Post*, February 7, 1943.

Reddaway, W. Brian. 1951. "Rationing." In *Lessons of the British War Economy*, edited by Daniel Norman Chester. Cambridge University Press.

Reed, Stephen B. 2014. "One Hundred Years of Price Change: The Consumer Price Index and the American Inflation Experience." *Monthly Labor Review* 137, (April): 1.

Reich, Robert B. 2011. "The Limping Middle Class." *New York Times*, September 4, 2011.

"Remembering Our Veterans." 2014. *History San José*. Accessed December 18, 2019. http://historysanjose.org/wp/remembering-our-veterans/.

Reston, Sally. 1943. "British Boys Clad by Clothing Swap." *New York Times*, September 21, 1943.

Reynolds, Helen. 1999. "Your Clothes Are Materials of War: The British Government Promotion of Home Sewing During the Second World War." In *The Culture of Sewing: Gender, Consumption and Home Dressmaking*, edited by Barbara Burman, 327–39. New York City: Berg.

Richards, Jeffrey. 1987. "Wartime British Cinema Audiences and the Class System: The Case of 'Ships with Wings' (1941)." *Historical Journal of Film, Radio and Television* 7, no. 2: 129–41.

Rivoli, Pietra. 2009. *The Travels of a T-Shirt in the Global Economy*. Hoboken, NJ: John Wiley & Sons Inc.

Robb, Linsey. 2017. "'Fighting in Their Ways'? The Civilian Man in British Culture, 1939–1945." In *Home Fronts: Britain and the Empire at War, 1939–45*, edited by Mark J. Crowley and Sandra Trudgen Dawson, 146–63. Woodbridge, UK: The Boydell Press.

Roberts, Helene E. 1977. "The Exquisite Slave: The Role of Clothes in the Making of the Victorian Woman." *Signs: Journal of Women in Culture and Society* 2, no. 3: 554–69. Accessed April 14, 2021. http://www.jstor.org/stable/3173265.

Roberts, Sam. 2015. "Mary Keefe, 92, Model for Rockwell's 'Rosie the Riveter." *New York Times*, April 25, 2015.

Rockwell, Norman. 1943. "Rosie the Riveter." *Saturday Evening Post*, Philadelphia, PA: G. Graham (Cover), May 29, 1943.

Roodhouse, Mark. 2013. *Black Market Britain, 1939–1955*. Oxford: Oxford University Press.

Rostow, Walt Whitman. 1942. "Price Control and Rationing: Some Aspects of Price Control and Rationing." *American Economic Review 32, no. 3,* Part 1 (September): 486–500.

Rothermund, Dietmar. 1996. *The Global Impact of the Great Depression, 1929–1939*. London and New York: Routledge.

Ruffner, Kevin Conley. 2002. "You Are Never Going to Be Able to Run an Intelligence Unit: SSU Confronts the Black Market in Berlin." *Journal of Intelligence History* 2, no. 2: 1–20. Accessed April 13, 2021. https://doi.org/10.1080/16161262.2002.10555067.

Rupp, Leila J. 1978. *Mobilizing Women for War: German and American Propaganda 1939–1945*. Princeton, NJ: Princeton University Press.

"Rush for Clothing Alarms Retailers: Women's 'Buying Spree' in Face of Assurances by OPA Is Seen as 'Type of Insanity.'" 1943. *New York Times*, February 25, 1943.

Sage, Robert. 1945a. "Rioting Spreads as Ex-Captives March in Paris: 400 Crash Thru Police Lines; Unrest Grows." *Chicago Daily Tribune*, May 20, 1945.

Sage, Robert. 1945b. "Seize All Clothing in Paris Stores." *Chicago Daily Tribune*, June 1, 1945.

"Sales Begin Today of Nylon Hosiery." 1940. *New York Times*, May 15, 1940.

Sawyer, Corinne Holt. 1987. "Men in Skirts and Women in Trousers, from Achilles to Victoria Grant: One Explanation of a Comedic Paradox." *Journal of Popular Culture* 21, no. 2 (September 1): 1–18.

"*Searching for the Girl Who Wore This Dress Made out of a Nazi Banner after WWII Ended.*" 2016. National Post, (Toronto, ON). November 7, 2016. Accessed April 13, 2021. https://nationalpost.com/news/world/searching-for-the-girl-who-wore-this-dress-made-out-of-a-nazi-banner-after-wwii-ended.

"Scarcity to Continue Well into Next Year." 1945. *New York Times*, December 9, 1945.

Schipani, Sam. 2020. "If You Run out of Toilet Paper, Here's What You Can Use Instead." *Bangor Daily News*, March 21, 2020. Accessed April 13, 2021. https://bangordailynews.com/2020/03/17/health/if-you-run-out-of-toilet-paper-heres-what-you-can-use-instead/.

Schmidt, Karl M. 1960. *Henry A. Wallace: Quixotic Crusade 1948*. New York: Syracuse University Press.

Schoenstein, Vincent. 2019a. *End of the War in Europe*. Unpublished.

Schoenstein, Vincent. 2019b. *Moira's Recycled Wedding Gown*. Unpublished.

Selcer, Richard F. 2010. "From Tara to Oz and Home Again: Home Sweet Movies." *Journal of Popular Film and Television* 18, no. 2 (July 14): 52–63. Accessed April 13, 2021. https://doi.org/10.1080/01956051.1990.9943655.

"Sewing with Cotton Bags." 1935. *The Textile Bag Manufacturers Association*, Chicago, IL.

Seyferth, Mimi. 2014. "Andriani Chalkiadakis and Her Parachute Wedding Dress." *Piecework*, (January-February).

Shalett, Sidney M. 1943. "Shoe Ration Put at 3 Pairs a Year," *New York Times*, February 8, 1943.

"Sheean Sees Jap Invasion: Attack on West Coast Predicted If Foe Gains Mastery of East Asia." 1942. *Los Angeles Times*, February 17, 1942.

Sheridan, Dorothy. 1991. *The Mass-Observation Diaries: An Introduction*. Brighton: Mass-Observation Archive and the Centre for Continuing Education, University of Sussex.

Shirer, William L. 1960. *The Rise and Fall of the Third Reich: A History of Nazi Germany*. New York: Simon and Schuster.

Shlaim, Avi. 1974. "Prelude to Downfall: The British Offer of Union to France, June 1940." *Journal of Contemporary History* 9, no. 3 (July 1): 27–63.

Shukert, Elfrieda Berthiaume, and Barbara Smith Scibetta. 1988. *War Brides of World War II*. Novato, CA: Presidio Press.

"Silk Boycott Is Urged: The Nation Would End Invasion of China by Injuring Japan." 1937. *New York Times*, September 30, 1937.

Sims, Shari. 2015. "White." In *Fashion Photography Archive*. London: Bloomsbury.

Sladen, Christopher. 1995. *The Conscription of Fashion: Utility Cloth, Clothing, and Footwear, 1941–1952*. Aldershot, UK; Brookfield, VT: Scolar Press; Ashgate Pub. Co.

Smith, Meredith. 2010. "The Civilian Experience in German Occupied France, 1940–1944." *History Honors Papers* 6. Accessed April 14, 2021. https://digitalcommons.conncoll.edu/histhp/6.

Smithies, Edward. 1982. *Crime in Wartime: A Social History of Crime in World War II*. London: George Allen & Unwin.

"So It Is up to Us Chaps." 1942. *Women and Home*. London, October 1942.

Solmssen, Kurt. 1943. "Secrets of the Black Market." *New York Times*, April 11, 1943.

Soskin, Betty Reid. 2018. *Sign My Name to Freedom: A Memoir of a Pioneering Life*, edited by J. Douglas Allen-Taylor. Carlsbad, CA: Hay House.

Steele, Valerie. 1998. *Paris Fashion: A Cultural History*. Oxford, UK and New York: Berg.

Steele, Valerie. 2001. *The Corset: A Cultural History*. New Haven, CT and London: Yale University Press.

Stevens, Susan. 2016. "Golden Age of Sewing." *Pasadena Museum of History*, March 26, 2016. Accessed April 14, 2021. https://pasadenahistory.org/exhibitions/golden-age-sewing/.

Stoller, Debbie. 2003. *Stitch'n Bitch: The Knitter's Handbook*. New York: Workman Publishing.

Strasser, Susan. 1999. *Waste and Want: A Social History of Trash*. New York: Metropolitan Books.

Street, Sarah. 1997. *British National Cinema*. National Cinema Series. London and New York: Routledge.

"Students Burn Clothes to Spur Silk Boycott" 1938. *Life*, January 10, 1938.

Summers, Julie. 2016. *Fashion on the Ration: Style in the Second World War*. London: Profile Books.

Summers, Julie. 2020. *Dressed for War: The Story of Vogue Editor Audrey Withers, from the Blitz to the Swinging Sixties*. London and New York: Simon & Schuster UK.

Talon Corporation. 1942. "Today, You've Got to Look Ahead When You Buy a Corset!" *Good Housekeeping*. New York, Hearst Magazines, April, 1942.

Taplin, Ian M. 1997. "Struggling to Compete: Post-War Changes in the US Clothing Industry." *Textile History* 28, no. 1: 90–104. Accessed April 14, 2021. https://doi.org/10.1179/004049697793711012.

Tarbell, Ida M. 1938. "The Old Sewing Room." *The North America Review* 245, no. 1 (Spring): 154–58. Accessed April 14, 2021. http://www.jstor.org/stable/25114967.

Taylor, Frederick. 2013. *The Downfall of Money: Germany's Hyperinflation and the Destruction of the Middle Class*. New York: Bloomsbury Press.

Taylor, Lou. 2002. *The Study of Dress History*. Manchester UK: Manchester University Press.

Taylor, Lynne. 1997. "The Black Market in Occupied Northern France, 1940–4." *Contemporary European History* 6, no. 2 (July): 153–76. Accessed April 14, 2021. http://www.jstor.org/stable/20081623.

Temin, Peter. 1989. *Lessons from the Great Depression: The Lionel Robbins Lectures for 1989*. Cambridge, MA: MIT Press.

The Board of Trade. 1941. "Patriotic Patches." *Woman and Home & Good Needlework Magazine*. London: Amalgamated Press, December.

The Editors of Encyclopedia Britannica. 2020. "Vulcanization: Rubber Manufacturing." *Encyclopedia Britannica*, June 8, 2020. Accessed April 14, 2021. https://www.britannica.com/technology/vulcanization.

"The History of Rubber." n.d. World War II and Rubber. Accessed December 17, 2019. https://historyofrubber.weebly.com/wwii.html.

"The Men at Good Housekeeping Say: If You Must Wear Slacks." 1942. *Good Housekeeping*, New York, Hearst Magazines, April 1942.

Thompson, Lisa S. 2018. "Nelly Don: An Educational Leader." Doctor of Education, Lindenwood University, ProQuest Dissertations Publishing.

Tobin, Shelley, Sarah Pepper, and Margaret Willes. 2003. *Marriage À La Mode: Three Centuries of Wedding Dresses*. The National Trust.

Tokatli, Nebahat. 2008. "Global Sourcing: Insights from the Global Clothing Industry—The Case of Zara, a Fast Fashion Retailer." *Journal of Economic Geography* 8, no. 1 (January): 21–38. Accessed April 14, 2021. https://doi.org/10.1093/jeg/lbm035.

Toles, Edward B. 1944. "Toles Sees Chicagoans Blast Nazis in Brittany." *The Chicago Defender (National Edition)*, September 2, 1944.

Toles, Edward B. 1945. "Cost of Living (Black Market): $300 Month." *The Chicago Defender (National Edition)*, October 6, 1945.

Turner, Kathleen J. 1977. "Comic Strips: A Rhetorical Perspective." *Communication Studies* 28, no. 1: 24–35. Accessed April 14, 2021. https://doi.org/10.1080/10510977709367916.

Turner, Nan. 2019. "Costumes Go to War: British Propaganda Films Influence Women to Do Their Part." *Dress: The Journal of the Costume Society of America* 45, no. 2: 153–71. Accessed April 14, 2021. https://doi.org/10.1080/03612112.2018.1551293.

Twigger Holroyd, Amy. 2021. *Amy Twigger Holyroyd*. Accessed March 27, 2021. https://amytwiggerholroyd.com/.

Ukai, Nancy. 2021. "Michiko and Ki's Wedding Photos: The Mystery Photographer." *50 Object Stories: The American Japanese Incarceration*. Accessed April 13, 2021. https://50objects.org/object/michiko-and-kis-wedding-photo/.

WW2 USO Preservation Association: Living History Group. Accessed April 14, 2021. http://www.ww2uso.org/links.html#SEWING.

Veillon, Dominique. 2002. *Fashion Under the Occupation*. Translated by Miriam Kochan. Oxford New York: Berg.

Vickers, Emma, and Emma Jackson. 2017. "Sanctuary or Sissy? Female Impersonation as Entertainment in the British Armed Forces, 1939–1945." In *Gender and the Second World War: Lessons of War*, 40–49, edited by Corinna Peniston-Bird and Emma Vickers. London, UK: MacMillan Education.

"*Vogue* Designs for Dressmaking: Dressmaker Dresses." 1947a. *Vogue*, New York: Condé Nast Publishers, September 15, 1947.

"*Vogue* Designs for Dressmaking: Spring Sewing." 1947b. *Vogue*, New York: Condé Nast Publishers, February 15, 1947.

von Studnitz, Hans-George. 1963. *While Berlin Burns,* translated by R. H. Stevens. London: Weidenfeld and Nicolson.

Wadsworth, Henry Ewart. 1949-50. "Utility Cloth and Clothing Scheme." *The Review of Economic Studies* 16, no. 2: 82–101.

Wagner, Carolyn. 2015. "Material Memories: The Parachute Wedding Gowns of American Brides, 1945–1949". PhD. dissertation, University of Cincinnati. Accessed April 14, 2021. http://rave.ohiolink.edu/etdc/view?acc_num=ucin1428065407.

Waldinger, Roger D. 1986. *Through the Eye of the Needle: Immigrants and Enterprise in New York's Garment Trades*. New York and London: New York University Press.

Walford, Jonathon. 2008. *Forties Fashion: From Siren Suits to the New Look*. New York City: Thames & Hudson.

"Warns Wool Blending Only Way to Forestall Rationing of Clothing." 1942. *Wall Street Journal*, June 11, 1942.

Warren, Elizabeth, and Amelia Warren Tyagi. 2004. *The Two Income Trap: Why Middle-Class Mothers and Fathers Are Going Broke*. New York: Basic Books.

"Wasteful Long Skirts." 1947. *The Times* (London), September 26, 1947.

Weiner, Zoe. 2020. "Wonder What to Do with Old T-Shirts? Here Are 15 Things Beyond Turning Them into Rags." *Sustainable Fashion*, January 20, 2020. Accessed April 14, 2021. https://www.wellandgood.com/good-looks/what-to-do-with-old-t-shirts/.

"What Suits the Sirens Wore." 1939. *The Times* (London), October 10, 1939.

Wicker, Alden. 2016. *Fast Fashion Is Creating an Environmental Crisis*. NYC: Newsweek, September 1, 2016. Accessed April 14, 2021. https://www.newsweek.com/2016/09/09/old-clothes-fashion-waste-crisis-494824.html.

Wilkerson, Isabel. 2010. *The Warmth of Other Suns*. New York City: Random House.

Wilson, Elizabeth, and Lou Taylor. 1989. *Through the Looking Glass: A History of Dress from 1860 to the Present Day*. London, UK: BBC Books.

Wilson, Eric. 2002. "Teal Traina, SA Legend, Dies at 85." *WWD.com*, New York City, April 15, 2002. Accessed April 15, 2021. https://wwd.com/fashion-news/fashion-features/article-1168823/.

Withers, Audrey. 1944. "Fashion: Fashion in England." *Vogue*, New York: Condé Nast Publishing, October 1, 1944.

"Women Everywhere Taking to Slacks." 2021. *YesterYear Once More: Life as it was Reported Back Then*, May 3, 2012. Accessed April 15, 2021. https://yesteryearsnews.wordpress.com/2012/05/03/women-everywhere-taking-to-slacks/.

"Women Lose Pockets and Frills to Save Fabrics." 1942. *Life,* April 20, 1942.

"Women Stampede for Stockings as Result of Government Silk Ban: Extra Salesgirls and Guards Called to Handle Crowds in Big Stores." 1941. *New York Times*, August 5, 1941.

Wood, Maggie. 1989. *We Wore What We'd Got.* Warwick: Warwickshire Books.

Woods, Judith. 2020. "Make Do and Mend? Children Don't Know What That Even Means." *The Telegraph*, February 24, 2020. Accessed April 15, 2021. https://www.telegraph.co.uk/news/2020/02/24/make-do-mend-children-dont-know-even-means/.

Woolston, Maxine Y. 1941. *The Structure of the Nazi Economy*. New York: Russell & Russell.

Woolton, Frederick James Marquis. 1959. *The Memoirs of the Rt. Hon. The Earl of Woolton.* London: Cassell.

Worth, Rachel. "Window-Shopping: Rachel Worth Visits the John Lewis Archives." *Selvedge: The Fabric of Our Life.* London: Selvedge Ltd, no. 79 Luna, November 1, 27.

Wrap. 2012. *Valuing Our Clothes: The True Cost of How We Design, Use and Dispose of Clothing in the UK.* Accessed August 18, 2021. https://www.wrap.org.uk/sustainable-textiles/valuing-our-clothes%20. https://www.fairact.org/wp-content/uploads/Wrap_Valuing_our_clothes_30pourcentsVoC_FINAL_online_2012_07_11.pdf

WWII Escape Maps. Accessed December 17, 2019. http://www.escape-maps.com/.

Wynn, Neil A. 1995. "War and Racial Progress: The African American Experience During World War II." *Peace & Change* 20, no. 3 (July): 348–63. Accessed April 15, 2021. https://doi.org/10.1111/j.1468-0130.1995.tb00238.x.

Zweiniger-Bargielowska, Ina. 2000. *Austerity in Britain: Rationing, Controls, and Consumption, 1939–1955*. Oxford, UK: Oxford University Press.

Index

1

1270th Engineer Combat Battalion ix, 2, 81
161th Field Artillery Band 2
489th Bomb Group Museum, Halesworth, UK 142

A

A. A. Milne
  Winnie the Pooh 176
Adlington, Lucy 70
Airborne and Special Operations Museum, Fayetteville, NC, USA 142
Ambrose, Stephen 141
Amies, Hardy 27, 28
apparel workers 18, 30, 180
Armistice, The 29, 155, 194
army surplus 104, 210
artificial silk 51, 52, 183
  See also rayon
Aubrac, Lucie 30
Auxiliary Territorial Service (ATS) 71, 160, 162, 165, 166–67

B

baby boomer generation 198
balaclava 117
  See also knitting
Balcon, Sir Michael Elias 161
bartering 14, 91, 173, 179, 188, 191
  city dwellers 178
  clothing 176
  kimonos 188
Baum, Frank L. 156–58
  See also movies
  Maud 156
Beebe, Joy (UK) 92, 115, 117, 184, 211–12
  Snapshots of a War Bride's Life 71, 160
Bemis Bag Company 121, 123
black market 20, 32, 103, 105, 173
  blackout cloth 182
  coupons 184
  France 180–82
  fueled by scarcity 179
  Germany 182, 189
  Japan 187–88
  illegal 14, 178
  military 189–90
  Philippines 174, 188–89
  punishment 182, 184, 191
  scare buying 185
  stockings 53, 183
  United Kingdom 179, 182–84
  United States 180, 182, 185–86
  unpatriotic 179
Blumenthal Lazan, Marion 11
Board of Trade 25–26, 29, 109, 113, 177, 184
Brady, Lydia (DE) 20, 31, 96–97, 105, 179, 196, 199, 209
Bravo, Tony 212, 214
Brewer Zurovcik, Rae (UK) 160, 165–67

Brieda, Lois 126
British Land Girls 72
Brooks Brothers 198
Brown, Sass 202
Buelow Alm, May (USA) 72, 74

C

California Museum, Sacramento, CA, USA 118
Cannell, Kathleen, dance and fashion correspondent 181
Cassell's Household Guide 109
Cenotaph, The 5
chilblains 31, 90
children's clothing,
  clothing exchange 177
  feed sacks 121, 123, 126
  hand-me-down 109–10, 113
Cholowski, Thom 1–2
Chouinard Art School 71
Churchill, Winston 42, 81
civvies 8, 111
Cline, Elizabeth L. 193, 198, 201
Coile, Ellen Miller (UK) 7, 117, 149, 151, 212
Coile, Jennifer 117, 151
comforts, knit 117
  See also knitting
concentration camp 7, 11, 30, 118, 130
  Bergen-Belsen 11
  Minidoka War Relocation Center 118
  Topaz War Relocation Center 138
crafting 14, 202–04, 209
Cramer, Jo 200

D

darning 57, 199
  egg, 199
D-Day 5, 73
Dietrich, Marlene 80–81
Dior, Christian 37, 195–97, 215
  New Look 48, 87, 195–96, 215–16
  tailleur bar 215
Do-It-Yourself (DIY) 14, 171
domestic arts 193–94, 197, 202–03
Dorothy of Oz 154, 158, 171
  See also movies
  gingham dress 154–55, 158–59, 171
  ruby slippers 159
Doyle Keefe, Mary
  model for Rosie the Riveter 79–80
dressmaker 8, 10, 37, 93, 100, 103–04, 108, 146, 197
Dust Bowl 154, 156, 157
  refugees 157

E

Earhart, Amelia, 80
Eastlake family (UK) 3, 4, 15, 101, 214
  Kath 3–5, 8, 12, 81–2, 100–01, 111, 177
  Sarah 6, 111, 196
  Sophie 3, 5, 81–3, 100–01, 111, 177
Edelkoort, Li 215
Edillo, Antonina B. (PH) 40, 140
Emporia, Kansas 51, 63, 88–89, 91, 122
Eric, French fashion illustrator 83
escape maps 60–61
Evans, Redd 76–77, 82

F

facemask 211–12, 214
fashion 2, 5, 27, 28, 32, 35–38, 44, 80, 130, 214–16
  1920s flapper 64
  comfort 45
  eco-fashion 209
  fashion show 32, 50, 65, 80
  fashion trends 44, 48, 113, 117, 130–31, 212, 214
  fast fashion 14, 194, 200–02, 209

French fashion 32–33, 80, 130, 195–96
frozen during WWII 36–37, 207
gendered 87
Hollywood influence 80, 131
parade 93–94, 163
post-war 48, 86, 195
trousers for women 65
United Kingdom 26–28, 38
United States 37–38
feed sacks 13, 121–27
See also sewing
aprons made from 121
broom skirt 125
clothing made from 121–22
dish towels 125
floral printed 122, 124, 126
International Sewing Bag Queen 125
patriotic 124
post-war 125
rick rack trim 124–25
RIT dye 123
stigma 121–23
underwear made from 121, 123
feminist 48, 197, 202
France 9, 17, 20–21, 29–33, 55, 65, 95, 115, 179–81
development of rayon 51
couture ration cards 32
fashion 32–3, 80, 130, 195–96
Haute Couture 32–3, 196
militarization of women 92
rationing 29, 31
sewing classes 94
System D 30–31
Friedman, Vanessa 214

G

Gainsborough Pictures 161–62, 164
Garbo, Greta 79
garment longevity 207–08
gender 2, 12, 63–90, 162
appropriate shoes 84
binary definition 65
defined by dress 64, 71, 87, 165
men dressed in women's clothing 85–86
norms 65
women in men's clothing 83–85
women's military service 71–3, 163–64, 170
General Limitation Order L-85 34–40
Germany 1, 7, 11, 20–25, 29–33, 40, 97, 177, 179–80
concentration camps 30
economic hyperinflation 155, 176
foreign workers 21
implemented rationing 17–23, 30
moving haute couture to Germany 32, 130
siphoned French production 29
stock market 155
Goebbels, Joseph 21
gray market 177–78
marche amical 178
Great Depression 16, 22, 64, 91, 113, 122–26, 137, 154–61, 186, 209, 216
Greer, Betsy, craftivism · 203

H

Habit, Franklin 199–200
handcrafts 91–119, 196, 202–04, 207, 211
hand-me-down 1, 8, 17, 134, 154
Hargrove, Charles 29
Harris, Sylvia (UK) 142
Haute Couture 32–33, 196
Hepburn, Katherine 80
Hitler Youth 11
Hitler, Adolf 20–23, 32–33, 79, 112, 155, 171

hoarding 14, 19, 173–76, 188, 211
- increased scarcity 35, 185
- caused by rumors of shortages 173, 179, 212
- considered evil 163, 174–76, 191

Hobson, Fern 179
Hodgson, Grace 22
Hollywood 13, 31, 80–81, 131, 146, 154–57, 161, 204
Hollywood Costume exhibit 154–55
Home Guard 162, 165
home sewing 10, 91, 93, 123–26, 146–47, 197, 201
homemaker 13, 64, 92, 109, 193, 203
Howard, Leslie 165, 169

I

interviews (pseudonyms)
- Adelaide (NL) 31, 85, 104, 109, 148, 178, 211
- Adina (AT) 10, 67, 178
- Alice (EE) 176
- Carla (IT) 10, 102–03, 108
- Doreen (UK) 26, 117
- Doris (USA) 54, 70–71, 148–49
- Eileen (USA) 12
- Elizabeth (UK) 8, 193
- Emma (NZ) 1, 71, 209
- Gennie (USA) 68–69, 71
- Gwen (USA) 68
- Hazel (AU) 67
- Ilene (USA) 51, 53, 55, 69–70, 109, 110
- Jean (UK) 51, 53, 105, 109–10, 146–47, 159–60, 183–84
- Jeanne (FR) 31, 55, 92, 104, 115, 210
- Joan (AU) 134
- Keiko (JP) 188
- Laney (USA) 68, 125–26
- Leslie (USA) 89
- Lisbeth (UK) 193
- Lucy (UK) 86, 110, 160
- Lynn (UK) 23, 55, 132–33
- Maier, Ingrid (DE) 1–2, 98, 177
- Maier, Valerie (DE) 1, 98
- Margaret (UK) 8
- Margo (USA) 187
- Margot (DE) 68
- Marianne (USA) 68–69, 71
- Nancy (USA) 68
- Natasha (FR) 9–10, 152
- Nobue (JP) 188
- Ruby (AU) 193
- Vera (UK) 104, 154, 179
- Vivian (USA) 68

Imperial War Museum, London, UK 94, 96, 115, 141, 208
Italy 7, 10–11, 102
- development of rayon 51

J

Japan 7, 17, 33, 40, 43, 48–50, 61, 67, 87, 108, 176, 187–88
- commerce with USA 50
- economic hyperinflation 176
- embargo of natural rubber 12
- enemy attack 40
- implemented rationing 17
- natural rubber production 12, 43
- Pearl Harbor 33, 42–43
- postwar 198
- silk exports 48–50, 61
- victory over Japan 87

John Lewis, department store 199

K

Kanemoto, Marian 118
Kibbey, Jason, Sustainable Apparel Coalition 202
Killerton, National Trust, Exeter, UK 134–35

knitting 13, 24, 52, 91–92, 114–19, 147, 174, 193, 208, 212
patriotic knitting 116, 161
relief knitting 114
revival of interest 202, 204
sea boot stockings 117
string used for knitting 119
unraveling sweaters 115
vintage patterns 204–08
washcloths, knitted 119

L
Ladies Home Journal (magazine) 64
Lange, Dorothea 137–38, 158
Last, Nella 81, 96, 194
Law, Dan 101
Stanley, Norman and Carol Law 101
lend-lease 33
Levi Strauss 70
Lady Levi's® jeans 70
Lindley, Edna Hannell (AU) 144–45
lisle 50–51, 93
Loeb, John Jacob 76–77, 82

M
Mahlendorf, Ursula 11, 82
Make Do and Mend 14, 94–96, 109, 193–210
sewing classes 94–95
Marcus, Stanley 35, 38
Marion Jr., George 55–56
Maritime Museum of Crete, GR 147
marriage bar 87
Mass Observation Project 81, 96
Maynard, Mary McKay 118–19, 188–89
mending 13–14, 17, 47, 60, 91, 100, 109–112, 119, 154, 193, 197, 199–201, 204, 212, 215
renewed interest 206–07, 209
socks 193, 199
T-shirt 201, 204, 207
visible 206
military 42–62
apparel workers moved to military production 18, 93
pinks and greens 105
priority over civilian production 12, 15, 16, 18, 20, 23, 25, 35, 61, 91, 96, 108, 115
repurposing uniform 20, 105
textiles, need for 42–43, 45, 50–51, 53–54, 60, 61, 115, 124, 141
women in uniform 71–74, 133, 161, 163, 165–70
Miller, Bob J. 4, 6
Miller, J. Howard
Rosie the Riveter 78
Mindanao Mother Lode Gold Mine 188
Minidoka National Historic Site 118
See also concentration camps
Molyneux, Edward 27, 65, 78, 83, 89
Monument to the Women of World War II 165–66
mores, social 53
movies 114, 154–72
A Letter from Bataan 174
attendance during WWII 159–60
escape from stress of war 159–60
Hollywood fashion influence 131
Millions Like Us 155, 161–65, 171
morale building 159–60, 171, 212
propaganda films 14, 94, 160–62, 171, 174
The Gentle Sex 155, 161, 165–71
The Plow that Broke the Plains 157
The Third Man 187
The Wizard of Oz 154–57, 171
mufti 8

N
Nadoolman Landis, Deborah 155
National Cotton Council 91, 123, 125

National Museum of the U.S. Navy, Washington DC, USA 37
National WWII Museum, New Orleans, USA 141
needle skills 196–97
negative rationing 21
  See also rationing
New Look 37, 48, 87, 195–97, 215–16
  See also Dior, Christian
non-rationed fabrics 100–04
  black-out fabric 100
  drapes 104
  fabric scraps 100
  remnants 100
  tablecloth 100
Normandy Veteran's Association 5
nylon 18, 33, 43, 53–61, 101, 130, 140, 143, 189, 190
  mending 60, 110
  parachutes 18, 53, 61, 101, 130, 140–42
  stockings 43, 52–56, 58, 61, 110, 143, 189, 190, 199

O
overalls 65, 68, 71, 76, 78–79, 87, 165, 195

P
pandemic 14, 211, 215–16
  fashion influence 212, 214–15
Panek, Tracy 70–71
paper 97–99, 113, 123–24, 211–12
  bags 124, 126
  salvaged 203
  shortages 97–99, 211–12
  towels 201, 209
  wedding dress 148
parachute 18, 48, 51, 53–54, 61, 100–04, 133, 140–41
  Baldwin, New York parachute factory 102
  military use 18, 51, 53, 61
  repurposed for clothing 48, 100–04, 133, 140–42, 147, 212
Pass, Victoria 214
patch pockets 38
patches 7, 13, 17, 91, 108, 112–14, 154, 157, 196, 206–07
  patriotic badge of honor 17, 91, 113
  sign of poverty 113
Pearce, Peggy 4, 6
Pearl Harbor 33, 42–43, 118, 137, 188
Pegler, Westbrook 21
Pence Berry, Dorothy E. (AU) 138
Philippines 40, 67, 118, 139–40, 188–89
  bakya 139
Piguet, Robert 83
Post Exchange (PX) 68, 105, 144, 189, 190
Princess Margaret Rose of York 115

Q
Queen Elizabeth 114–15, 165
Queen Victoria, wedding 131

R
rags 13, 91, 112–14, 182, 196, 201, 204, 209
  ragman 113
rationing 6, 8, 11–40, 45, 92–93, 105, 128, 139, 144, 147–49, 152, 155, 161–65, 173–74, 177–86, 196, 208–09
  children's clothing 177
  clothing 6, 18–20, 23–35, 165, 173, 185, 196
  coupons 13–14, 18–19, 22, 25, 27, 29, 35, 94, 100, 104, 119, 128, 133–35, 149, 164–65, 173, 176–79, 182–85, 187
  definition 17
  food 19, 23
  patriotic duty 17
  shoes 18, 25, 31, 34–35, 174, 177, 179, 187
  social class 17, 19

rayon 35, 43, 51–52, 56–59, 61, 113, 139, 148, 179, 183, 190
origin of name 51
stockings 51–52, 57–58, 183
Reid Soskin, Betty 135–36
repurposing 13–15, 17, 92, 104, 119, 126, 130, 138–42, 193, 203–04, 211
army blanket 103–04, 210
bed sheets 13, 20, 102, 105
butter muslin (mesh) 100
carpet 100
Chesterfield topcoat 106
curtains 13, 103, 128, 130, 211
fabric scraps 91, 100, 177, 188
home furnishing fabric 100
man's clothing 104–07
mosquito net 13, 130, 139
parachutes 48, 100–04, 130, 133, 140–42, 147
tablecloth 100, 130
Reston, Sally 177, 191
RIT dye 123
Rockwell, Norman 78–80
Roosevelt, Eleanor 115
Roosevelt, Franklin Delano 55, 118, 137
Rosie the Riveter 76–80, 82, 136, 211
Rosie the Riveter World War II Home Front National Historical Park 136
rubber 12, 18, 31, 33, 42, 43–45, 48, 61, 159
bands 159
boots and shoes 18, 31, 33–35, 85
elastic 8, 12, 15, 48, 211–12
girdles 43–48
rationing 33–34, 45
Ruddick, Leila (USA) 51, 91, 122

S
Schoenstein, Vincent (USA) 111, 143
Sekules, Kate 207
sewing 10, 12–14, 25, 67, 91–114
patterns 98, 197, 203
remnants 100, 155
shoddy 113
shoes 8–9, 21, 23, 30–35, 38, 83, 108, 139, 158–59, 165–66, 173–74, 182, 187
bakya 139
imported 9
men's 83–85
military 18, 20, 165–66
rationing 33–35, 38, 173–74, 187
repair 193
ruby slippers, *Wizard of Oz* 158–59
saddle shoes 87
scarcity 8, 23, 30, 182
wedding 139, 144, 149
whale skin 108
wooden 30–32, 34, 139, 181
work 33, 35
silk 13, 18, 29, 33–35, 42, 48–52, 60–61, 100–03, 110, 130–33, 145, 181
See also parachutes *and* stockings
kimonos 188
parachutes 18, 48, 61, 100–03, 130, 133, 140–41
powder bags 49, 61
rationing 33
silk stockings 49–53, 110, 133, 190, 206
scarcity 29, 33–35, 49–51, 53
wedding dresses 13, 60, 130–31, 133, 137, 140, 145
siren suit 81–84, 214
slacks 12, 51, 63–89, 165–179
appropriateness for women 66–67
comfortable 72
factory work 76–80, 165
farm wear 53, 69
gender 63–89
Hollywood movie star influence 80–81, 165
men's, opinion 65–66, 72

slacks (*Continued*)
- military, worn by women serving in 51, 65, 71–74, 169–70
- school wear 68, 71
- social class 171
- teenagers 87–89

Sleigh, Rosemond Rowe x
Smithsonian Museum of American History, Washington DC, USA 82, 105, 141
Snow, Carmel 195
Sparkle, Betty 204–06
sports 53, 64
- bicycling 64
- tennis 64

Squitieri, Kathryn, fashion historian 108
Stewart, Francesca Sorvillo (IT) 128
stockings 24, 43, 48–62
- *See also* nylo*n and* silk
- latch tool 110, 206
- mending runs 62, 110

Stoller, Debbie, *Stitch'n Bitch, The Knitter's Handbook* 202–04
System D, débrouille 30–32

T

Taylor, Lou, fashion historian 92, 129
Tangmere Military Aviation Museum, Chichester, West Sussex, UK 60–61
teenager 35, 89, 100, 102, 109, 113, 187
textile waste 201
thread, shortage 25, 30, 112
Tillie the Toiler 74–76
Toles, Edward 181
Traina-Norell 67
Turner, Joseph Earl 2, 3, 86
twice-turned 106–09
Twigger Holroyd, Amy 207–08

U

Uchida, George and Michiko 137–38
underwear 8, 12, 21, 26, 48, 73, 103–04, 121–23, 164, 212
- elastic shortages 8, 12, 15
- homemade 12, 48, 121, 212
- made from feed sacks 121–23
- made from parachutes 48, 93, 103–04, 212
- military 21, 35, 73, 113
- passion killers 167
- shortages 8, 12
- social class 164

United Kingdom 7–9, 23–29, 42, 182–85
- development of rayon 51
- domestic science class 93
- escape map wedding dress 61
- Incorporated Society of London Fashion Designers 27–29
- lend-lease 33
- rationing 17, 23–29, 38
- silk boycott 51
- Utility System 26–29
- women in military service 71–73
- Women's Voluntary Service 194

United States 11–12, 33–40, 147, 148, 185–87, 197–98
- employment of women 45
- entered WWII 50
- Executive Order 9066 118–19, 137
- isolationist 42
- military textile demand 43
- nylon, development of 53–56
- Pearl Harbor 42–43, 118
- rationing 33–40, 174–76
- rayon, development of 51–52
- silk imports from Japan 48–49
- stock market crash 155
- women in military service 71–74

USA Holocaust Memorial Museum, Washington DC, USA 142
Utility System 16, 26–28, 38, 135

V
Van Dyne, Luise (JP) 108, 144
Veillon, Dominique 2, 5, 180
Victoria and Albert Museum, London, UK 141, 204

W
Waller, Thomas Fat's 55–56
Warren, Elizabeth 197
wedding 3–4, 6, 9–10, 13, 51, 53, 60–61, 74, 94–95, 102, 111–12, 126, 128–153
 borrowed 9, 133, 142–44, 150–51
 color 131–133
 escape map wedding dress 60–61
 fashion trends 130–31
 from bed sheets 102, 128
 from parachutes 130, 133, 140–42
 furlough 129, 143
 hand knit 147
 Hollywood movie influence 131
 made from a parachute 60, 130, 140–42
 military uniform 133, 137
 paper 148
 repurposed 94, 140
 symbolic meaning 129–30, 134–35
 wedding veil, repurposed 128, 139
 white satin 131–32, 137, 140, 142, 145–47
Wells, Orson 187
Weston-super-Mare 3–5, 8, 48, 81, 50, 99, 100–01, 111, 177, 196, 214
 Holy Trinity Church 4
Westover, Russ 74–76
Wiggins, Celia 93, 103
Wile, Dennis 73
Wilkerson, Isabel 137
Withers, Audry 28, 38
Woolton, Frederick James Marquis, 1st Earl of Woolton 182
World War II War Brides Association 6, 130, 145, 165
 Bay Area WWII War Brides Past & Present exhibit 130, 142, 147
Worth, Rachel 199, 201

Y
Yount, Karin 100–01, 105, 177